The Vocation of the Catholic Philosopher

From Maritain to John Paul II

PUBLICATIONS OF THE

AMERICAN MARITAIN ASSOCIATION

General Editors:
Anthony O. Simon (1990 – 2004)
Michael Torre (2009 –)

Jacques Maritain: The Man and His Metaphysics
Edited by John F. X. Kansas, 1988
ISBN 0-268-01205-9 (out of print)
Distributed by the University of Notre Dame Press

Freedom in the Modern World: Jacques Maritain, Yves R. Simon, Mortimer J. Adler
Edited by Michael D. Torre, 1989, Second Printing, 1990
ISBN 0-268-00978-3
Distributed by the University of Notre Dame Press

From Twilight to Dawn: The Cultural Vision of Jacques Maritain
Edited by Peter A. Redpath, 1990
ISBN 0-268-00979-1
Distributed by the University of Notre Dame Press

The Future of Thomism
Edited by Deal W. Hudson and Dennis Wm. Moran, 1992
ISBN 0-268-00986-4
Distributed by the University of Notre Dame Press

Jacques Maritain and the Jews
Edited by Robert Royal, 1994
ISBN 0-268-01193-1
Distributed by the University of Notre Dame Press

Freedom, Virtue, and the Common Good
Edited by Curtis L. Hancock and Anthony O. Simon, 1995
ISBN 0-268-00991-0
Distributed by the University of Notre Dame Press

Postmodernism and Christian Philosophy
Edited by Roman T. Ciapolo, 1997
ISBN 0-8132-0881-5
Distributed by the Catholic University of America Press

The Common Things: Essays on Thomism and Education
Edited by Daniel McInerny, 1999
ISBN 0-9669226-0-3
Distributed by the Catholic University of America Press

The Failure of Modernism: The Cartesian Legacy and Contemporary Pluralism
Edited by Brendan Sweetman, 1999
ISBN 0-9669226-1-1
Distributed by the Catholic University of America Press

Beauty, Art, and the Polis
Edited by Alice Ramos, 2000
ISBN 0-9669226-2-X
Distributed by the Catholic University of America Press

Reassessing the Liberal State: Reading Maritain's Man and the State
Edited by Timothy Fuller and John P. Hittinger, 2001
ISBN 0-9669226-3-8
Distributed by the Catholic University of America Press

Faith, Scholarship, and Culture in the 21st Century
Edited by Alice Ramos, and Marie I. George, 2002
ISBN 0-9669226-5-4
Distributed by the Catholic University of America Press

Jacques Maritain and the Many Ways of Knowing
Edited by Douglas A. Ollivant, 2002
ISBN 0-9669226-4-6
Distributed by the Catholic University of America Press

Truth Matters: Essays in Honor of Jacques Maritain
Edited by John G. Trapani, Jr., 2004
ISBN 0-9669226-6-2
Distributed by the Catholic University of America Press

The Human Person and a Culture of Freedom
Edited by Peter A. Pagan Aguiar and Terese Auer, O.P., 2009
ISBN 978-0-9669226-7-7
Distributed by the Catholic University of America Press

Maritain and America
Edited by Christopher M. Cullen, S.J. and Joseph Allan Clair, 2009
ISBN 978-0-9669226-8-4
Distributed by the Catholic University of America Press

The Renewal of Civilization: Essays in Honor of Jacques Maritain
Edited by Gavin T. Colvert, 2010
ISBN 978-0-9669226-9-1
Distributed by the Catholic University of America Press

The Vocation of the Catholic Philosopher: From Maritain to John Paul II
Edited by John P. Hittinger, 2010
ISBN 978-0-9827119-0-3
Distributed by the Catholic University of America Press

The Vocation of the Catholic Philosopher

From Maritain to John Paul II

Edited by

John P. Hittinger

AMERICAN MARITAIN ASSOCIATION

Distributed by the Catholic University of America Press

Washington, D.C. 20064

Library of Congress Cataloging-in-Publication Data

The vocation of the Catholic philosopher: from Maritain to John Paul II / edited by John P. Hittinger.

p. cm.

Includes bibliographical references and index.

ISBN 978-0-9827119-0-3

1. Catholic Church and philosophy. 2. Catholic philosophers. 3. Maritain, Jacques, 1882-1973. 4. John Paul II, Pope, 1920-2005. I. Hittinger, John.

BX1795.P47V63 2011

261.5'10922--dc22

2011006764

Manufactured in the United States of America

Distributed by the Catholic University of America Press
620 Michigan Avenue, N.E. /240 Leahy Hall
Washington, D.C. 20064

Acknowledgements

I wish to thank Geoffrey Meadows for his assistance in the preparation of the manuscript and for his work with the authors. I am grateful to Sister Mary Roberta Connor, F.S.E., for the cover design.

The Maritain Association owes a great debt of gratitude to John Trapani and to Michael Torre for their determination and commitment to produce the series of books after a hiatus. Although the conference was held six years ago, I would like to acknowledge the hospitality of the Catholic University of America, especially the School of Philosophy and the School of Law.

Contents

PART III
Pope John Paul II's *Fides et Ratio*

PART IV
Contemporary Challenges

DEDICATED

to

THE DECEASED MEMBERS OF THE
AMERICAN MARITAIN ASSOCIATION

especially:

DONALD GALLAGHER, RALPH NELSON, AND RALPH MCINERNY,

and to

ALL YOUNG PILGRIMS OF THE ABSOLUTE

"The task which the new age we are entering expects of Christians is so difficult that they can not possibly accomplish it unless there are multiplied, in the very heart of and throughout the world, constellations of spiritual energy composed of humble stars invisibly shining, each a contemplative soul given over to the life of prayer.... Without contemplative love and infused prayer, and the participation of souls given over to them in the redeeming Cross, and without the invisible support which they bring to the work of all in the mystical body, and to that strange traffic which Providence carries on here below, the task demanded of the Christian, of all Christians, would be too heavy, and the great hope which is rising would be in vain. This hope will not be in vain, for the humble stars I am speaking of have begun secretly to glimmer; there are many more of them than one realizes strewn across the world."

—Jacques Maritain,
The Peasant of the Garonne

INTRODUCTION:
ODYSSEUS' BOW AND THE CATHOLIC PHILOSOPHER

> *"To epitomize the intellectual task confronting Thomas, and which he set for himself, I must use the image of Odysseus' bow, which was so difficult to bend that it took almost superhuman strength to draw the ends closer together. I have said that almost as soon as Thomas awoke to critical consciousness he recognized that it was his life's task to join these two extremes which seemed inevitably to be pulling away from one another."*
>
> —Josef Pieper,
> *Guide to Thomas Aquinas*

The theme of this collection of essays, *The Vocation of the Catholic Philosopher,* is inspired by the life and work of Jacques Maritain, especially his work *The Peasant of the Garonne.*[1] Written immediately after Vatican Council II, the book set out a vision for renewal of the Church and society through the kindling of "true new fires" of love and wisdom: "the true new fire, the essential renewal, will be an *inner* renewal."[2] The renewal will incorporate genuine discoveries and "Christian consciousness will penetrate deeper and further into the truth by which it lives and the evangelical reality."[3] Maritain understood the intention of the Council to be that accomplishment achieved by Aquinas centuries earlier. Pope Paul VI said of Thomas Aquinas: "Without doubt, Thomas possessed supremely the courage of the truth, a freedom of spirit in confronting new problems, the intellectual honesty of those who allow Christianity to be contaminated

---

[1] Jacques Maritain, *The Peasant of the Garonne: An Old Layman Questions Himself About the Present Time*, trans. Michael Cuddihy and Elizabeth Hughes (New York: Holt, Rinehart and Winston, 1968).

[2] Ibid., 65. (Jacques Maritain was present at the closing of Vatican Council II, on December 8, 1965; the preface to *The Peasant* was written on December 31, 1965, with the work being first published, in French, in the year following.)

[3] Ibid.; see also the opening chapter of Karol Wojtyła, *Sources of Renewal: The Implementation of Vatican II* (San Francisco: Harper and Row, 1980): "The implementation of Vatican II, or the process of Conciliar renewal, must be based on the principle of the enrichment of faith.... In the present study, designed to help towards the realization of Vatican II, we shall concentrate on the consciousness of Christians and the attitudes they shall acquire."

neither by secular philosophy nor by a prejudiced rejection of it. He passed therefore into the history of Christian thought as a pioneer of the new path of philosophy and universal culture. The key point and almost the kernel of the solution which, with all the brilliance of his prophetic intuition, he gave to the new encounter of faith and reason was a reconciliation between the secularity of the world and the radicality of the Gospel, thus avoiding the unnatural tendency to negate the world and its values while at the same time keeping faith with the supreme and inexorable demands of the supernatural order."[4] Josef Pieper suggested the image of "Odysseus' bow" to indicate the tremendous tension inherent in such a vocation.[5] In his own way, Maritain was just such a pioneer of the new path of philosophy combining the "secularity of the world and the radicality of the Gospel." And Vatican II put forward a grand vision for lay spirituality and the universal call to holiness as the source for the renewal of the Church and the temporal structures of the world.

Thus, Maritain tied the vocation of the Catholic philosopher to the meaning and import of the Council. Does the position of the Church in the modern world require the abandonment of the philosophy of Thomas Aquinas and the embrace of modern philosophy? Does respect for the autonomy and progress of the secular world require a separation from the guidance of doctrine and the formation of faith? Is it the fate of Catholic philosophers to be absorbed into the professional cadres of academia and fragmented into the rival ranks of secular philosophies? Must the great tradition of Catholic philosophy disappear, with but a faint trace in the journals of the historically minded? Not according to the man who fermented Catholic intellectual life for decades prior to the Council and who was considered a mentor by Pope Paul VI, namely Jacques Maritain. And not according to the man who was present at the Council and who worked to craft one of its key documents (*The Church in the Modern World*), one who later became the

---

[4] See John Paul II, *Fides et Ratio* #43, note #47, quoting Paul VI's Apostolic Letter *Lumen Ecclesiae* (20 November 1974), 8: *AAS* 66 (1974), 680.

[5] See Josef Pieper on a theologically founded worldliness as the heart of "the west," in *Guide to Thomas Aquinas*, trans. Richard and Clara Winston (New York: Random House, 1962), chaps. 11, 12.

Pope who steadied the Church in its post-Conciliar wavering, namely Karol Wojtyła.

According to their lights, the Church and the world need the philosophy of St. Thomas now more than ever. The efforts of the laity to "build the earth" and discover the excellence of the everyday call for the aid of divine grace and the light of faith. Catholic philosophers and thinkers—however dispersed throughout the ranks of academia and wherever present in the deliberations of the councils of the world or engaged in dialogues in galleries and assemblies—must retain the strong flavor of the salt of the gospel. Neither giddy with the superficial hopes of the progressives nor embittered with the shrill despair of the traditionalists, Maritain and Wojtyła brought the strength of their philosophical character (habitus) to confront the many challenges that face the Church in the modern world.

In 1966, Maritain offered his book, *The Peasant of the Garonne,* as a corrective, a rebuke to the two extremes he playfully named the "Sheep of Panurge" and the "Ruminators of the Holy Alliance," the so-called progressives and traditionalists, both of whom shunned the Council and distorted its fundamental meaning and significance. Maritain attempted to stabilize the core meanings of the Council in light of history, spirituality, and philosophy.[6] Pope John Paul II has accomplished the corrections and he has stabilized the core meanings much in the vein traced by Maritain in *The Peasant*. But much still waits to be discovered. The call for renewal is still waiting for intelligent and generous responses. Maritain's account of the intellectual and spiritual conditions for a true renewal provides us with much to consider. Pope John Paul II's encyclical *Fides et Ratio* expands and deepens these considerations. So what is the vocation of the Catholic philosopher in their view of the post-Conciliar era?

---

[6] Pope Paul VI also made such attempts on the theological front with his post-conciliar writings; see especially Pope Paul VI, *On the Mystery of Faith* (Boston: Daughters of St. Paul, 1966) and *On Saints Peter and Paul* (Boston: Daughters of St. Paul, 1967). See also Candido Pozo, *The Credo of the People of God: A Theological Commentary,* trans. Fr. Mark A. Pilon (Chicago: Franciscan Herald Press, 1980).

1. What Is Philosophy?

What is philosophy? Maritain said: "Philosophy is the science which by the natural light of reason studies the first causes or highest principles of all things—is in other words, the science of things in their first causes, in so far as these belong to the natural order."[7] Maritain's philosophical efforts must be traced back to his metaphysical habitus, especially his notion of the intuition of being.[8] Maritain feared that the emphasis upon efficacy and pragmatism had obscured the fundamental principles and dynamic of philosophy. In the age of an increasing influence of technology, the love of truth, the superior value of truth, will have a liberating effect on the human heart and mind. Men look for substitutes in myths and fables, because science itself is unable to answer the deeper personal questions about man, God and the world.[9] Maritain entitled one collection of his *The Range of Reason* to signify the full sweep of philosophical achievement as it encompasses an approach to God, the soul, justice, and truth. Science will try to extrapolate from science to create fables and myths to answer these questions. Maritain was critical of Teilhard de Chardin because he viewed his efforts as an extrapolation, a poetic myth of science, covering over the deeper yearning for a true philosophical approach to the big issues. Also, he criticized the forms of contemporary philosophy because they bracket the question of being. As forms of epistemological idealism, they trap the thinker within his own mind and never experience the relish of true being. The great vision of Christian renewal of temporal structures, the true activation of the temporal mission of the lay Christian, requires a preparation in the order of philosophy and

---

[7] Jacques Maritain, *An Introduction to Philosophy* (New York: Sheed and Ward, 1930). See the discussion in *The Peasant*, 136, on the theological light proper to theology and the need for a renewal of Thomism through the proper light of philosophy. Cf. *Fides et Ratio* §9.

[8] See Jacques Maritain, *The Peasant*, 99-101, 110-11, 132-35. See also John P. Hittinger, "The Intuition of Being: Metaphysics or Poetry?" in *Jacques Maritain: The Man and His Metaphysics*, ed. John F. X. Knasas (Notre Dame, Indiana: American Maritain Association, 1988), 71-82; reprinted in *Liberty, Wisdom and Grace: Thomism and Democratic Political Theory* (Lanham: Lexington Books, 2002).

[9] Ibid., 112-20.

spirituality. It requires "a great and patient work of revitalizing in the order of intelligence and the order of spirituality."[10]

Philosophy aims at spiritual renewal through the search for wisdom. Philosophers must respect the work of scientific inquiry; but science for its part must exercise self-discipline and refrain from extrapolating from its findings a new mythology or ideology. The search for wisdom begins with its enduring sense of wonder; the philosopher lies in between beasts and gods in a position of the metaxy. [11] Modern intellectuals tend to enclose themselves within a rational self-sufficiency and assume the position of a god-like autonomy. The ever-recurring temptation of science is the one first initiated so well by Lucretius—the poeticizing of the mechanisms of the world. Edward Wilson consciously invokes this same muse.[12] The great questions of meaning about man, God, and the world must lie beyond the scope of science. But science will make its poetic attempts to generate a comprehensive account, often doing bad theology rather than doing none at all. As Maritain says, the bad money chases out the good. The great hunger of the soul goes unfed. What is needed is an attention to the very intrinsic order of human intelligence, not an indiscriminate mixing together of science, poetry, and philosophy.

On the Feast of the Triumph of the Cross, 1999, Pope John Paul II issued the encyclical letter *Fides et Ratio* (On the Relationship between Faith and Reason). The mystery of the cross plays a prominent role in the relationship between faith and reason—the cross is said to be a "reef" whose submerged mystery will either break up the relationship between faith and reason (actually, he says that reason may come to grief on the shoals of its devising) or reason will be freed through the mystery of the cross to set forth upon a "boundless ocean of truth." With such nautical metaphors, one thinks by way of contrast of both the timidity of a Locke and the temerity of a Nietzsche. Locke says at

---

[10] Ibid., 53.

[11] See the new translation of Josef Pieper, *Platonic Myths* (South Bend, Indiana: Saint Augustine Press, 2011).

[12] Edward O. Wilson, *Consilience—The Unity of Knowledge* (New York: Alfred A. Knopf, Inc., 1998), and his essay "Resuming the Enlightenment Quest," *The Wilson Quarterly* 22, no. 1 (1998): 16-27.

the outset of the *Essay* that we should avoid the "vast Ocean of Being" wherein a man has no sure footing; he recommends that the mind rest content with its short tether, because, if the mind is not suited for metaphysical speculation, it is suited for practical matters—"convenience" and "virtue," he says. Nietzsche, by contrast, explains that the death of God, in erasing all points of reference and orientation, allows one to embark on an unbounded sea. For John Paul II, the cross represents the mystery of love, which cannot be eliminated and which provides the "ultimate answer" reason seeks. Neither Locke nor Nietzsche would be characterized as philosophers of love. Jacques Maritain, on the other hand, was often characterized thusly. He saw fit to include a text of Raïssa in *The Peasant of the Garonne*: "The True Face of God, or Love and Law." Thus the last line of his book is Raïssa's—"Love creates trust." So much for the myth of the bitter old man's last testimony! Maritain was a philosopher who lived in the mystery of the cross. Maritain's was a Christian philosophy, a "philosophical speculation conceived in dynamic union with faith" (§76). The questions about the meaning, coherence, and desirability of Christian philosophy were a matter of much debate a generation ago. The Pope's encyclical provides a new stimulation for revisiting those debates and for overcoming the widespread denial of the relationship, the position Pope John Paul II called the "drama of the separation of faith and reason." These essays draw upon the resources of Maritain's work to understand the corresponding aspects of the urgent project to rediscover or re-found their proper integration. It is a project that Maritain, in *The Peasant of the Garonne*, calls a "vast labor of reason" and a life of prayer.

In *Fides et Ratio*, Pope John Paul II commends specific thinkers by name as examples of the proper relationship between faith and reason: Edith Stein, John Henry Cardinal Newman, Antonio Rosmini, Étienne Gilson, and Jacques Maritain (§74). They exhibited the "indispensable requirements" for an authentic philosophy "consonant with the Word of God" (§80-84). "One thing is certain," said John Paul II: "attention to the spiritual journey of these masters can only give greater momentum to both the search for truth and the effort to apply the results of that search to the service of humanity." Common to their lives as Catholic philosophers was an effort to destroy the firewall between faith and reason set up by many Catholics of their day and to find a living synthesis between them. Yves R. Simon, who could well be added to the list of exemplars of philosophers in faith, offered some interesting reflections of his own. Yves R. Simon studied, wrote and taught during the challenging era prior to and after World War II. "One of the brightest in the history of philosophy"—so Yves R. Simon described the period between the wars, referring in particular to his mentor Jacques Maritain and also Étienne Gilson:

> Having understood that philosophy needs the light of faith, the Christian philosopher is saved from entertaining two kinds of truths and risking the divorce of his intellectual from his spiritual life. In my opinion it is this union of philosophical intelligence and Christian faith, brought about by the labor of a few great minds, that makes this period one of the brightest in the history of philosophy.[13]

He pointed out that their work is premised on a rejection of the notion that a firewall separates philosophy and faith. Simon found too many scholars accepted some version of the "two truth theory," according to which one may compartmentalize one's science and scholarship and isolate them from faith, holding in effect "two truths," never bothering to verify "whether there was any agreement." Simon clearly understood that these trends of thought contradict the Catholic understanding of faith. Yet he encountered "university conformism" in the standard rejection of the role of faith in the life of the philosopher. Their strictures were demanding, such that "authors were to be read or not read, journals consulted or not consulted, questions raised or not raised—in short the whole style of research, thought and expression was preset," all in an effort to banish faith from academia. Then it was Descartes and French rationalism; today it is deconstruction, existentialism, or linguistic analysis. The question remains: does the philosopher make room for faith?

According to Vatican II's *Church in the Modern World*, the "split between the faith which many profess and their daily lives deserves to be counted among the most serious errors of the age" (§36). Virtually

---

[13] Yves R. Simon, "Philosophy and Faith: Extracts from the Memoirs of a French Philosopher," *Notes et Documents de l'Institut International Jacques Maritain* XIV (January-March 1979): 5-8.

every Catholic university and college in the United States, save those conspicuous few, is under the sway of this error, ironically in the name of renewal and Vatican II. Yes, philosophy, along with temporal matters in general, has its own proper autonomy, because "all things are endowed with their own stability, truth, goodness, proper laws and order. Man must respect these as he isolates them by the appropriate methods of the individual sciences or arts" (§36). So too, believers must "keep the laws proper to each discipline, and labor to equip themselves with a genuine expertise in their various fields" (§43). But the autonomy of temporal affairs, philosophy included, does not mean that "created things do not depend upon God or that they can be used without reference to their creator" (§36). Moreover, grace is needed to cling to what is good and achieve integrity even within the natural order (§37). All human activity must be purified and perfected by grace, philosophy no less than other works and virtues. The life and work of Maritain and Simon are a testimony to the unity of life, in this case rigorous academic and intellectual work with devout faith, envisioned by Vatican II.

In his later essays, Maritain coins a new term to replace "Christian philosophy." He says that he would put in its place the phrase "philosophy fully considered as such" or "philosophy forging ahead" as distinguished from "Philosophy considered simply as such" or "stumbling philosophy."[14] He abandons the term Christian philosophy because of the unfruitful debates of previous decades; but he further radicalizes it, in light of Vatican II. He fears that the term Christian philosophy "runs the risk of being completely misunderstood, as if the philosophy in question were more or less reined in by confessional proprieties." He claims that "the reality is quite different. Given the naturally high estate proper to philosophical problems and at the same time the limitations of human intelligence, as well as the wounds of nature which affect the human mind itself, we should not be surprised that even among the greatest minds philosophy *considered simply as such* might very well become a stumbling block. All the same we must feel sorry for those who have never felt the flame burn brighter in them on reading Plato or Plotinus.... Whether there is question of a philosopher

[14] Jacques Maritain, *Untrammeled Approaches*, trans. Bernard Doering (Notre Dame, Indiana: University of Notre Dame, 1997), 421.

or of any man of faith, that faith impregnates the Christian intelligence completely. It deputizes philosophical reason to the single search for Truth, delivering it from its subjection to the world and from any form of servility to the fashions of the times. This is why what we call 'Christian philosophy' is a philosophy set free, and ought to be called philosophy *understood fully* as such."[15] The fulfillment and completion of the tasks and vocation of philosophy leads to the life of faith, and "faith impregnates the Christian intelligence completely."

Pope John Paul II makes two overarching claims about the *relationship* between faith and reason: (a) "Each contains the other, and each has its own scope for action" (§17); (b) "Each without the other is impoverished and enfeebled" (§48). We must precisely avoid the danger of pursuing faith without reason because, "deprived of reason, faith has stressed feeling and experience and runs the risk of no longer being a universal proposition"(§48). But reason should not be deprived of faith, and so he challenges the Catholic philosopher to develop a "philosophy consonant with the word of God" (§81). What would it take for a philosophy to feed the fires of faith, hope and love, and contribute to the "true new fire" of renewal?

"To be consonant with the word of God," says Pope John Paul II, "philosophy needs first of all to recover its *sapiential dimension* as a search for the ultimate and overarching meaning of life." On this essential task for philosophy itself, the Word of God will actually assist in restoring philosophy to its original vocation. For "the fundamental conviction of the 'philosophy' found in the Bible is that the world and human life do have a meaning and look towards their fulfillment, which comes in Jesus Christ" (§80). The Pope notes how contemporary men and women, those to whom the Christian must be concerned for the new evangelization, are caught in a "crisis of meaning" because of a culture of doubt and deconstruction, leading to "skepticism, indifference and various forms of nihilism" (§81). The modern mind is deeply introverted and "locked within the confines of its own immanence without reference to any kind of transcendence" (§81). Faith can shock or snap the modern mind back to the ardor of its quest for meaning, to recover its wisdom, or sapiential dimension. Pope John

---

[15] Ibid., 266.

Paul II reminds us that "the mystery of the Incarnation will always remain the central point of reference for an understanding of the enigma of human existence, the created world and God himself" (§80). We also call to mind that hermeneutical key to Vatican II, *Gaudium et Spes* §22: in the mystery of Christ, man finds his true meaning. Thus, "the challenge of this mystery pushes philosophy to its limits, as reason is summoned to make its own a logic which brings down the walls within which it risks being confined." Finally, it will be the mystery of the cross, the mystery of love, which pushes philosophy to face directly, without illusion or posturing, the full mystery and meaning of human existence (§23).

The contours of a philosophy consonant with the word of God must be more fully laid out. Pope John Paul II lays down two more requirements for such a philosophy—epistemological realism and a full metaphysical range of thought. Thus he says that "this sapiential function could not be performed by a philosophy which was not itself a true and authentic knowledge, addressed, that is, not only to particular and subordinate aspects of reality—functional, formal or utilitarian—but to its total and definitive truth, to the very being of the object which is known. This prompts a second requirement: that philosophy verify the human capacity to know the truth, to come to a knowledge which can reach objective truth by means of that *adaequatio rei et intellectus* to which the Scholastic Doctors referred" (§82). Although the Pope does commend modern philosophy for its discoveries in the realm of subjectivity and in the differentiation of the sciences, he cautions against the loss of a sense of being that accompanies the modern philosophy. The Cartesian gambit must be thoroughly understood and its impact upon the subsequent centuries of thought be brought out for display. But the radical turn to subjectivity will not finally be consonant with the word of God, or to the original vocation of philosophy as a quest for truth, a quest for the divine ground of all being.[16]

Finally, the "two requirements already stipulated imply a third: the need for a philosophy of genuinely metaphysical range, capable, that is, of transcending empirical data in order to attain something absolute,

---

[16] See John P. Hittinger, "Exorcizing the Ghost of Descartes," in *Liberty, Wisdom, and Grace*, 189-201.

ultimate and foundational in its search for truth" (§83). We must form a philosophy that can confidently cover the great questions of philosophy, to treat adequately of "a solid and harmonious knowledge of the human being, of the world, and of God."[17] A solid and harmonious knowledge must range through philosophy of nature, anthropology, and ethics, reaching up finally to reach truths of a metaphysical order—"Wherever men and women discover a call to the absolute and transcendent, the metaphysical dimension of reality opens up before them: in truth, in beauty, in moral values, in other persons, in being itself, in God" (§83). These three themes mark the work and achievement of Jacques Maritain, as well as Yves R. Simon, from beginning to end.

2. What Is Vocation?

In what way may we speak of the vocation of the philosopher? Vocation has various meanings. It could mean the suitability for a person to a certain task. It is an important consideration how one is equipped or trained for the life of philosophy. But this is not its primary meaning. A second meaning is the call or confirmation by someone to some other person to accomplish a task or to assume a role. The professions take up this notion of calling and specify the nature of responsibility to society at large in the various professions. This also has significance for the philosopher, especially the relationship of philosophy to the city and political life. But the third, most proper meaning of vocation is the call from God to serve Him. Thus, Francis de Sales provides a classic definition as follows: "A true vocation is nothing other than the firm and constant will possessed by the person called, to want to serve God in the manner and in the place where the Divine Majesty calls her."[18] The Catholic must understand vocation in all three meanings of the term, but obviously the supernatural vocation is most important of all.

---

[17] John Paul II, *Fides et Ratio* §60, note #83, quoting Vatican II's *Decree on Priestly Formation* (*Optatam Totius*), 15.

[18] St. Francis de Sales, "*Spiritual Conferences*," conf. 16: *Œuvres de S. François de Sales*, vol. 6, 312. See Carl Franklin Kelley, *The Spirit of Love: Based on the teachings of St. François de Sales*, foreword by Jacques Maritain (London: Longmans, 1952), 89, 98-99, 103, 219-21.

Maritain speaks about the dual vocation, spiritual and temporal, of all lay Christians, and this has bearing upon the vocation of philosophy. The spiritual vocation is to live the life of grace; its final end is the kingdom of God and is not of the world. The temporal vocation is to live and work as laborer of the world for its progress, beauty, and well being ("building the earth").[19] The vocation of philosophy in its origin is a temporal vocation, especially as seen in its practical philosophy, ethics and politics. It is an examination of the human good available to natural capacity and rational power. Nevertheless, even in ancient philosophy, the vocation is an unusual one, since its end transcends the city and culminates in contemplation of the eternal order. It is a natural end, contemplation of the truth, knowledge of the causes of natural things, as knowable by reason. It is not a matter of infused grace or supernatural revelation. That is the nature of philosophical thinking. But the state of the Catholic philosopher, as a member of the Church in the modern world, makes it rise to the level of a supernatural vocation. Thus Maritain said "without contemplative love and infused prayer, and the participation of souls given over to them in the redeeming Cross, and without the invisible support which they bring to the work of all in the mystical body, and to that strange traffic which Providence carries on here below, the task demanded of the Christian, of all Christians, would be too heavy, and the great hope which is rising would be in vain."[20] Clearly Maritain envisions the Catholic philosopher of the future to respond to the initiative of divine grace.

In *Fides et Ratio*, Pope John Paul II makes three references to "vocation." Early in the work, he speaks about the failure of those whose vocation it is to educate the young about the meaning of life and to provide reference points for their learning. Philosophy must respond to this vocation or call to provide some foundation for personal and communal life: "those whose vocation it is to give cultural expression to their thinking no longer look to truth, preferring quick success to the toil of patient enquiry into what makes life worth living. With its enduring appeal to the search for truth, philosophy has the great responsibility of forming thought and culture; and now it must strive

[19] Jacques Maritain, *The Peasant*, 208.

[20] Ibid., 82-83.

resolutely to recover its original vocation" (§6). Later, he discusses the search for the "ultimate and overarching meaning of life" as the "sapiential dimension" or wisdom dimension. He says this search will stimulate "philosophy to conform to its proper nature." This aspect of vocation "is all the more necessary today, because the immense expansion of humanity's technical capability demands a renewed and sharpened sense of ultimate values. If this technology is not ordered to something greater than a merely utilitarian end, then it could soon prove inhuman and even become potential destroyer of the human race" (§81). The vocation to search for wisdom and meaning also lays down the requirement of a respect for truth and for the metaphysical range of philosophy, as we mentioned above.

In the final section of *Fides et Ratio*, John Paul II says "between the vocation of the Blessed Virgin and the vocation of true philosophy there is a deep harmony" (§108). He considers the life of Mary "a true parable illuminating the reflection contained in these pages." Mary lost none of her humanity in giving assent to Gabriel's word; so, too, "when philosophy heeds the summons of the Gospel's truth its autonomy is in no way impaired." All the more do its enquiries "rise to their highest expression." In other words, philosophy needs to embrace faith and find its culmination as philosophy in such an embrace. The life of faith will enhance the excellence of reason, not detract from it. John Paul II invokes the Seat of Wisdom in the concluding section of *Fides et Ratio* and he exhorts the reader to philosophize in Mary ("*philosophari in Maria*," §108).

We see this parable lived out in the life of Jacques Maritain, who heeded the summons of the Gospel truth, and who saw his inquiries rise to a very high expression. His devotion to Mary was intense. His devotion to Mary was learned from his godfather, Léon Bloy, and formed by the apparition at La Salette in 1846. In *We Have Been Friends Together*, Raïssa said that La Salette was the most important religious event in centuries.[21] Our Lady at La Salette formed deeply the hearts

[21] At La Salette, Mary appeared before two young shepherd children; she sat and wept and told them of the impending chastisement of France and the world for its blasphemies and its failures to honor the Sabbath. Maritain wrote a manuscript on the apparition which he personally delivered to the Vatican and discussed with Pope Benedict XV in a private audience. He was

and minds of the Maritains.[22] Jacques and Raïssa were deeply attracted to the image of the Virgin in tears and saw in the apparition at La Salette an event of "exceptional grandeur and beauty."

---

forbidden to publish the study and to discuss the apparition. The apparition had become controversial because of the secrets revealed by the shepherdess, Melanie Calvat. The secrets reveal a very harsh punishment from the hand of God and the clergy are censured for their misdeeds. Melanie lived a life in exile, persecution, and suffering. Léon Bloy and Maritain were among her defenders. In the *Notebooks* (Notre Dame, Indiana: University of Notre Dame, 1984), Maritain has an interesting reflection on the meaning of the apparitions-he had exclaimed to Pope Benedict XV that he would affirm the truth of the apparition and the secrets. In his later, mature, reflection, he uses the notion of the preconscious of the spirit to explain that the words are not to be taken literally in everything, but we must understand the tremendous gap between "the infinite transcendence of the perspectives of heaven in comparison with those of earth" (91). The words must be charged with mystery and will inevitably suffer "a kind of immoderation." But the essential purpose of an apparition is "not to tell our fortunes nor to *inform* us as a secret agent would, but, as is the case for all revelation under the New Law, to draw our attention, by great signs capable of stirring hearts everywhere, to things which are of importance to our action, and which, of ourselves, we see more or less badly—shortcomings too real, hopes or threats with which the times are burdened, purposes of God which when realized will doubtless appear very different from the image which we could form of them—all of this designated in terms essentially mysterious which, even reported exactly as they were heard, are true 'literally' as to the general practical sense which is intended to be communicated to us, but not as to the particular mental perspectives, nor to the particular imagery, nor to the words taken according to the human measure through whose instrumentality a transcendent thought is signified to us" (93).

[22] The Maritains received the sacrament of confirmation soon after they visited the holy mountain at La Salette. Bloy said that "it fell to the lot of a shepherd girl ... to proclaim to us integral, absolute Christianity in all its splendor." Raïssa said its "prophetic contents tower over the misfortunes of our times." There are many themes from Jacques' work that derive from this devotion to Mary at La Salette: the seeds of integral humanism, the judgment upon modern culture, the love of poverty and justice, the role of suffering in love. In order better to understand their mission and work, as well as to expand our horizon to the prophetic scope of the Church in the modern world, we

There is a striking affinity between Maritain's devotion to La Salette and Pope John Paul II's advice to "philosophize in Mary." In *Fides et Ratio*, John Paul II talks about the cross as providing the authentic critique of a self-sufficient reason (§23). The cross is a challenge to reason because "reason cannot eliminate the mystery of love which the cross represents, while the cross can give to reason the ultimate answer which it seeks." To philosophize in Mary requires one to stand there also before the cross, meditating upon the meaning of the sacrifice. For Jacques and Raïssa, as well as for Pope John Paul II, we find a deep confidence that Mary, the Seat of Wisdom, would be a sure haven for all who devote their lives to the search for wisdom. John Paul II ended the encyclical with this prayer: "May their journey into wisdom, sure and final goal of all true knowing, be freed of every hindrance by the intercession of the one who, in giving birth to the Truth and treasuring it in her heart, has shared it forever with all the world."

Whatever the specific tasks in academia or culture the Catholic philosopher may take on, whatever specialization the Catholic philosopher may cultivate; the embrace of revelation and a response in faith are essential to the vocation of the Catholic philosopher. The Catholic philosopher must philosophize in Mary. This is not a pious exercise to be draped over a secular endeavor, but a transforming spirituality that affects both the head and heart. Cardinal Newman articulated a similar theme in his *Oxford Sermons* §15 ("The Theory of Developments in Religious Doctrine") in which he said: "St. Mary is our pattern of Faith, both in the reception and in the study of Divine Truth. She does not think it enough to accept, she dwells upon it; not enough

---

should make an effort to revisit that apparition at La Salette so greatly overshadowed by Lourdes and Fatima. Léon Bloy wrote a profound and stirring account of the apparition and its meaning for the modern world; the book is entitled *She Who Weeps: Our Lady of La Salette*, trans. and intro. Emile la Douceur (Fresno, California: Academy of Library Guild, 1956), a few excerpts of which can be found in Léon Bloy, *Pilgrim of the Absolute*, selections by Raïssa Maritain, intro. Jacques Maritain, trans. John Coleman and Harry Lorin Binsse (New York: Pantheon Books, 1947). See also Jacques Maritain, *Notebooks*, 81-99, and Raïssa Maritain, *We Have Been Friends Together*, trans. Julie Kernan (New York: Longmans, Green & Co., 1942), 183-92, and its sequel, *Adventures in Grace*, trans. Julie Kernan (New York, Longmans, Green & Co., 1945), 220-23, 241-45.

to possess, she uses it; not enough to assent, she develops it; not enough to submit the Reason, she reasons upon it; not indeed reasoning first, and believing afterwards, with Zacharias, yet first believing without reasoning, next from love and reverence, reasoning after believing. And thus she symbolizes to us, not only the faith of the unlearned, but of the doctors of the Church also, who have to investigate, and weigh, and define, as well as to profess the Gospel; to draw the line between truth and heresy; to anticipate or remedy the various aberrations of wrong reason; to combat pride and recklessness with their own arms; and thus to triumph over the sophist and the innovator."[23]

3. Lay Apostolate and the Vocation of the Catholic Philosopher

The vocation of the philosopher, considered from the standpoint of the tasks to be performed, serves as an example or species of "Catholic action," because it serves both the city and the Church. In an essay in *Scholasticism and Politics*, Maritain explains that the notion of "Catholic action" opens up for purview three levels of action: (1) the activity of the Church as such, concerned with the spiritual and the kingdom of God; (2) the temporal or political action, concerned with the political temporal common good; (3) the realm of Catholic action—the intersection of the spiritual and temporal.[24] Catholic action is situated in-between the temporal and the spiritual, between Caesar and the Church. On this third level of action, where "the spiritual is considered as joined to the temporal," belongs the apostolate, "but to the apostolate as touching things of earth; I mean so far as it has for its purpose to infuse evangelical vitality into the temporal life." Although philosophy is a secular activity, and it directly aims at a good of the natural, or natural finalities, it is also a matter for an apostolate. One can see this already in the concluding words to his second published essay, written in 1910 and later published in *Antimoderne*: "And now if

---

[23] John Henry Newman, *Oxford Sermons Preached Before the University of Oxford between A.D. 1826 and 1843* (London: Rivington, 1980); new edition with Mary Katherine Tillman (Notre Dame, Indiana: University of Notre Dame, 1997), 313-14.

[24] Jacques Maritain, *Scholasticism and Politics*, ed. Mortimer J. Adler (New York: Macmillan, 1940).

philosophy is anything at all, it has as its first duty to prepare there the pathways of grace. Undoubtedly it will preach in the desert."[25] His embrace of the faith and the guidance of Thomas Aquinas indicate his self-understanding as an apostle; for Aquinas was the "Apostle for our Time" because the disease afflicting the modern world is in the first place a disease of the mind. Aquinas' thought will get to the roots of the disease. At the heart of the disorder is a rupture of the proper relationship of faith and reason, the "organic link" commended by Pope John Paul II in *Fides et Ratio.* Maritain saw the split of faith and reason as the seed of an impending nihilism. Man has been "split asunder" and "nothing in human life is any longer made to man's measure, to the rhythm of the human heart." Man is at the center of a world "inhuman in every respect."[26] Maritain and John Paul II both considered the greatest sign of the time to be the capacity of technology to dominate, oppress and ultimately degrade human life, rather than to serve human flourishing.

In order to engage this modern culture at its root, Maritain envisioned the philosopher's role in Catholic action. He acknowledged the great role of Pope Pius XI; he "precisely stated its meaning and made its applications explicit, the central, essential importance which he attaches to Catholic action, his affirmed will to develop it everywhere, the solicitude with which he watches over it." Maritain said: "These words, which should be retained and carefully weighed, show how far, in the thought of the Pope, Catholic action is a thing of the Church and has the same finalities as the Church's pastoral ministry itself: laymen are called to assist the Church in the integral fulfillment of her pastoral office; *they are called to the apostolate, to that same apostolate with which Christ has charged the Twelve and their*

[25] Jacques, Maritain, "La Science moderne et la raison," originally published in *Revue de Philosophie* XVI (June 1910), 577-603, and then republished as the first essay of *Antimoderne* (Paris: Éditions de la Revue des Jeunes, 1922), 68; translation by Richard Lemp for the forthcoming volume in the Notre Dame *Collected Works of Jacques Maritain.*

[26] Jacques Maritain, *The Dream of Descartes*, trans. Mabelle L. Andison (New York: Philosophical Library, 1944), 146.

successors; and they receive for this an explicit mission."[27] The interest in lay apostolate anticipated Vatican II. One-time associate of the Maritain circle, Yves Congar explained that since the French Revolution the idea and practice of Catholic action has been underway as a way to confront "aggressive and widespread unbelief, the disappearance of props to the faith provided by political power." The structures of the world are separated from Christ by "hostility or indifference," full of new forces, unknown values, heedless, often ignorant of Catholic faith.[28]

In a previous chapter in *Scholasticism and Politics*, Maritain connects contemplation with Catholic action, as he will also do in *The Peasant*—"I have always insisted that all souls are called in some degree to the contemplation of the saints, which, because it is a contemplation of love, abounds in action. But now, and as corresponding to this call of God deep in our hearts, we are to meditate on another call, the call to action, apostolic action, which the Church addresses in some degree to all the faithful." But Catholic action depends upon contemplation. As an apostolic work, by its very nature, Catholic action must "proceed from a superabundance of contemplation." It may not be contemplation in its "typical and sublime form," but at least "*masked* contemplation."[29] It is the Holy Spirit who must form Catholic action.

Maritain presented a very eloquent and important statement about the spirit of Catholic action: "Behold of what spirit they are, who enter

---

[27] Jacques Maritain, "Catholic Action" in *Scholasticism and Politics*, 185-89, referencing Pope Pius XI's "Discourse to the Committee on Italian Catholic Action" (March 9, 1924), and his Encyclical *Non Abbiamo Bisogno* (June 29, 1931); my italics.

[28] Yves Congar, *Lay People in the Church*, (Maryland: Newman, 1956), 359. Both Maritain and Congar acknowledge the work of Pius X. But Congar credits Pius XI most of all because with him Catholic action took on a new tone and meaning, along three lines: "i. the insistence on the properly apostolic nature of Catholic action; ii. the generalized character of the appeal and the wide scope of the movement; iii. the pronounced aspect of a lay task, corresponding to the Christian's engagement in the more clearly recognized secular field," 362.

[29] Jacques Maritain, "Action and Contemplation" in *Scholasticism and Politics*, 177-78.

the lists for Catholic action. This spirit requires them to turn first toward wisdom and contemplation. This spirit is by definition an evangelical spirit. It does not ask us to train troops so as to execute orders at beck and call, disregarding or denying the 'interior man' and his conscience in order to act, to speak, to write or vote as the journal of a party prescribes; it asks us to prepare human persons to understand in the depths of their conscience the word of the Church herself and to discern the meaning of it." The second thing Maritain observes about Catholic action is that it will overcome the "*separatism* and *dualism* which have reigned too long in the Christian world." Modernity has fractured life such that "the Christian world obeyed two opposed rhythms, a Christian rhythm in matters of worship and religion, and, at least among better men, in things of the interior life; and a naturalistic rhythm in things of the profane life, the social, economic and political life, things too long abandoned to their proper carnal law."[30] An "organic and vital unity" must be restored.

The preparation for Catholic action requires prayer; it is inspired by love. But Maritain notes that "the most sincere love risks not performing any good, or even performing a great deal of evil, unless it passes through the Word and through Truth." The lay apostle must be intellectually formed. This is the work of Maritain's intellectual life: "An immense and difficult task here imposes itself upon Christian intelligence.... the effort must be freed from these myths and errors" of the day. The achievements of the modern age must be radically challenged, not to create some new synthesis, but to purify them through Catholic doctrine. "Let us not forget that the social, the economic, and the political, are intrinsically dependent on ethics, and that, *by this title,* for this formal reason, the social, the political, and the economic, are concerned with eternal life, and therefore with the pastoral ministry of the Church."[31] The Catholic mind must be illuminated by a doctrinal firmament and so relies upon theological wisdom. It was again in *Antimoderne* that he said: "By the Faith, intelligence

---

[30] Jacques Maritain, "Catholic Action" in *Scholasticism and Politics*, 190-91.

[31] Ibid., 192.

directly and infallibly receives the divine substance without which it dies of hunger; by the Faith it possesses the Truth."[32]

This philosophy formed by and consonant with the word of God will equip Catholic laity for the new evangelization. Vatican II speaks about the transformation of culture insofar as the Church "fosters and takes to herself, in so far as they are good, the abilities, the resources and customs of peoples. In so taking them to herself she purifies, strengthens and elevates them" (*Lumen Gentium* §13). The effect of her work is that "whatever good is found sown in the minds and hearts of men or in the rites and customs of peoples, these not only are preserved from destruction, but are purified, raised up, and perfected for the glory of God, the confusion of the devil, and the happiness of man" (*LG* §17).

Maritain's life and work is a prophetic witness to the vision of Vatican II on lay apostolate. What first emerged as Catholic action developed through the twentieth century under the influence of Catholic laymen such as Maritain to become the more specific notion of "lay apostolate" used in the documents of Vatican II. Whereas Catholic action places the laity directly under the guidance of clergy for the achievement of the goals of the hierarchy, lay apostolate pertains to the freedom of the laity as they perform their daily activities in the ordinary labors of the world. The new, central and vital role for lay people emerges from the original intention for the Council and from the deepest aspirations for reform and renewal. They provide the backdrop for the notion of lay apostolate put forward in the document *Decree on the Apostolate of Lay People* (*Apostolicum Actuositatem*). The nature of the apostolate and the variety of possibilities for its implementation are quite challenging. But the document provides very concrete and specific plans for education and training. Indeed, the document states that "a training, at once many-sided and complete, is indispensable if the apostolate is to attain its full efficacy" (§28). *Lumen Gentium* presents an affirmation of lay apostolate : "The laity, however, are given this special vocation: to make the Church present and fruitful in those places and circumstances where it is only through them that

---

[32] This is also from "Science moderne et la raison" in *Antimoderne*, 38: see note #25.

she can become the salt of the earth. Thus, every lay person, through those gifts given to him, is at once the witness and the living instrument of the mission of the Church itself 'according to the measure of Christ's bestowal' (Eph. 4: 7)" (§33). The laity are said to share in the kingly, priestly, and prophetic ministry of Christ. But the exercise of these ministries is primarily in the world, in secular activities, structures, and communities: "Even by their secular activity they must aid one another to greater holiness of life, so that the world may be filled with the spirit of Christ and may the more effectively attain its destiny in justice, in love and in peace. The laity enjoy a principle role in the universal fulfillment of this task. Therefore, by their competence in secular disciplines and by their activity, interiorly raised up by grace, let them work earnestly in order that created goods through human labor, technical skill and civil culture may serve the utility of all men according to the plan of the creator and the light of his word"(§36).

The scope of the work and apostolate is vast; *Gaudium et Spes* outlines and elaborates upon key areas such as family, culture, economics, politics, and international cooperation. A sound education is vital because the lay apostolate requires both faith and reason—one must know the matters of faith so that by a "well-formed Christian conscience" they may "see that the divine law is inscribed in the life of the earthly city." But also they must develop their own competence and training and make a unique contribution to the problems at hand—"Let the layman not imagine that his pastors are always such experts, that to every problem which arises, however complicated, they can readily give him a concrete solution, or even that such is their mission. Rather, enlightened by Christian wisdom and giving close attention to the teaching authority of the Church, let the layman take on his own distinctive role." What is demanded of the lay person is a "vital synthesis" of "humane, domestic, professional, social and technical enterprises" with religious values, under whose "supreme direction all things are harmonized unto God's glory" (§42). Therefore, in *Apostolicum Actuositatem*, the training of lay people is said to require "an integral human education" (#29). The foundation for this education must be "living by faith in the divine mystery of creation and redemption." The knowledge of revelation through scripture and tradition (*Dei Verbum*) must come first in the education for lay apostolate. And the training must include participation in the liturgy (*Sacrosanctum Concilium*). In addition to this spiritual formation, the lay people need to be educated in theology, ethics, and philosophy (*Apostolicum Actuositatem* #29). The vocation of the Catholic philosopher serves to benefit both the city of man and the city of God. The life and work of both Maritain and Wojtyła show to us that the vocation of the Catholic philosopher is defined by lay apostolate to culture.

4. The Essays in this Volume

The authors of these essays display the vital connection between faith and reason, and they explore many of the themes we have noted above. The essays were first presented at the 2005 annual meeting of the American Maritain Association on "The Spiritual Conditions of Renewal" held at the Catholic University of America. The conference was held in order to commemorate the 40 year anniversary of the conclusion of the Second Vatican Council (December 8, 1965) and the completion of Maritain's *The Peasant of the Garonne* (whose preface was written on December 31, 1965).

In Part I, "Spiritual Renewal and the Apostolate of Philosophy," the essays establish the importance of the spiritual context for understanding the vocation of Catholic philosophy. Richard Schenk, O.P., provides a masterful account of the significance of the recent council in his essay, "Vatican II and Jacques Maritain: Resources for the Future? Approaching the Fiftieth Anniversary of the Council." Rev. Daniel B. Gallagher, in his essay "'The Obedience of Faith' in *Dei Verbum*: A Pauline Phrase and its Implications for Catholic Intellectual Life," explains the precise meaning and significance of faith; it is crucial for any use of a formula about "faith and reason." As Pope Benedict XVI has said, we must refer to "ecclesiastical faith," the faith of the Church, as expounded by the documents of Vatican II. Sr. Prudence Allen, R.S.M., in "Mary and the Vocation of Philosophers," shows just what a profound notion is contained in Pope John Paul II's encouragement for philosophers to "philosophize in Mary."

Part II, the "Vocation of the Philosopher," gathers essays on the various aspects of the vocation of the philosopher as a thinker. The first essay, "Yves R. Simon: A Question of Calling," by Ralph Nelson, explores the life and thought of Yves R. Simon in order to come to a better understanding of the precise philosophical demands on the vocation.

This volume is dedicated in part to Ralph Nelson, a Catholic philosopher who was dedicated to the legacy of Maritain and Simon. He died in 2009; this essay is a excellent tribute to his contribution to the Association, his colleagues, and students. Michael Torre, in his "To Philosophize *for* the Faith: Jacques Maritain's Intellectual Vocation," argues that Maritain's whole work is better seen as that of lay theologian than of a philosopher only. In the essay by Cornelia A. Tsakiridou, "'Redeeming Modernism': Jacques Maritain and the Catholic Vocation," we come to a better understanding of Maritain's impatience with traditional Thomism and his pioneering efforts to engage modern philosophy, a task that Pope John Paul II would also take on as a Catholic philosopher. John G. Trapani, Jr., in "Gatekeeper of Small Mistakes: An Example of the Philosopher's 'Other' Vocation,'" explains how one may engage the intellectual currents of the day in a style that characterized Maritain.

In Part III, on "Pope John Paul II's *Fides et Ratio*," the first essay by Msgr. John F. Wippel, "*Fides et Ratio*'s call for a Renewal of Metaphysics and St. Thomas Aquinas," provides a masterful analysis of the text to show the manner in which Pope John Paul II renewed the Church's affirmation of the role of Thomas Aquinas in the intellectual life of the Church, and in philosophy specifically. Lawrence Dewan, O.P., in "St. Thomas and the Renewal of Metaphysics," considers why the full metaphysical range of philosophy must come to learn from Thomas Aquinas. Both of these essays are important for understanding the vocation of the Catholic philosopher according to both Maritain and Wojtyła. Both are committed to the restoration of the thought of Thomas Aquinas and the centrality of a realistic metaphysics of being. Finally, John F. Morris, in "*Fides et Ratio* and Pope John Paul II's Call to Catholic Philosophers: Orthodoxy and/or the Unity of Truth," explains that the classic understanding of the unity of truth continues to serve as a foundation for the life of reason.

Part IV, containing the concluding essays on "Contemporary Challenges," gives some indication of the lay apostolate of the Catholic philosopher at work. Edmund D. Pellegrino, professor and physician, makes the case against the secularist understanding of human nature and medicine in "Humanism and Bioethics: The Prophetic Voice of Jacques Maritain (1882-1973)." James Hanink turns to the crisis in the contemporary world concerning the family, in "Vocation, Family, and the Academy: *Signa Perscrutandi*." Both of these essays show the importance of Catholic action/lay apostolate where the temporal and spiritual intersect. In the final essay by Heather McAdam Erb, "Chosen for Glory: Aquinas on Vocation to the Supernatural," we conclude with an appreciation of man's highest vocation to supernatural life in heaven. It would thus be fitting to end with the justly famous motto of the Maritains, taken from their spiritual master Léon Bloy: "there is but one sadness, not to be a saint."

5. Conclusion: On the Paradoxes of Vocation

The meaning of the vocation of the Catholic philosopher has suffered the same confusion as the Church at large did after Vatican Council II. More often than not, the distinctive Catholic identity was lost. Many Catholics yearned to become contemporary and "up to date." But, in following the trends of the secular world, it was all too easy to vulgarize the *aggiornamento* of Popes John XXIII and Paul VI. The trends of the modern world diversified and threatened to fragment the common purpose of the Church and destroy the communion of faith. Maritain and Wojtyła, by holding fast to a Christocentric faith and the metaphysical realism of Thomistic philosophy, envisioned a renewal of Catholic life and purpose. Both men understood that Vatican II was above all about "progress in evangelical awareness and attitudes of heart rather than with defining dogmas." They understood the need for a more profound synthesis of faith and reason. They understood that the key to a renewal of Catholic philosophy would require a deeper unity of faith and life in the person, in the subjectivity of the philosopher. To bring into a vital synthesis, in heart and mind, life in all of its diversity and richness and the faith in its mystery of revealed truth would require conversion of heart and philosophical vigor. Such a vision of Catholic philosophy is hard to realize because of its paradoxical character. Much like Odysseus' bow, the paradoxes pose a formidable challenge. Catholic philosophy must be secular and religious; it is guided by both faith and reason. Catholic philosophers are free to develop an open philosophy and they will exhibit a pluralism of method and schools, as they also acknowledge the work of Thomas Aquinas. Finally, the vocation to Catholic philosophy will be intensely personal and free in its decisions and directions, but it must remain "ecclesial." As Pope Benedict XVI recently said at The Catholic University of America, "each and every aspect of your learning communities reverberates within the ecclesial life of faith. Only in faith can truth become incarnate and reason truly human, capable of directing the will along the path of freedom (cf. *Spe Salvi*, 23)."[33]

It is a vocation both secular and religious. The vocation to philosophy must be defined in terms of its secularity. Philosophy arises from the stirring of wonder within human experience and it is constituted by precise logical demands. The disciplines of philosophy, such as ethics, philosophy of nature, anthropology, and metaphysics emerge out of human practice and speculation. The vocation of philosophy is clearly differentiated from that of the theologian. Philosophy has its own discourse and its own methods. In the contemporary world, philosophy has its own profession, organization, and standards. But, as it follows its own course, as it is true to its Socratic roots and to its sapiential goal, philosophy cannot but reach out to theology. Grace provides moral steadiness and personal illumination. A higher wisdom provides a point of orientation and a promise of the perfection of its mission.

A second paradox defines Catholic philosophy, that of using both reason and faith. The Catholic philosopher discovers that each without the other is "impoverished and enfeebled." Reason pursues its own life and possesses its "autonomy," but it is stimulated from within to act ever more strongly as such. In the contemporary world, "the parrhesia of faith must be matched by the boldness of reason" (*Fides et Ratio* §48). The paradoxical assertion of both faith and reason, each calling for and demanding the specificity and strength of the other, is hard to grasp, let alone to practice. Rationalism and fideism are constant temptations.

Two more paradoxes face the Catholic philosopher today. It is an age of pluralism. There are many routes to the same goal; there are 1001 goals. The philosophy of St. Thomas is no longer the exclusive philosophy of choice for Catholic thinkers today. His presence in Catholic universities and departments of philosophy has dwindled, if not disappeared. The reading of the signs of the times has led many to study and embrace diverse currents of thought, from analytic philosophy to phenomenology. And yet, if a philosopher responds to

---

[33] Benedict XVI, "Address to Catholic College Presidents" (Washington, D.C.: April 17, 2008).

the inner need for a philosophy "consonant with the Word of God," one inevitably returns to Thomas Aquinas. One understands the reason why Thomas Aquinas receives the continual endorsement of the Church. A Catholic philosopher along the lines of Wojtyła and Maritain today will be Thomistic in spirit and in appreciation, if not in fact. Thomism is systematic, but not a system; it is open to further development and engagement with truth.[34] Aquinas represents the paradox of Catholic philosophy at its most fundamental level: "a reconciliation between the secularity of the world and the radicality of the Gospel" (*Fides et Ratio* §43).

Catholic philosophy serves the essential aim of the Church—evangelization. But it does so in its own way: not by proselytism, not by serving up a crypto-theology, but by the authentic search for truth in everyday life and in all secular venues of truth seeking. Pope John Paul II refers to these venues as the "Areopogai of culture."[35] Philosophy is and must be a free response and it is therefore under the sign of personal freedom. And yet the intensely personal decision to set out on the path of philosophy bears an ecclesial orientation; as Pope Benedict XVI said, "the ecclesial life of faith" is to reverberate in our life and work. The words of the prophet Isaiah (55:10-11) ring true: "as the rain and snow come down from heaven, and return no more thither, but soak the earth, and water it, and make it spring, and give seed to the sower, and bread to the eater: so shall my word be which shall go forth from my mouth: it shall not return to me void, but it shall do whatsoever I please, and shall prosper in the things for which I sent it."

Maritain explained that the spiritual and supernatural vocation and the temporal and secular vocation involve the same work; the object of

---

[34] See Maritain, *The Peasant*, 208-10; Josef Pieper, *The Silence of St Thomas* (South Bend, Indiana: St. Augustine Press, 1999); and Ralph M. McInerny, *Thomism in an Age of Renewal* (Notre Dame: University of Notre Dame, 1968).

[35] "The modern world reflects the situation of the Areopagus of Athens, where Saint Paul spoke. Today there are many 'areopagi', and very different ones: these are the vast sectors of contemporary civilization and culture, of politics and economics. The more the West is becoming estranged from its Christian roots, the more it is becoming missionary territory, taking the form of many different 'areopagi'." *Tertio Millennio Adveniente* §57; cf. *Redeemer of Man*, §33; *Mission of the Redeemer*, §37.

work is the temporal vocation; whereas the manner or mode of work is the spiritual vocation. If a Catholic philosopher lives from Christ that should change the manner or mode or the spirit in which philosophy is done. Maritain refers to the "radiance of the gospel shining through the daily task itself."[36] Vatican II called for an end to the duality of faith and life, a great error of our day. Maritain insists upon the concrete unity of the person: vocation in some way must ultimately be one. He says of the temporal and spiritual callings, as a philosopher and as a Catholic, that "the two vocations are distinct, they are not separate." For one is "not a laborer of the world with a certain portion of his being, and a member of the church with another portion." The Catholic philosopher also must be "a member of the Church who is a laborer of the world, sent to the land of the things which are Caesar's." A vocation is a call to mission. Sent into the "land of Caesar," or into the realm of the temporal and secular, the "modern world," a Catholic philosopher is a citizen of two cities: a pilgrim in the one, seeking his true home in the other.

We must conclude with that oft-quoted passage from Maritain's *Notebooks* for a parting thought about the vocation of the Catholic philosopher. May we always cherish Maritain's deep sense of mission, combined with his stubborn sense of independence!

> What am I, I asked myself then. A professor? I think not; I taught by necessity. A writer? Perhaps. A philosopher? I hope so. But also a kind of romantic of justice too prompt to imagine to himself, at each combat entered into, that justice and truth will have their day among men. And also perhaps a kind of spring-finder who presses his ear to the ground in order to hear the sound of hidden springs, and of invisible germinations. And also perhaps, like every Christian, despite and in the midst of the miseries and the failures and all the graces betrayed of which I am becoming conscious in the evening of my life, a beggar of Heaven disguised as a man of the world, a kind of secret agent of

[36] Jacques Maritain, *The Peasant*, 208.

the King of Kings in the territories of the prince of this world, taking his risks like Kipling's cat, who walked by himself.[37]

John P. Hittinger,
Feast of the Annunciation, 2011:
"Ecce ancilla Domini: fiat mihi secundum verbum tuum." Lk. 1:38

---

[37] Jacques Maritain, *Notebooks* (Notre Dame, Indiana: University of Notre Dame Press, 1984), Preface. The reference is to Rudyard Kipling, "The Cat that Walked by Himself," in *Just So Stories* (1902).

PART I

Spiritual Renewal and the Apostolate of Philosophy

Vatican II and Jacques Maritain: Resources for the Future? Approaching the Fiftieth Anniversary of the Council[1]

Richard Schenk, O.P.

Let us seek with the desire to find, and find with the desire to seek still more.

—*Saint Augustine*

On the last day of the Second Vatican Council, December 8, 1965, as part of the council's final pageantry and symbolic conclusion, messages were addressed by Pope Paul VI and the bishops to several groups representative of those segments of the cultural world that the council most hoped to engage. Jacques Maritain was asked to accept the message for "thinkers and academics" ("les hommes de la pensée et de la science"). Not only did Maritain enjoy the personal admiration and support of Paul, not only had Maritain influenced the council in matters such as religious liberty and human rights, but he represented the kind of echo that the council fathers were hoping to elicit from academics and other intellectuals. At the heart of the council's message was the maxim ascribed to Augustine: "Let us seek with the desire to find, and find with the desire to seek still more."[2] The message combined moments of humility and criticism, admitting that the Church was still searching for her own way forward, but also

---

[1] This essay also appears in *Logos: A Journal of Catholic Thought and Culture*, 13.1 (Winter 2010), 79-106.

[2] *Acta Apostolicae Sedis* (LVIII 1966), 10–11. Cf. Augustine, *De Trinitate* IX 1: "Sic ergo quaeramus tamquam inventuri; et sic inveniamus, tamquam quaesituri." As Brian Daley has pointed out, a similar notion is found near the end of the first chapter of Anselm's *Proslogion*: "Quaeram te desiderando, desiderem quaerendo. Inveniam amando, amem inveniendo." The text of the message has been translated into English by Richard Lemp and John P. Hittinger in Timothy Fuller and John P. Hittinger, *Reassessing the Liberal State: Reading Maritain's Man and the State* (Washington, D.C.: American Maritain Association, 2001), 245.

expressing the need for the intellectual world to open its eyes to the light of faith. "Do not forget that, if thinking is something great, it is first a duty. Woe to him who voluntarily closes his eyes to the light. Thinking is also a responsibility, so woe to those who darken the spirit by the thousand tricks which degrade it, make it proud, deceive and deform it."[3]

That mix of hope and warning belonged to what arguably was best about the council. This article argues that where the council and its reception in the postconciliar Church were the weakest, it was caused by a failure to achieve this studied ambivalence, due to an exaggeration and isolation of the hopes for or the suspicions about our times.[4] To ask what Maritain and the council can contribute today to the intellectual and spiritual conditions for renewal is to remember where they got that mix right and to accept today together with Maritain's legacy this conciliar commission to engage the world with both hope and critique.

Admittedly, there are reasons prima facie for skepticism that the search for a renewal of Church or society could profit by the study either of Vatican II or of Maritain, much less of the two in tandem. Haven't these mines been exhausted long ago? Is there anything we could conceivably "desire to find" in them that would intensify "the desire to seek still more"? Were they even in their heyday perhaps more a source of impoverishment than enrichment? Do we need to choose between the spirit of the council and that Garonne Valley peasant who was so dismissive of novel postconciliar developments? All of these reasons for doubting the potential for renewal to be found in Maritain *and* the council have less to do with individual doctrines than with fundamental perspectives and broader decisions about the hermeneutics of genuine interpretation. As Maritain himself put it in *The Peasant of the Garonne*, the decisive questions here have less to do

---

[3] See Timothy Fuller and John P. Hittinger, *Reassessing the Liberal State*, 245.

[4] For a more detailed account cf. Richard Schenk, "*Officium signa temporum perscrutandi.* New Encounters of Gospel and Culture in the Context of the New Evangelisation," in *Scrutinizing the Signs of the Times in Light of the Gospel*, ed. Johan Verstraeten, *Bibliotheca Ephemeridum Theologicarum Lovaniensium*, CCVIII (Leuven: University Press and Leuven/Paris/Dudley, Peeters, 2007), 167–203.

with "particular clarifications" than with "general approach."[5] Correspondingly, this article deals with some of these necessarily broader issues of our "general approach": first, as regards the council; then, as regards Maritain; both, in the context of the question about our potential today to draw upon these two legacies in order to make a contribution to renewal.

I. THE SECOND VATICAN COUNCIL

As is widely accepted, we no longer can speak "innocently" of the council; innocent, that is, of our views of the postconciliar development and of our own designs to move beyond it. The attempt to unfold so complex a situation in the short space of an article is a task impossible to fulfill well and yet even more impossible to neglect altogether. One aid is provided in this case by John Henry Cardinal Newman's third note of genuine Church development, the power of assimilation, which Newman positions between isolation on the one hand (the inability to assimilate what had originated elsewhere) and, on the other hand, the loss of identity and unity (being assimilated to what must remain alien to one's genuine identity).[6] Another aid is provided by Maritain's largely non-polemical use of the categories of Right and Left, the characteristics of which I will presume here; the central difference consisted for Maritain in the answer to the question of whether change is sought over the retention or restoration of the present or past status quo.[7] Maritain distinguished and then reunited a political and a temperamental meaning of Right and Left. I review here two of the leading interpretations of the council by those on the political Left and two by those on the political Right, together with postconciliar developments, in order to argue that the genuine renewal of the council and philosophy demands our moving *per modum remotionis*

---

[5] Jacques Maritain, *The Peasant of the Garonne* (Toronto: Macmillan, 1968), 64.

[6] John Henry Newman, *An Essay on the Development of Christian Doctrine* (Garden City, New York: Image/Doubleday, 1960).

[7] Maritain, *The Peasant of Garonne*, 31, drawing on his *Letter on Independence* from 1935, cited here according to Jacques Maritain, *Integral Humanism, Freedom in the Modern World*, and *A Letter on Independence*, Collected Works 11 (Notre Dame, Indiana: University of Notre Dame, 1996), 119–39, esp. 131.

beyond all four of these well-known interpretations. We need to develop the suggestions already made by considering a fifth reading. The two interpretations on the political Left share with one another the goal of departing from many of the concrete forms and formulations of earlier Catholicism, whereas the two interpretations on the political Right seek chiefly to retain and/or retrieve select shapes of the older tradition. Let us begin with the positions most devoted to change.

1. Assimilated Neo-Modern Theology

On the political Left there are especially older proponents (who surprisingly often were temperamentally of the Right),[8] insisting upon what was arguably the majority view at many Catholic faculties in the first two decades of the postconciliar era: that the only prophetically obligatory voice of the council, despite nonobligatory voices of "conservative opposition," called the Church to assimilate herself to the Enlightenment legacy in secular culture as regards all three *munera ecclesiae*: in doctrine, with a greater stress on the nonbinding dimensions of the doctrinal tradition and the actual magisterium; in prayer, with a substitution of social service and community building for the direct veneration of God;[9] and in governance, in an approximation of Catholic social thought to the late Enlightenment hopes for the universal progress of a prosperity driven by the expansion of technology. This movement saw the council as a mandate to seek partnership in global progress and a global ethic through the progressive relativization of specifically Catholic belief and practice.[10]

---

[8] The impact of a now familiar brand of "intolerant liberalism" upon the theology faculties of the postconciliar period often seemed to confirm Maritain's formula: "There are no more terrible revolutions than revolutions of the Left made by temperaments of the Right." Maritain, *Integral Humanism*, 132.

[9] The classical formulation was provided by Karl Rahner in the final year of the council: "Über die Einheit von Nächstenliebe und Gottesliebe," first in *Geist und Leben* 38 (1965), 168–85, then immediately as "Über die Einheit von Nächsten- und Gottesliebe," in: Rahner, *Schriften zur Theologie. Bd. 6: Neuere Schriften* (Einsiedeln: Benziger, 1965).

[10] The late modern concern for universal justice has often been in tension with postmodernization in the theology of religions. Enthusiastic proponents of the pluralistic theology of religions, a phenomenon of postmodern theology,

Because of the conviction that the Enlightenment agenda of modern society did ensure progress, this interpretation's stance toward secular politics was more progressive than revolutionary.[11] This interpretation of the Left was propagated in those first two decades typically by the "intolerant liberal," politically on the Left but temperamentally of the Right. In the philosophical world, this reading found its parallel and support in the older works of Jürgen Habermas during that phase when thinkers of one stripe, largely oblivious to the traditionalism behind

---

have criticized the global ethic program of Hans Küng for its unwillingness to be thoroughly pluralistic in its judgment of religions; cf. P. F. Knitter, "Nochmals die Absolutheitsfrage," *Evangelische Theologie*, 49 (1989): 505–16; Knitter, "Interreligious Dialogue: What? Why? How?," in L. Swidler et al., ed., *Death or Dialogue?*, 19–44; Knitter: "Suche nach Einheit in Unterschiedenheit. Jüngste Ansichten zum Religiösen Pluralismus," *Dialog der Religionen* I (1991): 230–37; and the literature noted by Richard Schenk, "Zwischen *Projekt Weltethos* und *The Clash of Civilizations*. Religioese Identitaet im Zeitalter der Globalisierung," in *Nationale und kulturelle Identität im Zeitalter der Globalisierung*, ed. A. Rauscher (Berlin: Duncker & Humblot, 2006): 111–24; Schenk, "Debatable Ambiguity: Paradigms of Truth as a Measure of the Differences among Christian Theologies of Religion," in *Jahrbuch für Philosophie des Forschungsinstituts für Philosophie Hannover*, vol. 11, ed. R. Schenk, V. Hoesle, and P. Koslowski (Vienna: Passagen, 2000): 121–51. Whatever might be the best evaluation of Küng's *Weltethos* vis-à-vis his theology of religions, there is no reason to doubt in principle the possible legitimacy of hybrid forms of thought in addressing the very mixed reality of religious thought and practice.

[11] For this reason, key elements of this interpretation, such as the dominant reading of the conscience prior to *Veritatis Splendor*, could be indifferent to geopolitical issues. While no one dreamt of answering the question as to the morality of South African apartheid or South American oligarchy by posing the counter-question as to the good intentions of its proponents and practitioners, that is what is most telling of all: the political paradigm was understated in the theory of conscience dominant in the first postconciliar decades. The rise of political theology did much to end the Rahnerian era; however, this does not indicate that the dominant theologies of those first decades after the council had been completely disinterested in political advocacy, but merely that theologies inclined in this way had assumed that their advocacy would be effectively advanced by the ongoing dynamic of the Enlightenment project, the dialectic of which went largely unnoticed. The strategy was chiefly to join that project, not to challenge it.

their shared "rationality," still made up the majority of members in the clubs of ideal communication. Transformed directly into a theological interpretation, this style of vision often views the last twenty-five years of postconciliar development (1985–2010) as frustrating the genuine goals of the council and their consistent interpretation in the mold of the majority trends in the theology of the 1960s and '70s. This optimistic position toward the Enlightenment legacy in the council and its immediate postconciliar reception implied the robust rejection of Maritain's legacy, viewed chiefly as a criticism of Cartesian modernism and as an advocate of conciliar hopes for the renewal of the direct veneration of God inside and outside the liturgy.[12] Not Vatican II, considered now as irretrievably highjacked, but only a prospective Vatican III is seen here as a potential basis for renewal, which would consist in shoring up the disintegrating Enlightenment and then assimilating the Church to it.

2. Assimilated Postmodern Theology

Further removed from the memory of the world wars, but also following the growing insight into the limitation of natural resources and the limited possibilities of universal consumerism, there is on the political Left a second and younger interpretation of the council's dynamics. Its proponents are temperamentally to the left of their predecessors, though their desire for institutional change is now restricted even more exclusively to the Church. Their program for change in the realm of social justice is arguably the weakest among the four interpretations to be discussed here; and this qualifies their political Leftism: it is political chiefly with reference to the Church, especially with regard to any universal or perennial teachings in faith and morals. This reading shares with its predecessor much the same narrative of the council's secular redefinition of the *munera ecclesiae*. While even the older interpretation had more suggestions on how to change the Church than on how to change society, this younger postmodern theology, unlike its late-modern predecessor, is skeptical about society's own potential for generating universal progress, world-

[12] Cf. the interpretation of Maritain in Gerald A. McCool, *The Neo-Thomists* (Milwaukee: Marquette University, 1994).

wide prosperity, or justice for all.[13] The theology of postmodern assimilation sees more clearly than the earlier proponents of neomodernist assimilation that the secular society to which it seeks to conform itself had changed radically within a decade after the council. In the philosophical world, this second interpretation has its parallel and support in the vision of postmodernity articulated by Richard Rorty and J. F. Lyotard. At its worst, chauvinistic, at its best, resignative, this branch of postmodern theology calls in effect for the accommodation of faith to the secular culture of the affluent West (in its less militant forms), to which Christian theology should assimilate itself and for which it should provide assurance and confirmation. As society has lost the metanarrative of progress, it, too, is no longer a theology of those who clamor for international justice. It sees the council itself and the first twenty years of its reception *materialiter* as hopelessly marked by the delusional optimism in technological progress, a brief final glow of the last embers of a dying Enlightenment. What it sees as the only abiding message of the council is the formal side of *aggiornamento*, the alleged call of the council to assimilate itself to the spirit of its time, whatever the time, today the time of postmodern regionalism. In this interpretation, the texts of the council belong, together with the likes of Maritain, largely to the past and provide at best a picture of what not to seek to become in our inevitably fragmented future.

3. Unassimilated, Metaphysically Grounded Theology

There is a standard interpretation on the Right (both politically and temperamentally), understandably eager to safeguard the council itself, the affirmation of which is indeed necessary for the affirmation of any vital sense of ecclesial magisterium. This stance recognizes the deficiencies of the first two decades of postconciliar theology in accommodating the *munera ecclesiae* so closely to secular society. Yet, ignoring much of the historical data, worked out largely by the studies occasioned by the fortieth anniversary of the council, it interprets the

---

[13] Cf. Lieven Boeve, "*Gaudium et spes* and the Crisis of Modernity: The End of Dialogue with the World?" in *Vatican II and its Legacy*, ed. M. Lamberigts et al. (Leuven: University Press and Peeters, 2002), 82–94; Boeve, *Interrupting Tradition: An Essay on Christian Faith in a Postmodern Context* (Louvain: Peeters and Eerdmans, 2003).

council itself benevolently but almost exclusively in terms of its continuity with the past, while attributing most innovative aspects to its postconciliar misunderstanding and misinterpretation.[14] There has been more understanding for Maritain as metaphysician and as *The Peasant of the Garonne* in this interpretation than in any of the other three views, but it glosses the fact that Maritain's criticism of certain trends, formulated already in the early months of 1966, could hardly have known the scope and depth of postconciliar development. As I argue later, Maritain's praise and critique of postconciliar developments have to do with forces evident at the council itself, even though Maritain does not say so explicitly. This interpretation, intending to embrace something like the maxim of the young Newman—"speak gently of thy sister's fall" —finds itself today in a quandary as to how to develop the council for future renewal; and even Maritain seems to offer little here outside a nostalgic citation of the past. The relative novelty of the council and its necessity for any future renewal is most often left underdeveloped here.

4. Unassimilated Postmetaphysical, Postmodern Theology

Highly critical of Maritain the metaphysician and of Maritain the proponent of human rights and religious liberty, a younger

---

[14] One could glean this reading from isolated essays even of the usually even-handed and circumspect Avery Cardinal Dulles, e.g. in his otherwise helpful article, "True and False Reform," in *First Things* 135 (August/September 2003): 14–19, where ill-conceived developments are traced back to postconciliar interpretations of the council, but never explicitly to texts or debates of the council itself. And yet, reading more widely in the Cardinal's reflections, we find the complementary admission: "The council did ... adopt a rhetoric of consensus, service, openness to change and inclusiveness. But that rhetoric did little to prepare people for cases in which consensus could not be reached, or in which people did not want to hear what the church was obliged to preach, or in which ecclesiastical institutions are not subject to change, or in which inclusion would destroy the necessary unity of the flock of Christ. By their tone, if not their content, the council documents exuded optimism and perhaps raised unrealistic expectations. The calls for submission and compliance were so muted that readers could easily overlook them. The difficulty was increased by the condition of Western culture in the years when the council was being received." Avery Cardinal Dulles, "Vatican II, Substantive Teaching," in *America* 188, no. 11 (March 31, 2003).

interpretation on the political (but not the temperamental) Right describes itself as postmodern, but embodies more of the *Antimoderne* than its postmodern cousin on the institutional Left. Despite their self-assigned label of radical orthodoxy, the proponents of this interpretation deviate predictably not only from Maritain's sketch of the temperamental Right, which he had described as more concerned with order than with justice; but, more crucially, the proponents of non-assimilated postmodern theology often also harbor more intense political ambitions to reverse the injustices of neoliberalism than their postmodern cousins on the Left:[15] an example of where the terminology has become "confounded," as Maritain had admitted it would.[16] Both branches of postmodern theory share the rejection of the Enlightenment myths of progress and universality, but the would-be orthodox postmoderns show a more consistent concern for faith-based political advocacy, aimed at a reawakening of Christendom. Although this pathos for political reform does not always carry over to the realm of individual moral theory, it owes much to the Calvinist revival of the later Karl Barth.[17]

Postmodern orthodoxy emphasizes the corruption of human nature, reason, and will, but allows God to begin again by a new revelation and

---

[15] Cf. Stanley Rosen, "Rorty and Systematic Philosophy," in Rosen, *The Ancients and Moderns: Rethinking Modernity* (New Haven/London: Yale University, 1989), 175–88. It is in good part Lieven Boeve's continued dependence upon positions such as Rorty's that makes his otherwise attractive claim to have transcended not only the modern/antimodern alternatives, but also the modern/postmodern ones, difficult to accept: cf. Lieven Boeve, "Beyond the Modern and Antimodern Dilemma: Theological Method in a Postmodern Theological Context," in *Scrutinizing the Signs of the Times in Light of the Gospel*, ed. Johan Verstraeten (Louvain: Peeters, 2007), 150–66, esp. 165.

[16] Maritain, *A Letter on Independence*. For the reasons Maritain offers there, it is also a justified expectation that the political impact of this brand of Anglo-Catholic communitarianism will confirm his observation that "there are no more feeble governments than governments of the Right led by temperaments of the Left."

[17] Cf. James H. Olthuis and James K. A. Smith, eds., *Radical Orthodoxy and the Reformed Tradition* (Grand Rapids, Michigan: Baker, 2005), and the foreword by John Milbank to James K. A. Smith, *Introducing Radical Orthodoxy, Mapping a Post-Secular Theology* (Grand Rapids, Michigan: Baker, 2004).

the community of believers, distinct from nonbelieving society; in this context, the position embraces a moment of communitarianism, even sectarianism. While it finds its positive philosophical resources in thinkers like Alasdair MacIntyre and Stanley Hauerwas, it seeks when dealing with the sources of postmodern nihilism to follow roughly the pattern once modeled by Barth in his appropriation of Ludwig Feuerbach: as Barth suggested that Feuerbach's "projection critique" had unmasked the egotism of all religions, but had not called into serious question the possibility of a "religionless faith," or one that at least yearned to be such, so, too, writers such as Laurence Paul Hemming have sought to portray Heidegger's critique of the Christian God and the spiritually gifted human person as a helpful critique of the metaphysical God and the (allegedly) autonomous-Pelagian subject à la Maritain.[18] This interpretation, rejecting as well the advocacy of human rights by Maritain and the council, sees both as already far too accommodating to the Enlightenment project.[19] Unlike the previous

---

[18] Laurence Paul Hemming, *Heidegger's Atheism: The Refusal of a Theological Voice* (Notre Dame: University of Notre Dame, 2002); and Hemming, "Nihilism, Heidegger and the Grounds of Redemption," in, *Radical Orthodoxy*, eds. John Milbank, Catherine Pickstock, and Graham Ward (London: Routledge, 1999/2003), 91–108; and Hemming, "In Matters of Truth: Heidegger and Aquinas," in *Contemplating Aquinas: On the Varieties of Interpretation*, ed. Fergus Kerr (London: SCM Press, 2003), 85–104.

[19] Cf. Tracey Rowland, *Culture and the Thomist Tradition After Vatican II* (London: Routledge, 2003), where Maritain is seen as a principal voice within "Whig Thomism," particularly in his "efforts to reconcile Thomistic natural law with the Liberal natural right doctrine and his endorsement of the natural rights in the United Nations' *Declaration on Human Rights* in 1948" (16). Following Alasdair MacIntyre (148 et passim), Rowland sees Maritain's efforts in this regard as a failure and the chief cause to be named for the tragic weakness of the understanding of culture in *Gaudium et Spes*, which "bear(s) witness to Maritain's general political project of *rapprochement* with the Liberal-humanist tradition" (22; for the centrality to the argument of the book of identifying this alleged mistake cf. 11). This example of radical orthodoxy is unable to differentiate "the affirmation of the secular in Rahner and Maritain" (30–32), despite its stereotype dismissal of Maritain as a representative of "implicit extrinsicism" (of which Rahner could hardly be accused) and despite its claim to pay constant attention to the provenance of thinkers (need one compare their respective debts—and those of Anglo-

interpretation on the Right, it sees the first twenty years of postconciliar development as the direct fruit and the genuine, if unfortunate, continuation of the council itself. Of all four interpretations, it is the most critical of the council. De facto, its proponents have in common with the interpretations on the Left the global rejection of Maritain, joining their postmodern cousins in spurning metaphysics and the language of universal rights.[20] As a whole, they gloss over what they might have claimed as common ground with Maritain: the concern for the revival of Christendom and the renewal of Christian worship,[21] the insight into the irreligious and

---

Catholic communitarians—to Hegel?). One need only recall the peasant's critique of Teilhard to suggest the distance between Maritain and Rahner in their evaluations of the council. For Rahner's postconciliar stance of the 1970s toward the relationship of his own evolutive worldview to Teilhard's evolutionary programmatic cf. *Grundkurs des Glaubens* (Sämtliche Werke 26, Zürich/Düsseldorf/Freiburg: Benziger/Herder, 1999), 176: "Wir suchen Theoreme zu vermeiden, die von Teilhard de Chardin her geläufig sind. Trefffen wir uns mit ihm, ist es gut, und wir brauchen das nicht absichtlich zu vermeiden." No other authors are named here as sources of or parallels to this central *Motiv* of Rahner's thought.

[20] Tracey Rowland's neglect of Joseph Ratzinger's (resp. Benedict XVI's) concern for human rights discourse makes even her newer and in many ways kinder view of *Gaudium et Spes* and its reception more difficult to accept; cf. Tracey Rowland, *Ratzinger's Faith: The Theology of Pope Benedict XVI* (Oxford: Oxford University Press, 2008), especially 30–47; for Rowland on Boeve cf. 41, 44, 144ff; and again on Maritain as the naive "flagship of neo-Thomism," "Natural Law: Neo-Thomism to Nuptial Mysticism," *Communio: International Catholic Review* 35 (Fall 2008): 374–96.

[21] For a plausible theory of how to complement Maritain's concern for universal human rights with MacIntyre's Christian communitarianism, cf. Deborah Wallace on Jacques Maritain, and Alasdair MacIntyre, "The Person, the Common Good and Human Rights," in Brendan Sweetman, ed., *The Failure of Modernism: The Cartesian Legacy and Contemporary Pluralism* (Washington, D.C.: American Maritain Association, 1999), 127–40. A more extreme position, claiming Maritain as a communitarian, is offered by Michael Moreland, "Jacques Maritain, Thomism, and the Liberal-Communitarian Debate," in Sweetman, *The Failure of Modernism*, 141–54. For an opposing view cf. John Milbank's gentle but firm dismissal of Maritain for (just) missing the Blondelian denial of secularism and exerting a pernicious influence on Y.

pernicious character of bourgeois liberalism,[22] and the dismissal of the modern project in the tradition of Descartes and Kant along with the far-reaching, if selective, retrieval of premodern wisdom.

5. A Fifth Interpretation: The Theology of Critical Engagement

Prescriptive as well as descriptive in intention, none of these four well-known readings of recent Church history is without merit, and each of them would deserve its own conference: the zeal for justice in the social action of the first; the "disillusioned" realism of the second; the dedication of the third to the Church and to human rationality; the pious impatience and the awareness of initial human finitude in the fourth. Three of the four see the first twenty years after the council as its genuine development, although only one of them desires to perpetuate its concrete agenda. Two of the four miss the power of assimilation by excess, the other two by defect. All four, however, share a common feature—while knowing of the debates at the council between majority and minority positions, they see its genuine interpretation and its legitimate postconciliar development in, at most, one of the opposed forces. An alternative to all of these interpretations would have to integrate much of their individual strengths, even while avoiding their particular weaknesses, striving to the greatest degree possible, as Maritain put it, "to be neither [merely] of the Right nor of the Left" in a political sense,[23] or, more concretely:

> In the application required by the present state of things, a sane Christian politics (I mean inspired by Christian principles

---

Congar et al., *Theology and Social Theory: Beyond Secular Reason* (Oxford: Blackwell, 1990/2004), 223ff.

[22] Jacques Maritain, *The Person and the Common Good* (New York: Scribner's, 1947), 87ff.

[23] Maritain, *A Letter on Independence*, 132ff.; *The Peasant of the Garonne*, 31–38, especially 32ff. The title of the *Letter* refers to independence from both political extremes. To the options of being Right, Left, neutral to both, or combining both, Maritain adds a fifth variant in the conclusion to his *On the Church of Christ* (Notre Dame: University of Notre Dame, 1973), 240: "I have an idea that this book will displease everybody, I mean all those who today have taken position 'on the right' or 'on the left.' (And this does not displease me, although I certainly did not have this intention in writing it.)"

> but appealing to all non-Christians who would find it just and humane) would doubtless appear to go very far to the Left as regards certain technical solutions, in appreciation of the concrete movement of history and the need for the transformation of the present economic system—all the while having absolutely original positions and proceeding in the spiritual and moral order from principles very different from the conceptions of the world and of life, of the family, and of the city that are held in honor by the various parties of the Left.[24]

A fifth interpretation, though articulated soon after the council, has gained wider currency only in the last twenty-five years (1985–2010) of the nearly fifty years since the beginning of the council; but it seems to offer the interpretation of recent history most capable of the synthetic task that Maritain was calling for. This theology of critical engagement takes the two sides of the debates at the council as defining together the parameters of ideal postconciliar faith: an expansion into religious and societal discourse beyond the narrow boundaries of the Church, but in critical conversation with these non-Catholic worlds. It seeks to avoid both the isolation and the assimilation of Catholicism. Like all but the third interpretation, this position sees the immediately post-conciliar trends rooted in the council itself. Like the two postmodern trends, it sees the folly of hoping for the self-perfecting of the *saeculum*. It shares with the interpretations of the Left the desire to engage the non-Catholic world of its time in its "gaudium et spes," but it shares with the analysis of the Right the greater sensitivity to the "luctus et angor" of our day.

This fifth option, prepared in the conciliar and immediately postconciliar writings of Karol Wojtyła and Joseph Ratzinger (despite the seemingly opposite temperaments of the authors), suggests a way for post-Rahnerian theology to be in dialogue with the world without "kneeling before it," to borrow a phrase from the Garonne valley. Rejecting conformity to both secularism and sectarianism, avoiding the extremes of left and right that Maritain had described in archetypes as the lemming-like sheep of Rabelais's Panurge and the Manichean Ruminators of the Covenant, the fifth reading sought to embrace the

---

[24] Maritain, *A Letter on Independence*, 133.

legacy of the council as pointing the way toward promoting dialogue with secular forces, with philosophies of non-Christian provenance, and with non-Christian religions, even while affirming the eschatological importance of Christ and our faith in him: *Fides et Ratio*, *Veritatis Splendor*, interreligious dialogue within and because of the horizon of *Dominus Jesus*.[25] This understanding of the council's commission suggests the need to correct and complement the reasoning of the speculative and practical intellect as it is given prior to faith, but not a need to start all over again by bracketing the world outside the Christian tradition; indeed, it called upon theologians to profit from the contributions of philosophical and historical disciplines. It finds its philosophical parallel and support in thinkers such as Robert Spaemann, who confronts many of the more problematic conclusions of our age with the ordinary moral intuitions that perdure beneath them.[26] As in what has been at least the mainstream of Catholic faith, the human intellect appears here wounded, not hopelessly corrupted. Because of these remnants of health, the council deemed it right to engage the non-Catholic world, to listen to its voice for more than just an admission of contemporary depravity and bankruptcy, for more than just a confession of the complete loss of metaphysics and the natural law. But because of human woundedness, the council was also right to caution against self-assimilation to the age or ultimate reliance upon it. According to this interpretation, the council must be read today in continuity with both sides of its debates, one of which, in relative isolation, dominated its theological and pastoral reception in the first two decades after its conclusion, before in the last twenty years the two currents could begin to be brought back together again in greater continuity with the council's historical reality and textual legacy.

The council must be read today again as what it most closely was, taking as prescriptive the duality often merely described in it, and

---

[25] Cf. Maritain, *The Peasant of the Garonne*, 36, using the two images as "Archetypes" of the extremes on the Left and the Right; cf. F. Rabelais, *Gargantua et Pantagruel* IV (resp. *Pantagruel* III), 6–8.

[26] Cf. Richard Schenk, "The Ethics of Robert Spaemann in the Context of Recent Philosophy," in Brian J. Shanley, ed., *One Hundred Years of Philosophy* (Washington, D.C.: Catholic University of America, 2001), 156–68.

working out by debate a dual hermeneutic of modernity: conjoining a hermeneutic of making sense of the grand projects of modernity to a hermeneutic of harboring suspicion about them. It is reminiscent of Kant's dictum that concepts without experience are empty; and experience without concepts, blind. Without the innovative call to engage the concrete, contingent world of our time, the council would have been empty of forces for renewal. Lacking continuity with the doctrinal resources of its past, the council would have been too blind to offer orientation and support to its own age. The only historically adequate and pastorally responsible reading of the council demands attention to the two sets of voices in the debates and the final texts of the council, a dual hermeneutic that joins engagement to criticality in the approach to our times, a disciplined ambivalence that calls for both retrieval and suspicion of the modern and premodern projects in searching for the renewal of a humane world. A reading that isolates one or the other voice of the council will necessarily be either blind (not knowing how to provide orientation to our times) or empty (not knowing how the times concretize, individuate, and make urgent the faith: *caritas Christi urget nos*).

In one of his several published reflections on *Gaudium et Spes* in the mid- and late-sixties, the not-yet forty-year-old Professor Joseph Ratzinger portrayed the Pastoral Constitution as articulating the theological anthropology necessary not only for education, but for a genuinely Christian engagement of culture.[27] In its interpretation of a technological world, the council is shown here as having explicated an aspect of the Church's mission both novel and important. In Ratzinger's reading of 1966, the council also had addressed here a novel ambivalence of the human situation in our day. Despite accurately

[27] Joseph Ratzinger, "Das Menschenbild des Konzils in seiner Bedeutung für die Bildung," in Kulturbeirat beim Zentralkomittee der deutschen Katholiken, ed., *Christliche Erziehung nach dem Konzil: Berichte und Dokumentation* (Cologne: J. P. Bechem, 1967), 33–65. Less than five months after the close of the council, Ratzinger, then professor of dogmatics and the history of dogma at the Catholic theology faculty in Tübingen and just returned from the council, took up here the question of the significance of the council's understanding of the human being (i.e., its theological anthropology) for education (April 23, 1966 at Bad Honnef).

perceiving and criticizing the self-delusion that often accompanies contemporary talk of the historical character of humanity and the new humanism of our own age, the council also acknowledged our characteristically modern need and opportunity to develop global responsibility and solidarity as the necessary but not sufficient condition of fulfilling the abiding vocation of full humanity. As Ratzinger insisted, this was a relative and important *novum* of the council. Whereas the patristic period knew of the development of the one Adam of humanity through the six epochs of its history, the modern view of historical humanity has interpreted the new duties of the globalized future in strongly technological terms. The ambivalence of our times is reflected in "the danger and the possibility" of speaking today of the human being as a project of history.[28] "The thorough presentation of this (modern) situation and the conscious acceptance of its ambivalence as danger and possibility, as threat and promise, is decisive, because the acceptance of the contemporary situation in both its faces provides anthropology from the start a historical index."[29] Ratzinger's central thesis was that not every change calling for a new embrace of global responsibility is humanizing, but the task of humanization will not be fulfilled without embracing the historical demands of our epoch for greater global responsibility (the necessary but not sufficient condition of genuine humanization).[30] The cultural and educational mission of the Church must be viewed, he argued, in this qualitatively new anthropological context. This conscious acceptance of the ambivalence that is implied in accepting the modern situation both "as danger and possibility, as threat and promise," characterized Ratzinger's other commentaries on the council as well.[31]

---

[28] Ratzinger, "Das Menschenbild des Konzils in seiner Bedeutung für die Bildung," 36.

[29] Ibid.

[30] Ibid., 34-37

[31] As an example of the Tübingen professor's affinity to the peasant's analysis from the same time cf. especially Joseph Ratzinger, *Die letzten Sitzungsperiode des Konzils* (Cologne: J.P. Bachem, 1966), from the central section on "The Battle about Schema XIII" (25–58), notably the paragraph on "The chief substantive problem: belief within the technical world" (39–43), e.g. 40ff. with reference to the "tendency towards Teilhardism": "As for the Council's final draft [of *Gaudium et Spes*], there remained even there, despite all the

A close study of the writings of the man who would become Benedict XVI reveals at least two flaws in the usual way in which his development as a theologian is understood: the early work contains an expressed critical potentiality in reference to the modern world, inside and outside the Church, and the later work retains its affirmation of the relative novelty and importance of the council's advice on engaging modern culture. His interpretation of the council still offers us the help of Ariadne's thread to escape the labyrinth into which the council would be banned by the first four interpretations discussed above.

II. MARITAIN AS A MODEL OF A CONCILIAR RENEWAL: "UN BRAS D'ATHLÈTE ET UNE HAUTE VOIX DE LAMENTATEUR"

1. Maritain and the Council: The True New Fire

As the interpretations of the Right mentioned above had recognized, Maritain's praise for the council was not ingenuous. "The true new fire" that he expected from the council with regards to the *munera ecclesiae* shone for Maritain all the more brightly in contrast to

---

distancing from such ideas, an almost naive sounding pleasure in the idea of progress, in that little was said of the ambivalence of all external progress that the human race might make. In dismantling that resentment against technological civilization which previously had dominated attitudes influenced by the medieval orientation of ecclesial thought, there was something grand in the Council, a step forward of decisive historical significance, which may not and should not be reversed. But at the same time one will have to add that such resentment will only be fully dismantled when we have become free to see soberly what is negative and what is regressive in that "progress" and to recognize without glossing the distance between technological and genuinely human progress. The authentically decisive question at stake here goes deeper still. This question can be formulated with the alternative: How are technological salvation and the salvation of faith related to one another? How are technological progress and Christian hope related to one another? The solution offered by a crass form of Teilhardism answers that the two are identical. The weakness of the draft text on the Church in the world of our times was that, put simply, it failed to distance itself sufficiently from that identification."

the "masked Manicheanism ... superimposed" on that preconciliar Church that the peasant describes in terms no less bitter than those referring to many of the postconciliar excesses that, in his view, had followed directly from previous ecclesiastical inexperience in engaging the non-Catholic world. Indiscriminate affirmation had followed indiscriminate condemnation; assimilation had been facilitated by prior isolation. Maritain hoped that the "true new fire," if ignited by the council, would bring light and warmth to the Church from a comparatively dark and frozen state in her relationship to non-Christians (chapter 4), in the dialogue of minds capable of the truth in conversation with both contemporary (chapter 5) and medieval thought (chapter 6), as well as in genuine veneration and sanctity (chapter 7). At the same time the peasant knows that the world has a "fundamental ambivalence,"[32] that "history progresses at the same time in the line of evil and in the line of good,"[33] and that in the latter days of the Enlightenment "logophobia" and "chronolatry" are twin dangers (so much so that in the postmodern world they can move beyond that love-hate relationship of Enlightenment reason to fuse into one as a trendy irrationalism).[34]

What was perhaps somewhat ingenuous, if well-intended, was Maritain's ascription of the excessive affirmations of Enlightenment hopes exclusively to the misinterpretations of the council, when in those early months of 1966 it was evident that there were important voices in the debates and final texts of the council itself, which, when taken in isolation, would amount to much the same positions. Maritain asserts that the Pastoral Constitution was well aware of this ambivalence and dedicated to avoiding the dual dangers of "practical Manicheanism and Pelagianism," even while observing closely the resurgence of these dangers in the first months of the postconciliar era.[35] To choose one example, Maritain's sustained criticism of the "Teilhardian" belief in self-propelled, technological progress is discussed in much the same sense, if at greater length and in more

---

[32] Maritain, *The Peasant of Garonne*, 39.

[33] Ibid., 13.

[34] Ibid., 21ff.

[35] Ibid., 61.

polemical terms, as Ratzinger, who, writing in that same spring of 1966, understands these overly optimistic passages as unfortunate remnants of an earlier phase of the discussion that remained, though not without counter-texts, in parts of the final text of *Gaudium et Spes.*[36] What the peasant seems to be reaching for throughout his affirmation of the council, coupled as it is to warnings of its aftermath, is arguably close in substance to that fifth interpretation mentioned above, so too in his desire to engage in novel but critical ways the non-Catholic world. Maritain's ambivalence toward the council is often understated, such as when the council is portrayed as expressing a naive, so-called "Maritainian optimism," or when conversely Maritain is portrayed as simply rejecting the council and caricatured as being in contradiction to *Nostra Aetate*: "a metaphysical anti-Semite," simply because he affirms the eschatological mediation of Christ.[37]

The two other arguments prima facie for doubting the value of Maritain's legacy as a source for renewal in the genuine spirit of the council pull in opposite directions from one another: while his involvement in the human rights debate has been dismissed recently as a naive accommodation to modernity, his conversation with the modern project as a whole is often dismissed *in globo* as nostalgic and reactionary. Let us recall first the Maritain of the human rights movement.

2. Maritain at the United Nations: Facing Babel

In November 1947, as president of the French delegation to the Second UNESCO conference in Mexico that was to prepare the Universal Declaration on Human Rights, Maritain delivered one of the signature addresses of his life—"The Way of Peace" (La Voie de la

---

[36] Cf. Joseph Ratzinger, *Die letzten Sitzungseriode des Konzils*, 39–43.

[37] Cf. the late Leon Klenicki, "Jacques Maritain's Vision of Judaism and Anti-Semitism," in Robert Royal, *Jacques Maritain and the Jews* (Mishawaka/South Bend: American Maritain Association, 1994), 72–88; and the less differentiating contribution by John Hellman, "The Jews in the 'New Middle Ages': Jacques Maritain's Anti-Semitism in its Times," in Royal, *Jacques Maritain and the Jews*, 89–103.

Paix)[38]—a talk to which he returned repeatedly in later works from *Man and the State* to *The Peasant of the Garonne Valley*.[39] Not without a certain poignancy, this thinker, who had first made his start in fame and fortune as the semi-official philosopher of *Action Française*,[40] begins his reflections here by a generous and universalist interpretation of what might easily have sounded like chauvinist remarks delivered by Léon Blum at another UN conference held in San Francisco just three years before.[41] In keeping with his "second conversion" of 1926, Maritain seeks to confirm the best instincts of the age, whose memory of the recent past had sharpened the willingness of an increasingly polarized world to agree, despite itself, upon a list of human rights, the violation of which was widely acknowledged to produce injustice and profound suffering. In one of the most telling differences between Maritain and recent postmodernism, Maritain sums up the tendency to have only regional acknowledgements of rights as "Babelism," obviously without the undertone of Derrida's or even Herder's approval of Babel.[42] Maritain is far from thinking or pretending for his colleagues at UNESCO that this consensus is secure or self-evident to our times, much less to all times. Our times continue to suffer, Maritain thought, under the pragmatic perversion of justice (Machiavellianism or *Realpolitik*), under collective violations of justice, and under "the problem of human value [or dignity] and the human use of science and technology."[43] From our vantage point today, it is clear that these

---

[38] Jacques Maritain, *Œuvres Complètes*, vol. IX (Fribourg/Paris: Éditions Universitaires/Éditions Saint-Paul 1990/2000), 145–64.

[39] Cf. Jacques Maritain, *Man and the State* (Chicago: University of Chicago, 1951), 77–79; Maritain, *The Peasant of the Garonne*, 81.

[40] For the role of Léon Blum in the Dreyfus affair and for the weight and public meaning of Maritain's remarkable shift in 1926, cf. Ralph McInerny, *The Very Rich Hours of Jacques Maritain, A Spiritual Life* (Notre Dame, Indiana: University of Notre Dame, 2003), 60–65.

[41] Cited according to the translation of the revised version of that inaugural address, "The Possibilities for Cooperation in a Divided World," in Jacques Maritain, *The Range of Reason* (New York: Scribner's, 1952), 172–84, here 172ff.

[42] Contrast Maritain, *The Range of Reason*, 179, with James K. A. Smith, *The Fall of Interpretation, Philosophical Foundations for a Creational Hermeneutic* (Downers Grove, Illinois: InterVarsity, 2000), 57–60.

[43] Maritain, *The Range of Reason*, 178.

problems would not disappear in the second half of the twentieth century, so that Pope John Paul II in *Evangelium Vitae* (§4) could echo and intensify Maritain's analysis, while naming one of the practical irritations with our contemporary human rights discussion:

> Unfortunately, this disturbing state of affairs, far from decreasing, is expanding: with the new prospects opened up by scientific and technological progress, there arise new forms of attacks on the dignity of the human being. At the same time a new cultural climate is developing and taking hold, which gives crimes against life a new and—if possible—even more sinister character, giving rise to further grave concern: broad sectors of public opinion justify certain crimes against life in the name of the rights of individual freedom, and on this basis they claim not only exemption from punishment but even authorization by the State, so that these things can be done with total freedom and indeed with the free assistance of healthcare systems.

Maritain's answer was not to accept the nationalization, regionalization, confessionalization, or bourgeois privatization of rights, but to seek the codification of as many genuine and universal rights as the collective memory of suffering and the experience of totalitarianism could achieve. He openly admits that not all participants in the conference will have the same sense of the foundations of these rights, rooted as they are in natural law and eternal law; theirs will be a practical, not a theoretical or foundational agreement.[44] Maritain knows, too, that without this common and adequate foundation the danger of an eroding consensus is heightened.[45]

Maritain's rights' programmatic is evident in his development of a key, if imprecise, tool for defending rights in the public forum: the distinction between person and individual. Even prior to the critical

---

[44] Cf. already Jacques Maritain, *The Rights of Man and Natural Law* (New York: Scribner's, 1943).

[45] For Maritain's proximity to the fifth interpretation suggested above, cf. the address of now Pope Benedict XVI before the UN on April 18, 2008.

intervention by Pius XI,[46] Maritain had referred to a passage that he had discovered in the second edition of Réginald Garrigou-Lagrange's first major work, *Le Sens Commune, la Philosophie de l'être et les formules dogmatiques.*[47] Immediately after the 1907 condemnation of so-called "modernism" (a broad movement that, by its frequent reduction of thought to more voluntarist drives, often showed a greater affinity to postmodernism than to the Cartesian-Kantian project),[48] Garrigou-Lagrange had published this monograph,[49] citing the support found in *Lamentabili*,[50] and detailing his extensive critique of the Bergsonian theologian Édouard Le Roy (1870–1954),[51] whose life-philosophical or

---

[46] Cf. Jacques Maritain, *Three Reformers: Luther, Descartes, Rousseau* (New York: T.Y. Crowell, 1970), 25; Maritain, *The Person and the Common Good* (New York: Scribner's, 1947), 3, n. 2.

[47] Réginald Garrigou-Lagrange, *Le Sans Commune, la philosophie de l'être et les formules dogmatiques* (Paris: Beauchesne, 1909).

[48] In a recent work on the council, Hubert Wolf draws the convincing distinction between the modernism of the strong Cartesian subject and that of the far more voluntaristic "modernist" movement at the turn of the nineteenth to the twentieth century: "Einleitung: (Anti-) Modernismus und II. Vatikanum," in Wolf, ed., *(Anti-) Modernismus und Modernismus in der katholischen Kirche: Beiträge zum theologiegeschichtlichen Vorfeld des II. Vatikanums* (Paderborn: Schöningh, 1998), 15–41, here 20. The study uses the distinction to analyze the appeal in 1977 by Archbishop Marcel Lefebvre to his students at Ecône to continue their schism and reject what he claimed was the modernistic "liberalism" of the council and of Pope Paul VI, due in good measure to the influence of "the bad Maritain"; cf. Priesterbruderschaft Pius X, ed., *Damit die Kirche fortbestehe* (Stuttgart, 1992). Lefebvre implied here that there was also a "good Maritain," presumably both *Antimoderne* and anti-modernistic.

[49] Cf. the lengthy pre-study of 1908, the year of Maritain's break with Bergsonianism: Réginald Garrigou-Lagrange, *Le sens commune, la philosophie de l'être et le formules dogmatiques*, in *Revue Thomiste* vol. 16 (1908): 164–85, 259–300, 566–616, especially the third part.

[50] No. 26: "Dogmata fidei retinenda sunt tantummodo iuxta sensum practicum, id est tamquam norma praeceptiva agendi, non vero tamquam norma credendi" (DH 3426).

[51] Cf. Richard Peddicord, *The Sacred Monster of Thomism, An Introduction to the Life and Legacy of Reginald Garrigou-Lagrange* (South Bend: St. Augustine's Press, 2005). A portrait in broad, expressionistic strokes, this free-wheeling essay

pragmatic hermeneutic of doctrinal development exemplified the modernism of his day. Garrigou-Lagrange's study first appeared just as Maritain was distancing himself from Bergson's work. Recalling the dogmatic development of the notion of person, Garrigou-Lagrange's defense of the intelligible content in doctrine and of the spiritual dimension in the human person against their reduction to subspiritual aspirations for communal or individual existence recurred in the lengthy quotes found in *Three Reformers* (1925). Concerned chiefly with the anthropological distinctions, spiritual/material and intellectual/voluntative, Garrigou-Lagrange had mentioned only in passing the distinction of *totum/partes*, and this without reference to the state as *totum*, much less the totalitarian state. Already in 1925, Maritain developed the part/whole analysis of the person/individual distinction and its political implications for freedom of the person vis-à-vis the state.[52] After 1926, Maritain would come increasingly to dwell on the distinction between person and individual chiefly in terms of wholes and parts and to use the mereologically enhanced distinction as one of his chief arguments for the rights of the person against the totalitarian claims of those states that deemed their citizens and residents to be completely plastic to the goals and desires of the community. At the heart of Maritain's argument is his insistence that the person is more than merely a part of the state as *totum*. While not reducing the dogmatically clarified notion of person to this *sensus practicus* as a *norma agendi praeceptiva* (which would have violated the very point of *Lamentabili*), there is no doubt that Maritain's mereological analysis of the distinction between person and individual provided him with one of his principal tools for the defense of persons in an age of totalitarianism. It was a defense that carried weight not just with the faithful who believed in the persons of the Trinity, but with all those

---

makes no mention of Maritain's reception of this distinction nor, more importantly, of the controversy on the causality of sin that played so central a role in Garrigou's estrangement from Marín-Sola and Maritain. For a more detailed and penetrating but no less critical study cf. Michael D. Torre, *God's Permission of Sin: Negative or Conditioned Decree? A Defense of the Doctrine of Francisco Marín-Sola, OP, based on the Principles of Thomas Aquinas* (Fribourg: Academic Press Fribourg, Editions Saint-Paul Fribourg Suisse, 2009).

[52] Maritain, *Three Reformers*, especially paragraph 3 in the section on M. Luther: "The Individual and the Person," 14–28, here 24ff.

whose memory of recent suffering still enabled them to acknowledge the human person's practical rights, even if they lacked the conviction of their divine origins. Although the mereological analysis provided here was in many ways a rather blunt tool (for the state surely must provide for persons as such, just as persons with their properly personal needs and obligations need something like a state), Maritain discovered that this notional development could benefit those whose knowledge *quoad nos* still included the aversion to totalitarianism, not just in its communist and fascist forms, but also in "bourgeois liberalism," where the same "conflict between the whole and the part" recurs: "Bourgeois liberalism with its ambition to ground everything in the unchecked initiative of the individual, conceived as a little God, and the absolute liberty of property, business and pleasure, inevitably ends in statism."[53] He continues, "The moral crisis of our occidental civilization and the disastrous spasms of our liberal capitalist economy exhibit all too clearly the tragedy of bourgeois individualism."[54]

3. Maritain in Conversation with Modern and Postmodern Projects

The texts of Maritain on universal human rights do not support the interpretation of his work between 1926 and 1965 as an easy self-assimilation to contemporary culture; the critical voice is too strong, the identification of the open and hidden sufferings of the times too programmatic. But what about the opposing interpretation, the one that paints Maritain the metaphysician as too dismissive of the modern project to be a source for the renewal of our engagement of it, much less a source for the engagement of the postmodern movements on the Right and Left that share with one another the definition of our times as postmetaphysical?

Certainly there is no lack of texts in which Maritain sets his program for the revival of metaphysics against the whole modern development from Descartes on: texts where Maritain declines to choose, for example, between Kantian and Hegelian options, but simply claims to dismiss them all. This topic, too, would deserve its own conference, but I would like to suggest here briefly that this is not the only side of

---

[53] Maritain, *The Person and the Common Good*, 81ff.

[54] Ibid., 85.

Maritain's engagement with our age, nor the one that best promises renewal. Ralph McInerny has recently recalled how the Maritain of *Existence and the Existent* was offering an alternative to contemporary existentialism, itself a throwback to the attitude dominant between the wars and at the same time a foretaste of the postmodern reflex to come; for the leading brands of postmodernism today are little more than existentialism minus the pathos of authenticity, replaced now by the pathos of sub-personal (structuralist) or suprapersonal (post-structuralist), of regional, forces, traditions, and trends. Maritain affirmed the importance of human action and history in determining the shape of human existence, in appreciation of this side of existentialism, even while criticizing this newest exaggeration of the *homo faber* narrative and its axiomatic atheism (paradigmatically in Jean Paul Sartre).

The same study by McInerny recalls Maritain's cultural circle with its many difficult friendships, the search for conversion mingled with solidarity in the sense of living in difficult times: solidarity by which Maritain sensed that somehow the whole age shared in the plight of a Georges Rouault, born under the bombardment of modern warfare.[55] Maritain's advocacy for the human rights movement reveals this same critical solidarity. His critique of modernity and his search for the renewal of metaphysics, though surely at times overstated, was part of what *Gaudium et Spes* would say is true of all genuine Christians, that they share not only "the joys and the hopes," but also "the griefs and the anxieties" of this age, its *luctus et angor*, those forgotten words, the equally forgotten part of the intentionally mixed message of the Pastoral Constitution. Already by 1912, Bloy had recognized just this sort of necessary programmatic ambivalence in his godson, identifying in his philosophy this unique combination: "Un bras d'athlète et une haute voix de lamentateur": the powerful arm of what would become an advocacy for our times precisely by lamenting what was harmful within them.[56]

---

[55] Cf. Jacques Maritain, *Georges Rouault* (New York: H.N. Abrams/Pocket Books, 1954).

[56] Cited by Raïssa Maritain from Léon Bloy, *Le Pèlerin de l'Absolu*, October 17, 1912, in: *Les Adventures de la grâce*, cap. viii: *Œuvres Complètes*, vol. XIV (Fribourg/Paris: Éditions Universitaires/Éditions Saint-Paul, 1993), 1017; *We*

The legacy of Maritain seems to call us today to reject the claim, for example, that the priority of the right to life before the right to privacy is exclusively a religious, never a rational conviction: Maritain's example suggests that we should deny that such an insight requires *de iure* great sanctity or special revelation (although the experience of our times reminds us of just how much these can be of help de facto).[57] The right to life must rather be insisted upon with the tools of public advocacy and of reason: jurisprudential, historical, and metaphysical. How far this "paracletic" vocation of the philosophizing Christian can accommodate the postmodern demand for the "burial of metaphysics" need not be decided in advance; the cause of strong reason need not beat its chest and boast of its power. But in an age when the transcendental at the center of the loudest debates is the *verum* of things, Maritain's legacy leads us to ask: how much of a decline can metaphysics endure before we have lost even the ability to say that a claim is false, before we lose the age's (here not so postmodern) still-treasured ability to criticize injustice?[58] Domestic and international disputes about the hierarchy of rights discredit neither the very notion

---

Have Been Friends Together/Adventures in Grace (New York: Image), 338: "Everyone knows my lack of enthusiasm for philosophy, in my eyes the most boring way of wasting life's precious time; beside its Hyrcanian jargon discourages me. But with Jacques it is all singularly different. . . . I did not expect to see so strong an arm come forth from the tattered outfit of philosophy. The arm of an athlete and the lofty voice of a bewailer [of olden times: addition of the translator]. I felt at the same time something like a wave of sorrowful poetry, a powerful tidal wave coming from a far distance." I want to thank John Hittinger for his assistance in locating this passage.

[57] Cf. Robert Spaemann, "Is Every Human Being A Person?" *The Thomist*, 60 (1996): 463–74. On the significance of faith for attempts to preserve the sense of personal dignity in times of acute challenge cf. Richard Schenk, "Von der Hoffnung, Person zu sein. Theologische Überlegungen zur Diskontinuität von Verheißung und Vertrauen," in Schenk, ed., *Kontinuität der Person: Zum Versprechen und Vertrauen*, Collegium Philosophicum, vol. 2 (Stuttgart-Bad Cannstatt: Frommann-Holzboog, 1998), 147–77.

[58] Cf. Richard Schenk, "Praktische Unwahrheit und Metaphysik," in Schenk et al., ed., *Jahrbuch des Forschungsinstituts für Philosophie Hannover* (Schriftenreihe des Forschungsinstituts für Philosophie Hannover) vol. 7 (Hildesheim: Bernward, 1993), 11–44.

of rights nor our obligation to articulate and defend above all the rights of persons who are treated as mere instruments of more powerful interests. Maritain's life and works can help philosophers to renew the vocation that has been theirs at least since Socrates: to serve their cities by helping their fellow citizens to live well-examined lives.[59]

[59] In the year that he shifted from philosophical to theological studies, Karl Rahner, still some fifteen years shy of the decisive formulation of his theological system, said of Maritain's small monograph on *Religion and Culture* that it could serve as a basis for Christians' (but sadly not, Rahner adds, for Christendom's) examination of conscience. While Rahner's theology would manage to challenge the Church far more than it did the extraecclesial culture, Maritain's work would come to show ways to distinguish "is" from "ought" in both, expressing by this twin application of dialectic to the Church and the world of our times the genuine spirit of the council; cf. Karl Rahner's review of Jacques Maritain, *Religion and Culture* (1936), in Rahner, *Sämtliche Werke* 4 (Solothurn/Düsseldorf/Freiburg: Benziger/Herder, 1997), 453ff.

"THE OBEDIENCE OF FAITH" IN *DEI VERBUM*: A PAULINE PHRASE AND ITS IMPLICATIONS FOR CATHOLIC INTELLECTUAL LIFE

Rev. Daniel B. Gallagher, M.A., Ph.L., S.T.L.

The American Maritain Association convenes this year to commemorate several anniversaries. December 8th marks the Fortieth Anniversary of the solemn liturgy, celebrated by Pope Paul VI in Saint Peter's Basilica, which brought the Second Vatican Council to a close. The Pastoral Constitution *Gaudium et Spes* had been promulgated on the previous day. Twenty-three days later, Jacques Maritain would pen the preface to *The Peasant of the Garonne.* Each of these events is indeed worthy of commemoration. One would hope, however, that the *Divine Constitution on Divine Revelation (Dei Verbum),* promulgated on November 18th of 1965, would receive no less attention on the Fortieth Anniversary of its publication. "Because of its inner importance," Archbishop Ermenegildo Florit of Florence remarked, "as well as the many vicissitudes it has undergone, the history of the draft of the Constitution on Divine Revelation has fused with the history of this Council into a kind of unity."[1]

In what follows, I would like to revisit *Dei Verbum* with the intention of re-presenting its rich doctrine on Christian faith, a doctrine worthy of closer attention on the part of theologians and philosophers alike. The fathers at Vatican II offered the biblical notion of "obedience" as a privileged way of understanding the Christian response to divine revelation. Rather than entering into the many practical applications of "obedience" to the day-to-day work of professional philosophers and theologians, I will focus more narrowly on the reasons for which this Pauline term was adopted and then proceed to draw out some of its theological and philosophical implications.

My method will be the following. First, I compare the corresponding passages from Vatican I and Vatican II, which discuss the act of faith

---

[1] See the *Commentary on the Documents of Vatican II,* vol. 3, ed. Herbert Vorgrimler (New York: Herder and Herder, 1969), 155.

and consider briefly the evolution of the text in the latter. I then consider some of the more salient theological implications of the Pauline phrase. In the third section, I examine the work of scriptural exegetes on the phrase "obedience of faith" as we find it in Paul's Letter to the Romans. Finally, I turn to *Fides et Ratio* to illustrate the full import of the biblical phrase through Pope John Paul II's personalist analysis of the act of faith.

I

Vatican I: Dei Filius	Vatican II: Dei Verbum
Cum homo a Deo tamquam creatore et Domino suo totus dependeat et ratio creata increatae Veritati penitus subiecta est, **plenum revelanti Deo intellectus et voluntatis obsequium** fide praestare tenemur.	Deo revelanti praestanda est *oboeditio fidei*, qua homo se totum libere Deo committit **"plenum revelanti Deo intellectus et voluntatis obsequium"** praestando et voluntarie revelationi ab Eo data assentiendo.

Both *Dei Filius* and *Dei Verbum* orient the act of faith toward a specific object, the knowledge of which, albeit naturally accessible to man in an imperfect way, transcends all human faculties. In both cases, faith is directed toward the God who reveals *(Deo revelanti)*. However, we immediately notice a difference between *Dei Filius* and *Dei Verbum* in that the latter highlights the importance of conceiving the act of faith as a total and unmitigated personal commitment to God rather than a commitment of individual human faculties or powers. To describe the act of faith, Vatican I adopted the phrase "*plenum revelanti Deo intellectus et voluntatis obsequium fide praestare*."[2] The word *fide*, in the ablative case,

[2] Heinrich Denzinger, *Enchiridion Symbolorum*, ed. Peter Hünermann, 3008. Heinrich Fries notes that even though the dative *revelanti Deo* is present, the *obsequium* objectifies the dative of the response of faith and de-personalizes it. Consequently, the teaching of Vatican I is *Instructionstheoretische.* "...hier werde ein unpersonaler 'Es' - und Daßglaube vorgestellt - der 'Du-Glaube', die Wahrheit als Begegnung, gehe dabei verloren." *Fundamentaltheologie*, 310. Nonetheless, because of its invaluable contribution to a greater

describes the means by which the *obsequium* is offered. The meaning of *fide,* as an ablative of instrument, remains faithful to the Tridentine doctrine affirming the divine infusion of the theological virtues. We could say that faith, as a virtue infused by God, leads to the *obsequium* which man himself offers as a response to the supernatural gift of faith.

In paragraph 5 of *Dei Verbum,* however, the description of what is offered to God who reveals himself is significantly modified ("*obsequium*" in *Dei Filius* → "*totum se*" in *Dei Verbum*)[3], as well as the description of the way in which it is offered ("*fide*" in *Dei Filius* → "*oboeditio fidei ... quâ*" in *Dei Verbum*). The wording we find in *Dei Verbum* is a result of several petitions submitted by the bishops at the Council for a description of faith which might adhere more ostensibly to biblical formulations.[4] At the same time, there is an anthropological

---

understanding of the intellectual element of faith, "Das I. Vatikanum ist besser als sein Ruf." Ibid.

[3] Although "obedience" is not used in *Dei Filius* to describe the initial faith response to God who reveals, it is used in reference to the necessity of grace for the act of faith to occur. "Quare fides ipsa in se, etiamsi per caritatem non operetur (cf. Gal. 5.6), donum Dei est, et actus eius est opus ad salutem pertinens, quo homo liberam praestat ipsi Deo oboedientiam gratiae eius, cui resistere posset, consentiendo et cooperando." Heinrich Denzinger, *Enchiridion Symbolorum,* ed. Peter Hünermann, p. 3010.

[4] In the *Relatio* of the *Commissio Theologica* we read: "Plures postulant, ut praebeatur *descriptio fidei* magis biblica et personalistica, quae melius correspondeat descriptioni datae de revelatione ipsa." Francesco Gil Hellin, *Concilii Vaticani II Synopsis: Dei Verbum,* 697. I do not want to suggest that the term *obsequium* lacks biblical roots. Indeed, there are several examples of its use in the Vulgate. However, in the specific context of *Dei Filius, obsequium* was not explicitly chosen in view of its direct citation of scripture. In the Vulgate, *obsequium* is used to translate *latreia* from the Greek. Ratzinger and Rahner make direct reference to *obsequium* as *latreia* in Rom. 12.1 (see below). In the *Sentences,* Thomas Aquinas uses the term "obsequium" to refer to any general service of one person to another. Drawing from the Greek *latreia,* Thomas denotes the specific *obsequium* rendered to God as *latria.* Thomas interprets the use of *obsequium* in Rom. 12.1 as expressive of the offering of oneself through a life grounded in the virtues of faith, hope, and charity. Joseph Henchey, "La formula 'in obsequium' nel linguaggio di S. Tommaso," *Angelicum* 69 (1992): 454-56. *Obsequium* is also used in the New Testament to translate *leitourgia,* which, in Phil. 2.17, takes the genitive case *tēs pisteōs.*

shift underpinning the entire topic of revelation and faith in *Dei Verbum*. Man not only subjects himself to God through faith on the basis of his utter dependence on God, he also realizes what it means to be human precisely by committing himself to God through faith. In the final section, we shall turn to consider how this is fleshed out in Pope John Paul II's encyclical *Fides et Ratio.*

The dynamic response of faith as described in paragraph 5 of *Dei Verbum* might roughly be diagrammed as follows:

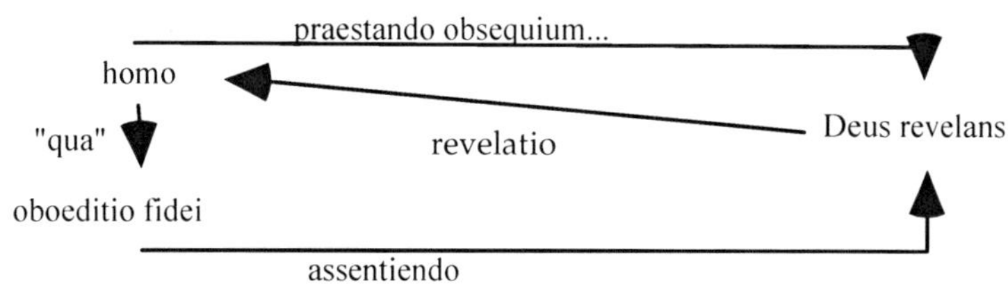

II

Far from promulgating a definitive, self-contained formulation of "faith," *Dei Verbum* opens a realm of possibilities for further theological and philosophical reflection. Rather than setting boundaries, a phrase as pregnant as "obedience of faith" allows us to investigate more deeply the spiritual, intellectual, and ethical aspects of Christian faith.

Juan Alfaro commends the selection of Romans 1.5 as a way of underscoring the essential notion of self-giving in faith.[5] Such an understanding attends to the continual re-commitment that takes place throughout one's life,[6] thus leaving open the possibility that the

---

Finally, *obsequium* is even used to translate "obedience" (*hupakoē*) in 2 *Cor.* 10.5.

[5] "Rinovando il concetto della rivelazione, il Vaticano II ha rinnovato logicamente anche quello della fede come risposta dell'uomo all'automanifestazione e autodonazione di Dio in Cristo." Juan Alfaro, *Rivelazione Cristiana, Fede e Teologia* (Brescia: Queriana, 1986), 116.

[6] "La fede cristiana richede la sua attuazione nelle circostanze della vita d'ogni giorno; è una decisione radicale, che esige sempre decisioni concrete nuove. La permanente tentazione di cullarsi nella decisione presa una volta è una

initial act of faith will wane if one fails to draw nourishment and strength from the sacraments, prayer, and upright moral living.[7]

Alfaro's distinctive theology of the supernatural virtues compliments the doctrinal formulation of faith found in *Dei Verbum*. A theology that considers faith, hope, and love as constitutive of Christian existence rises above the debate of how *fides informis* relates to the "obedience of faith" because it proposes a harmonious unity of the theological virtues understood as three "aspects" of Christian existence. While neither disparaging the supernatural origin of the infused virtues nor ignoring the legitimate distinctions among them, Alfaro chooses to focus on the dynamism of the concrete, willing human person and his of her experience of believing, hoping, and loving that flow from the life of grace. Each of the theological virtues

---

minaccia incombente sulla stessa fede." Juan Alfaro, *Rivelazione Cristiana, Fede e Teologia* (Brescia: Queriana, 1986), 113. "Faith answering to the Gospel can thus also be called obedience by Paul since an affirming posture necessarily results in the gospel itself determining the believer's life and action from then on ... Paul shows here that the affirming acceptance of the gospel does not just represent a one-time act which takes place at the beginning of being a Christian; that faith which stands at the beginning needs rather to be sustained in the entire life of the Christian." Hans-Jürgen Hermisson & Edward Lohse, *Faith* (Nashville, Tennesee: Abingdon, 1981), 146.

7 "Può capitare che un uomo sia considerato o consídersi se stesso non credente, mentre nell'atteggiamento profondo della sua libertà e nelle sue azioni ubbidisce a un valore assoluto (il cui vero nome, Dio, ignora senza colpa), e in questa scelta permanente e radicale riconosce il Dio della rivelazione, vivendo di conseguenza a livello esistenziale la decisione della fede, benchè non la esprime concettualmente nell'affermazione del messaggio cristiano." Alfaro, *Rivelazione Cristiana, Fede e Teologia*, 114. "In piena fedeltà al dato biblico, il concilio presenta la fede come risposta totale dell'uomo e mette in risalto la dimensione di dono fiducioso di se stesso alla grazia di Dio in Cristo, senza dimenticare *l'aspetto di prassi della fede come "obedienza"* e "testimonianza" che hanno compimento nell'azione del cristiano." Alfaro, *Rivelazione Cristiana, Fede, e Teologia*, 116-117. Alfaro also recognizes that unfortunately "la teologa cattolica e quella protestante continuano a parlare della prassi del credente come se fosse solo risultato ed espressione della fede e non una dimensione costitutiva della fede in se stessa." Ibid., 127.

entails a radical response to orient oneself toward God who reveals Himself in Jesus Christ.

Heinrich Fries also draws attention to the fecundity of Paul's phrase in Romans understood as the totality of man's response.[8] The self-abandonment of the person implicitly contained within it places in greater relief the divinity of its "object."[9] Rino Fisichella urges readers

---

[8] "The narrowing conceptions of faith as intellectual belief in dogmas or as fiducial faith are absorbed in the larger definition of faith as the total Yes of persons who, in the realization of their existence, give themselves over totally to God who is, in Jesus Christ, the way and truth of human beings." Fries, *Fundamental Theology,* 379. Dario Vitali also notes the importance of overturning a limited understanding of faith as *obsequium:* "Parlare dell'uomo che si abbandona tutto a Dio liberamente è ben altra cosa che parlare di pieno assequio dell'intelletto all verità rivelate, la formula conciliare recupera la totalità e la complessità dell'atto di fede, in correlazione all complessità del concetto di Rivelazione. Se, infatti, la Rivelazione non è unicamente un insieme di verità da credere, ma è anzitutto la libera e gratuita autocommunicazione di Dio all'uomo in Cristo – 'Piacque a Dio nella sua bontà e sapienza rivelare se stesso e far conoscere il mistero della sua volontà, mediante il quale gli uomini per mezzo di Cristo, Verbo fatto carne, nello Spirito Santo hanno accesso al Padre e sono resi partecipi della natura divina' – la fede non può essere unicamente un assenso intelletuale a delle verità, ma un atto che tocca e coinvolge l'uomo in tutto il suo essere. *In altre parole, il recupero della Rivelzione in tutta la sua profondità e complessità di evento trascina anche il recupero di una realtà altretanto articolota sul versante della fede.* La fede appare allora come il 'si' integrale dell'uomo a Dio, che lo introduce nella partecipazione alla divina natura" (*emphasis mine*). *Esistenza Cristiana: fede, speranza, e carità* (in publication), 20. Vorgrimler contrasts the response of the total person in faith with previous intellectualistic misconceptions. Herbert Vorgrimler, *Commentary on the Documents of Vatican II,* vol. 3 (New York: Herder and Herder, 1968), 177.

[9] "...it must be said that it is not without significance that the attempt to present the total character of faith primarily makes use of the idea of obedience and only secondarily takes up the idea of trust. This makes it clear that self-abandonment in faith is not without direction, but includes commitment to the word, and that this self-abandonment of faith means a readiness for the concrete manner of the encounter with God and his claim, as these are brought to me historically through the preaching of the Church. That this view is entirely in accordance with the Pauline *kerygma* has been shown impressively in the works of R. Bultmann." Vorgrimler, *Commentary*

of *Dei Verbum* not to miss the way the Pauline phrase aludes to an attentive listening to, and faithful proclamation of, the salvific Word of God.[10]

The primary motive for the insertion of the phrase "obedience of faith" into the *Dogmatic Constitution on Divine Revelation* was to broaden the conciliar teaching on faith by highlighting the personalist aspects of total self-giving and trust contained in the scriptural term.[11] The

---

on the Documents of Vatican II, 179. "La parola 'obedienza' perciò non deve sorprendere; essa deve essere intesa nel suo significato biblico. Da esso si ricava un contenuto molto ricco e intenso che fa della fede non un puro atto intelletuale, ma un atto vitale ed esistenziale, cioè la risposta che l'uomo dà a Dio con tutto il suo essere; meglio ancora, la fede è l'esperienza che l'umanità fa di Dio e della sua parola." Giovanni Cardaropoli, *Introduzione alla fede cristiana* (Bologna: Piemme, 1991), 151.

[10] "La fede si gioca sull'obbedienza e questa ne costituisce la sua forma più coerente; essa dipende dall'ascolto e viceversa, così come l'ascolto porta all'obedienza. In una parola, per Paolo, la fede è centrata nella formulazione cristologica che sintetizza il mistero pasquale: passione-morte-risurrezione del Signore." Rino Fisichella, *Quando la fede pensa* (Casale Monferrato: Piemme, 1997), 128. Fisichella also stresses the generous and free act of self-giving: "(La fede) costituisce l'atto mediante il quale con tutto se stesso, ognuno si abbondona obbedienzialmente all voluntà del Padre." Fisichella, *Quando la fede pensa*, 235. Compare Alfaro: "La frase del Concilio Vaticano II 'se totum Deo *committit*' dice, con lo stesso verbo, che l'uomo, nella fede, *si dà e si abbandona* a Dio." Alfaro, *Rivelazione Cristiana, Fede e Teologia*, 124.

[11] The documents leading up to the final draft of the *Constitution on Divine Revelation* reveal that the phrase "obedience of faith" found its way into the later *Schemata* by way of the document *De deposito fidei pure custodiendo* which was completed in July of 1961 and discussed by the *Commissio Theologica* in September of the same year. Brendon J. Cahill, *The Renewal of Revelation Theology (1960-1962): the development and responses to the fourth chapter of the Preparatory Schema "De deposito Fidei"* (Rome: Gregoriana, 1999), 71-107. At the beginning of chapter 4, we find the paragraph in which the "*notio catholica*" of revelation and faith is described. Dhanis' *De revelatione et fide*, which had been proposed prior to the drafting of *De deposito fidei pure custodiendo*, adopts the word *obsequium* found in *Dei Filius*, but does not contain the expression *oboedientia fidei* ("*...sapientissimus Deus voluit ut obsequium illius fidei rationi constentaneum est*"). Ibid., 309. Despite the absence of the term in Dhanis' text, he made a valuable contribution toward an understanding of the act of faith

conciliar fathers believed that the Pauline expression "obedience of faith" most fully captures this sense.[12] A study of the conciliar interventions shows that the bishops believed the phrase embraced both the initial response to God who reveals Himself and the continual, day-by-day living out of that response. Obedience is neither merely the addition of *obsequium* and *assensus* nor is it simply the "handing-over" of one's intellectual and voluntary faculties. It is a commitment of the entire self *quadam proportione* to God's own self-giving as revealed in Jesus of Nazareth. Consequently, the obedience of faith is intimately tied to the more personalist view of revelation that emerges from paragraphs 2 through 4 of *Dei Verbum.*

Let us now turn to consider briefly the original context of the phrase within Paul's letter to the Romans to appreciate further the remarkable affinity between the conclusions drawn by scriptural exegetes and the motives that drove the conciliar Fathers to adopt the phrase.

III

The body of Paul's letter to the Romans is sandwiched between two occurrences of the expression "obedience of faith" (*hupakoē pisteōs*) in verses 1.5 and 16.26, a term he uses to summarize the scope of his mission to the Gentiles, among whom are included the Romans. At the

---

in more personalized terms by suggesting a citation of *"fides ex auditu"* from Rom. 10.17 to render a more specifically Pauline understanding of faith. These two contributions paved the way to an understanding of faith as "obedience" even before explicit citations of Rom 1.5 and 16.26 were inserted into *Dei Verbum.*

[12] The following key intervention by Julius Cardinal Dörpfner best summarizes the reasons for adopting the wording found in *Dei Verbum*: "Haec paragraphus agit 'de fide revelationi praebenda,' i.e. de responso ab homine Deo sese revelanti dando. Quo in connexu pro necessitatibus praedicationis hodiernae et pro fine pastorali huius Concilii *non* sufficit tantummodo repetere conceptum fidei a Concilio Vaticano I traditum, licet verissimum, sed fere nonnisi apologeticum; potius necesse est iam inde ab initio prae oculis habere notionem biblicam fidei et efferre indolem eius personalem necnon influxum gratiae divinae." Francesco Gil Hellin, *Concilii Vaticani II Synopsis: Dei Verbum* (Rome: Editrice Vaticana, 1993), 533.

beginning of the letter, Paul directly links his commission to bring about the obedience of faith in his hearers to his own office of apostleship.[13] The same designation is repeated at the end of the epistle, this time in connection with the gospel of Jesus Christ, which "has been disclosed through the prophetic scriptures for the purpose of bringing about the obedience of faith among all the Gentiles" (Rom. 16.26).

Although it is highly significant that Paul designates the obedience of faith as the aim of his missionary activity at both the beginning and the end of the letter,[14] the precise import of the phrase is somewhat vague in respect to the teaching developed within the body of the letter. The much-debated point about the purpose of the epistle complicates the search for a precise meaning of "obedience," especially in reference to the Christian community in Rome.[15] Paul seems to imply that the Gentiles' ability to accept his preaching presupposes a type of obedience roughly understood as a willingness to listen. Elsewhere in the letter, however, as in 16.19, Paul suggests that the obedience of the believers in Rome is already exemplary at the time of the composition of the letter. Although this ambiguity may in part stem from the activity of subsequent redactors, we must also respect the coherence of the letter as a whole in the attempt to elucidate the meaning of "obedience."

---

[13] "Just as the Israel of old was virtually defined as the 'obedient nation,' practicing an obedience of fidelity to the law, so now Paul has been charged to gather from all nations a final people of God, defined solely on the basis of that obedience which stems from faith." Brendan Byrne, *Reckoning with Romans* (Wilmington: Michael Glazier Press, 1986), 37.

[14] "Wir haben es mit einer zusammenfassenden, missionarishcen Wendung zu tun, die dem Begriffe des Glaubensgehorsams entsprechen muß." Otto Michel, *Der Brief an die Römer* (Göttingen: Vandenhoeck & Ruprecht, 1978), 76.

[15] Byrne argues that, since Paul is sensitive to the fact that the community at Rome has already accepted the good news, his purpose in writing the epistle is that "it will bring about in Rome, prior to his visit and further expedition to the West, a deeper sympathy for the conformity to the specifically Pauline contours of the gospel: most notably the inclusion of the Gentiles as equal citizens in the eschatological people of God." B. Byrne, *Reckoning with Romans* (Wilmington: Michael Glazier, 1986), 19.

Pauline scholars continue to debate the central message of Romans. Stendahl summarizes recent developments as a shift in emphasis from individual justification—ostensibly present in the exegesis of the Reformers[16]—to salvation history and the fulfillment of God's promises to the Jewish people in the Old Testament.[17] Obedience is thus required from Jew and Gentile alike in light of what Jesus Christ has accomplished for the many rather than the few.[18] A polarity between that which is called for in faith on the part of the Jews and that which is

---

[16] "Instead of reading Paul in the context of the first century situation, where concern for the inclusion of the Gentiles in the messianic community was paramount, the Reformers had interpreted Paul's statements as answers to the quest for the assurance about man's salvation out of a common human predicament." Glen N. Davies, *Faith and Obedience in Romans: A Study in Romans 1-4* (Sheffield: Sheffield Academic, 1990), 11.

[17] Cf. Krister Stendahl, *Paul Among Jews and Gentiles* (Philadelphia: Fortress, 1977). Stendahl states that: "The doctrine of justification by faith was hammered out by Paul for the very specific and limited purpose of defending the rights of Gentile converts to be full and genuine heirs to the promise of God to Israel." Ibid., 2. "Paul's argument is that one does not have to go through Judaism into Christianity, but that there is a straight and direct way for the Gentiles apart from the law." Ibid., 18. "Paul's doctrine of justification by faith has its theological context in his reflection on the relationship between Jews and Gentiles, and not within the problem of how *man* is to be saved." Ibid., 26. Others have contributed to the recontextualizing of dikaiosuvnh Qeou within other themes in *Romans*. Garlington notes that "the subject matter of Romans announced by these verses (1:3-6) is not justification by faith as such but the revelation of the righteousness of God to everyone who believes." Don Garlington, *The Obedience of Faith: A Pauline Phrase in Historical Context* (Tübingen: Mohr, 1991), 250. For a review of the issue, see R. Y. K. Fung, "The Status of Justification by Faith in Paul's Thought: A Brief Survey of the Modern Debate," *Themelios* 6 (1981): 4-11.

[18] Garlington's study of the Jewish understanding of obedience reveals that *hupakoē* must be understood primarily within the scriptural tradition of the Old Testament. What is remarkable in Romans, however, is that this same obedience is rendered possible for "all nations" through the obedience of Jesus Christ. "Because of this denotation of the 'obedience of faith' in Jewish theology, Paul's phrase assumes the character of a 'manifesto' that 'the nations' can participate in God's (new) covenant apart from becoming and remaining Jewish." Garlington, 5.

required of the Gentiles would obfuscate both the purpose of Paul's office of preaching and his motive for writing the letter to the Romans.[19] The Gospel message implicitly contained in Rom. 1.5 and expounded in the body of the letter is that the same promises which had given hope and identity to the Jews through the centuries, by being fulfilled in Jesus Christ, are now open to the Gentiles as well.[20] Their obedience to the Gospel demonstrates that they were responding to God's plan in the way that Israel's forefathers also had responded in faith.[21]

The genitive case of *pisteōs* has given birth to a plethora of possible translations of Romans 1.5, but also a variety of interpretations of the theology of faith developed subsequently in the letter. While the entire doctrine of faith in Romans may be determined by a translator's rendering of the genitive in *hupakoē pisteōs*, more often one's understanding of the doctrine contained in the body of the letter determines the translation of the genitive case.

The majority of commentators since 1960 take the genitive case of "faith" in the expression *hupakoē pisteōs* as a genitive of apposition. Such an interpretation resists the tendency to give priority to one word over the other, or the specific placement of one word within the *genus* of the other. Examples of non-appositive interpretations include

---

[19] The fact that the Gentiles in the Roman community would be designated as *hagioi* underscores the singularity of obedience as the defining characteristic of believers who are genuinely living the faith. Dunn states that "the fact that Gentiles should count themselves *hagioi* when they offered no sacrifices, call no man 'priest', practiced no rite of circumcision, must have been puzzling to most pagans and offensive to most Jews." James D. G. Dunn, *Romans 1-8* (Dallas: Word Books, 1988), 20. It is their obedience, then, which proves that they are indeed called to share in the promises made to Jews and fulfilled in Jesus Christ.

[20] Minear, placing this text under the light of Gal. 3:28, states that "the only distinction which survived the resurrection of Jesus was the distinction of faith and unbelief." Paul S. Minear, *The Obedience of Faith: the Purposes of Paul in the Epistle to the Romans* (London: SCM, 1971), 48.

[21] "On this basis he is able to address the Romans *as though they were the ancient people of God,* because they have responded—and still do respond—to God's gospel with believing obedience." Garlington, *Obedience of Faith,* 242.

translations such as "obedience required by faith" or those which take the genitive "of faith" to mean simply "believing."[22]

A cursory reading of the different translations found in various versions of the Bible opens our eyes to the several hermeneutical difficulties presented by the passage. The major bibles in English, including the *New Jerusalem Bible,* the *New American Bible,* and the *New Revised Standard Version,* all opt for a literal translation of the phrase, i.e., "the obedience of faith." In a footnote to the verse in the *New Jerusalem Bible,* we read that obedience "is a virtue of faith rather than the obedience owed to the gospel message."[23] Other translators, however, interject a theological interpretation into the translation itself. The expression is thus rendered "the obedience which consists in faith," or "the obedience which springs from faith."[24] There are others who turn the entire meaning around and thus translate the phrase as "the faith which consists in obedience."[25] Some prefer to emphasize the attitude of obedience by translating the phrase as "believing obedience." J. J. Vincent offers a translation that expresses both the obedience by which one comes to faith, and the obedience which typifies faith.[26] Ernest Best is of the opinion that neither term should be given excessive priority.[27] The *Interpreters' Bible* of 1954 reads "the obedience (to Christ) which comes from faith." John Knox prefers "obedience *to* the faith," but as Patrick Boylan remarks, the lack of an

---

[22] The former translation places a certain species of "obedience" into the genus "faith," while the latter translation places the species "faith" into the genus "obedience."

[23] Cf. 1985 edition of *The New Jerusalem Bible,* 1867. In the 1966 version of this bible, the editors call this genitive a "subjective genitive" which they claim is an obedience "implicit in the virtue of faith."

[24] Archibald M. Hunter, *The Epistle to the Romans* (London: SCM, 1955), 29.

[25] Charles E. B. Cranfield, *A Critical and Exegetical Commentary on the Epistle to the Romans* (Edinburgh: T. & T. Clark, 1975), 50.

[26] "The obedience which characterizes and proceeds from faith." John J. Vincent, *Letter to the Romans* (London: Epworth, 1963), 39.

[27] "Faith and obedience go inextricably together. Only in obedience is there faith, for faith is not an emotional feeling or an intellectual acceptance, but an active response to a person: God. It is trust." Ernest Best, *The Letter of Paul to the Romans* (Grand Rapids: William B. Eerdmans, 1971), 41.

article preceding "faith" in the Greek, as well as the unlikelihood that faith was understood as a body of teaching at the time of the original composition of Romans, weakens the latter interpretation.[28]

Joseph Fitzmyer makes a provocative suggestion that "obedience" may not be the most auspicious translation of *hupakoē*. The Knox Bible suggests "homage," while the *New Biblical Commentary* suggests "trusting submission." Due to pejorative overtones of "obedience," Fitzmyer suggests that it may be more desirable to use a word such as "commitment."[29] Despite the risk of losing sight of the allusion to the importance of covenantal obedience in the Old Testament, "commitment" is advantageous in distinguishing the type of obedience found in the Old Testament from the complete submission to God in the person of Jesus Christ announced in the New Testament. If, however, we want to join Garlington and Davies in emphasizing the continuity of *hupakoē* with the tradition of the Old Testament,[30] "commitment" fails to communicate the link between obedience to the Old Covenant and that to the New. "Commitment" also seems to undermine the aspect of authority that "obedience" includes, as well as the etymological similarities between *hupakoē* and *oboedire*. Finally, it may blur the distinction between the Greek word *hupakoē* and other words in Greek such as *prothesis* ("devotion" in Acts 11.23) and even *hupomonē* ("steadfastness" in 1 Tm. 6.11 and Js. 5.11). In any event, Fitzmyer's suggestion is helpful in pointing out the flexibility of the term *hupakoē* in the letter to the Romans, as well as highlighting its descriptive function when found in conjunction with the genitive *pisteōs*.[31]

---

[28] Patrick C. Boylan, *St. Paul's Epistle to the Romans: Translation and Commentary* (Dublin: MH Gill, 1934), 5.

[29] Joseph A. Fitzmyer, *Romans: A New Translation with Introduction and Commentary* (New York: Doubleday, 1993), 327.

[30] "Obedience as evidence of and expressive of faith for Christians is not qualitatively different from that which is characteristic of believers before Christ, though the content of that obedience as it relates to the law may require some qualifications." Davies, *Faith and Obedience in Romans*, 19.

[31] Although it must be noted that "pistis" itself often carries a meaning of "commitment" as faithfulness or steadfastness in the New Testament (see 1 Tim. 6.11).

Fitzmyer's translation also strongly evokes the expression "*totum se Deo committit*" in *Dei Verbum* analyzed in the preceding section.

In short, "obedience" seems to be the most favorable translation of *hupakoē*. Most likely, Paul did not intend to restrict his use of the term to a single and exclusive meaning. In both his letter to the Romans and in other instances where he uses "obedience,"[32] the term refers to a total commitment to Christ, as well as the necessary dispositions of listening, submission, self-abasement, and fidelity that would have been just as clear to Paul's original audience as they are to us today. For these reasons, the fathers at Vatican II believed the inclusion of the Pauline expression and the rewording of the description of faith in *Dei Verbum* to be both a complement to and an improvement upon *Dei Filius.*

IV

In Pope John Paul II's encyclical *Fides et Ratio*, possibilities are opened for both the philosopher and the theologian to discern more keenly the role of the human will in the act of faith understood as obedience. John Paul presumes that there must be some analogical understanding of freedom in order both to preserve the reasonableness of the *obsequium* involved in the act of faith, and to hold obedience as the fulfillment of man's spiritual nature: a nature which antecedes the act of faith.

The discussion in *Fides et Ratio* concerning the act of faith contextualizes the faith/reason question within the history of Vatican I and Vatican II considered above. As stated previously, there is no abrogation of the will in the act of faith as described in *Dei Verbum.* Nonetheless, a difficulty remains: not only is the will *offered* to God through the obedience of faith, the will itself moves the subject to make this offering. For this reason the act of faith is impossible without the gift of supernatural grace. In order to commit his will, man must in fact employ his will, enabling him to offer himself *libere* and assenting to revelation *voluntarie.* This might seem paradoxical at first, but not quite

[32] 2 Cor. 10.5-6. *Hupakoē* also appears in Rom. 15.18, 5.19, 6.16, and 10.16.

in the way described by Rudolf Bultmann.[33] For there to be a fulfillment of that which man is by nature, there must be an analogous use of "freedom" as understood before and after the act of faith. This analogy allows man to realize his full freedom not only "after" the act of faith, but precisely "in" the act itself. It is in the act of faith that the full spiritual nature of man is realized.

Pope John Paul II's analysis in *Fides et Ratio* reveals the influence of the obediential model apparent in *Dei Verbum* 5 as well as in its underlying anthropology.[34] The biblical notion of obedience opens up a

---

[33] Bultmann places the question of freedom into the forefront of the discussion concerning obedience and faith. The will, rather than simply opening itself up to the workings of grace, must actually reverse itself in order to expunge all that it desires for its own sake. Rudolf Bultmann, *The Theology of the New Testament* (London: SCM, 1959), 314. Bultmann understands faith as obedience in the following way: "Faith is obedience, because in it man's pride is broken. What is actually a foregone conclusion becomes for man in his pride what is most difficult. He thinks he will be lost if he surrenders himself -if he surrenders himself as the man he has made of himself for the first time. Obedience is faith because it is the abandonment of pride, and man's tearing himself free from himself." *Glauben und Verstehen*, 2, 154 (translation mine). The reversal of the will is integral for the full realization of faith through obedience. Because faith is a reversal of the will, it can never constitute a foundation upon which the rest of Christian life can be built. This reversal, insofar as it is a "deed," is in constant need of renewal. "Faith is never a foundation upon which we set ourselves up, but rather an ever new deed, new obedience, always uncertain, as soon as we reflect upon it, as soon as we speak of it, it is certain only as deed." Bultmann, *Glauben und Verstehen*, I, 37; cf. *Kerygma und Mythos*, II, 202. It is this reversal, which assures the authenticity of faith so that it may be distinguished from a "work." Ibid., 315. Bultmann is of the opinion that perfect obedience was impossible for the ancient Jew since the very notion of obedience was a "formal" principle rather than a principle which involved the radical allegiance of the whole man. *Primitive Christianity in Its Contemporary Setting*, 68.

[34] "This statement (*Dei Verbum*, 5) reflects an awareness of the different emphases in Protestant and Catholic theology and an intention to include the sound elements of each. The dimensions of trust, obedience, and intellectual assent are here harmoniously integrated into an expression of full personal adhesion." Avery Dulles, *Assurance of Things Hoped For* (Oxford:

new horizon for understanding the relational aspect of the act of faith. Man exercises obedience through the act of faith, but, rather than offering an *obsequium*, he offers his very self to the other.[35] An offering of merely an *obsequium* would undermine man's potential to realize his freedom in the act of faith, for his very self would remain somehow "outside" the faith relationship. Indeed, man remains an "I" after the act of faith, but he is an "I" who has given himself completely and freely to a "Thou" who, in turn, actualizes the subject's fullest anthropological potential. Only when the "I" maintains its status as an active subject will personal freedom have a role to play in the dynamic faith-response.

Besides the personal dynamics of faith considered in paragraph 13 of *Fides et Ratio*, there are three points to be made regarding John Paul II's treatment of *oboeditio fidei*. First, the foundation of credibility is reaffirmed to be God who reveals Himself. God is the "pledge" of those things he reveals.[36] There is no external source apart from revelation which would determine the act of faith in such a way that would prevent the act from being an act of absolute obedience. The *preambula fidei* in no way precondition the subject such that he can exhaustively ascertain the credibility of revelation in Jesus Christ prior to coming

---

Oxford University, 1994), 185-86. For a review of the personalist philosophy of human action underlying John Paul's teaching on faith, see Rocco Buttiglione, *Il Pensiero dell'Uomo che divenne Giovanni Paolo II* (Milan: Mondadori, 1988), 147-210.

[35] Cf. *Veritatis Splendor*, 88: "It is urgent to rediscover and to set forth once more the authentic reality of the Christian faith, which is not simply a set of propositions to be accepted with intellectual assent. Rather, faith is a lived knowledge of Christ, a living remembrance of his commandments, and a *truth to be lived out*. A word, in any event, is not truly received until it passes into action, until it is put into practice. Faith is a decision involving one's whole existence. It is an encounter, a dialogue, a communion of love and of life between the believer and Jesus Christ, the Way, and the Truth, and the Life (cf. Jn. 14:6). It entails an act of trusting abandonment to Christ, which enables us to live as he lived (cf. Gal. 2:20), in profound love of God and of our brothers and sisters."

[36] "Hoc significat eum (hominem) plene integreque agnoscere rerum revelatarum veritatem, quoniam ipse se pignus illarum exhibet Deus." *Fides et Ratio*, 13.

into contact with that revelation through the Word of God. Such a position would in fact mitigate the role of freedom in the act of faith, for it would imply that there were externally grounded motives coercing the will rather than prompting it. Rather, the full realization of the spiritual freedom of the human person, perfected through faith, is in some perfect measure proportionate to the origin of credibility who is God himself.[37] Faith, as an obedient response, first recognizes the divinity and transcendence of God.[38] The *datum* of revelation in Jesus Christ is the "material" of credibility to which the predicate "credible" primarily refers, while the origin of that credibility is God himself.[39]

Second, the full surrender to God through the act of faith is ultimately grounded in truth, a transcendental which played an integral role in the thought of John Paul II's anthropology.[40] Absolute truth, including the truth about man, becomes the force that draws man toward divine revelation. This truth, like the credibility of revelation, is guaranteed by God Himself. Not only is truth a key transcendental in the analysis of the credibility of revelation and man's assent, it is also that which leads to the ultimate freedom attained through faith.[41] Man, who naturally tends toward freedom, is defined by John Paul II as *ille qui veritatem quaerit.*[42] The ultimate truth sets man

---

[37] "Usque ad extremum intellectus ac voluntas exercent spiritualem suam naturam ut subiecto humano permittatur actum perficere qui uniuscuiusque libertas pleno modo vivatur. In fide proinde non adest dumtaxat praesens libertas: etiam postulatur." *Fides et Ratio,* 13.

[38] "Id (responsio oboeditionis fidei) poscit ut Ille sua agnoscatur in divinitate, sua in trascendentia supremaque libertate." *Fides et Ratio,* 13.

[39] "Deus qui facit ut ipse cognoscatur ob suae absolutae transcendentiae auctoritatem, secum etiam adfert credibilitatem eorum quae revelat." *Fides et Ratio,* 13.

[40] Cf. John Paul II, *Redemptor Hominis,* 19; *Veritatis Splendor,* 64.

[41] Freedom, according to John Paul II, cannot be perfectly realized outside of faith. "Quomodo enim verus libertatis usus iudicari posset nulla sese aperiendi voluntas ad id quod sinit homines se totos explicare? Credendo namque persona humana actum suae vitae significantissimum complet." *Fides et Ratio,* 13.

[42] John Paul II, *Fides et Ratio,* 28.

free insofar as he is spared of enslavement to a series of merely apparent truths, the pursuit of which would drive him to frustration and despair.[43]

Third, the revelation of truth which calls for the obedience of faith is to be accepted as total gift. In this way the *oboeditio fidei* becomes the rendering of a gift in return for an even greater gift completely unmerited by man. If an attitude of obedience were lacking, man would presume ownership of the gift of salvation, rendering the full commitment of one's entire self impossible in the act of faith. Revealed truth, insofar as it is gratuitous, paves the way for an interpersonal communication that essentially consists in a relationship between the Giver of the gift in his giving and the receiver of the gift in his acknowledgment that God is indeed the giver. The underlying anthropology of the act of faith in *Fides et Ratio* renders this interpersonal communication possible, for it is the man Jesus Christ who communicates with man, revealing to him the fullness of truth about himself.[44] The encounter with Jesus Christ is always an encounter with the gift of truth which includes both the truth of God and the truth about man.

A reading of *Fides et Ratio* 13 reveals that the language of obedience is most appropriate to the act of faith. In order to apply it properly to the supernatural act by which one commits himself to God, it must be distinguished from all other natural instances of "obedience" by analogy. Only in this way can the paradox between freedom and obedience be resolved. An understanding of the nature of obedience in common experience, however, allows the subject to penetrate more deeply the meaning of one's relationship with God. As noted previously, it is quite possible that Paul adopted the expression to enable his listeners to concretize an understanding of the faith they had already received.

Although there are some essential differences between the ways obedience, faith, and justification interact in Protestant and Catholic thought, the common insistence upon a humble openness to the revelation of God opens the door to a fuller understanding of how the

---

[43] Ibid.

[44] Vatican II, *Gaudium et Spes*, 22.

entire self is offered in faith. It is not simply one apprehension among many, nor is it one decision to be made among many.[45] Rather, it is that unique act by which man most fully realizes his freedom.[46] The obedience/freedom paradox is only resolved when we take stock of the object of obedience, the one to whom the act of faith is directed: a God who totally transcends this world but nonetheless reveals Himself by becoming Man in the world.[47]

V

Before being elevated to the College of Cardinals, Avery Dulles noted that different theological currents have attempted to shed light on the polyvalence of faith by focusing on one particular way of viewing the supernatural act. He writes that "the biblical usage of terms such as the

---

[45] Cf. John Paul II *Veritatis Splendor,* 66: "There is no doubt that Christian moral teaching, even in its Biblical roots, acknowledges the specific importance of a fundamental choice which qualifies the moral life and engages freedom on a radical level before God. It is a question of the decision of faith, of the *obedience of faith* (cf. Rom. 16:26) 'by which man makes a total and free self-commitment to God, offering "the full submission of intellect and will to God as he reveals."' This faith, which works through love (cf. *Gal.* 5:6), comes from the core of man, from his 'heart' (cf. Rom. 10:10), whence it is called to bear fruit in works (cf. Matthew 12:33-35; Lk. 6:43-45; Rom. 8:5-10; Gal. 5:22)."

[46] Cf. John Paul II, *Crossing the Threshold of Hope* (New York: Knopf, 1949), 188-95. John Paul holds up Mary as the primary model of one who exercises and perfects her human freedom in the obedience of faith: "The Holy Spirit, who with his power overshadowed the virginal body of Mary, bringing about in her the beginning of her divine Motherhood, at the same time made her heart perfectly obedient to that self-communication of God which surpassed every human idea and faculty.... Mary entered the history of the salvation of the world through the obedience of faith. And faith, in its deepest essence, is the openness of the human heart to the gift: to God's self-communication in the Holy Spirit. St. Paul writes: 'The Lord is Spirit, and where the Spirit of the Lord is, there is freedom.' When the Triune God opens himself to man in the Holy Spirit, this opening of God reveals and also gives to the human creature the fullness of freedom. This fullness was manifested in a sublime way precisely through the faith of Mary, through the 'obedience of faith'." *Dominum et Vivificantem,* 51.

[47] Cf. John Paul II, *Redemptor Hominis,* 10.

Hebrew *'emunah,* the Greek *pistis,* and their cognates is sufficiently flexible to allow theologians to move in different directions."[48] Given this flexible notion of faith, the model of obedience, thoroughly grounded in scripture and elaborated by both Catholic and Protestant theologians, may prove to be particularly useful today. Obedience to the teaching of the Magisterium has a solid theological basis not only in the early Christians' obedience to the Word they had received through Paul, but also in Christ's filial obedience to his heavenly Father. To put it bluntly, obedience to the Magisterium of the Church is intimately tied to the obedience owed to Christ himself, who became obedient to show us the way to true freedom. In more recent years, Cardinal Dulles has drawn attention to this important aspect of obedience in the urgent task of reforming the Church: "Catholics should be trained to have a greater confidence in the Magisterium, which enjoys a special assistance from the Holy Spirit. They should willingly conform their private judgment to its teaching, even when no dogmatic definition has been made."[49]

Jacques Maritain, the self described "old layman," exemplified both the docility and the freedom that characterize the obedience of faith. We might call to mind his renunciation of *Action Française* following Pius XI's condemnation of the movement in 1926, or his somewhat reluctant assumption of diplomatic duties when called to serve both Church and country as ambassador to the Holy See in August of 1945. Maritain's obedience was, nonetheless, anything but unreflective. We have only to recall his ambivalence regarding the possible liceity of certain artificial means of contraception in his correspondence with

[48] Dulles, *The Assurance of Things Hoped For,* 170. At the beginning of his pontificate, John Paul II stressed the need for respectful cooperation between theologians and the Magisterium: "If it is permissible and even desirable that the enormous work to be done in this direction should take into consideration a certain pluralism of methodology, the work cannot however depart from the fundamental unity in the teaching of Faith and Morals which is that work's end. Accordingly, close collaboration by theology with the Magisterium is indispensable." *Redemptor Hominis,* 19. Cf. Avery Dulles, *The Splendor of Faith: The Theological Vision of Pope John Paul II* (New York: Herder and Herder, 1999), 68.

[49] Dulles, "True and False Reform," *First Things* 135 (August/September 2003): 17.

Charles Journet in the late 1940s. Notwithstanding Maritain's hesitations, however, Ralph McInerny suggests that "one can predict what his response to Paul VI's encyclical would have been: total acceptance....no reader of *The Peasant of the Garrone* could image Jacques Maritain questioning, either privately or publicly, such a document as *Humanae Vitae.*"[50]

I close with a cogent description of the informed, reasonable, and free obedience which is the hallmark of Christian faith made by a young conciliar *peritus* by the name of Father Joseph Ratzinger as he commented upon *Dei Verbum* 5 a year after its promulgation: "It is not without significance that the attempt to present the total character of faith primarily makes use of the idea of obedience and only secondarily takes up the idea of trust. This makes it clear that self-abandonment in faith is not without direction, but includes the commitment to the word, and that this self-abandonment of faith means a readiness for the concrete manner of the encounter with God and his claim, as these are brought to me historically through the preaching of the Church."[51]

---

[50] Ralph McInerny, *The Very Rich Hours of Jacques Maritain* (Notre Dame, Indiana: University of Notre Dame, 2003), 183-84.

[51] *Commentary on the Documents of Vatican II*, vol. 3, ed. Herbert Vorgrimler (New York: Herder and Herder, 1969), 179.

MARY AND THE VOCATION OF PHILOSOPHERS[1]

Sr. Prudence Allen, R.S.M.

Pope John Paul II said in *Fides et Ratio* "that between the vocation of the Blessed Virgin and the vocation of true philosophy there is a deep harmony" (#108).[2] This is an intriguing reflection because philosophers are usually associated with human reason, while Mary is usually associated with theologians, revelation, and faith. The encyclical also says that "all men and women ... are in some sense philosophers and have their own philosophical conceptions with which they direct their lives" (#31). Since many philosophers have written about personal encounters with Mary in ways directly related to their vocation, let us consider how their reflections might help us respond to the invitation to philosophize in Mary, *philosopharia in Maria.*[3]

1. The Call

Vocation is described in the *Catechism of the Catholic Church* as a call by God through Jesus Christ to everyone to enter the Kingdom of heaven and to the perfection of sanctity.[4] In the primary sense, vocation only concerns our final end, or union with God and the communion of saints. In a secondary sense, vocation concerns our state in life as consecrated religious, married lay, or ordained priest. Being a

---

[1] This paper was published previously in *New Blackfriars*, vol. 90, no. 1025 (January 2009): 50-72. With gratitude for suggestions for composition and revision of this paper by John Hittinger, PhD, Michael Torre, PhD, Marica Frank, PhD. Michael Woodward, PhD, Sr. Rita Rae Schneider, RSM, PhD, Sr. Mary Judith O'Brien, RSM, JD, JCD, Sr. Esther Mary Nickel, RSM, SLD, Mother Mary Quentin, RSM, Superior General, and Mother Mary McGreevy, RSM, Vicar General, Religous Sisters of Mercy of Alma, Michigan. It was presented at the American Maritain Association Conference, Washington, D.C., October 14, 2005.

[2] John Paul II, *Fides et Ratio*: *On the Relationship between Faith and Reason* (Boston: Pauline Books and Media, 1998), #108.

[3] Ibid., #108 note 132.

[4] *Catechism of the Catholic Church* (New York: Image, 1995), #1, 3, 543, and 825.

philosopher is a vocation in a tertiary sense, because it is only part of the means we use to reach our final end.

In Saint Paul's letter to the Romans 8.26-30 we read:

> We know that in everything God works for good with those who love him, who are called according to his purpose. For those whom he foreknew he also predestined to be conformed to the image of his Son.... And those whom he predestined he also called; and those whom he called he also justified; and those whom he justified he also glorified.[5]

Thomas Aquinas, in reflecting on this sequence of 'foreknown, predestined, called, justified, and glorified' distinguished God's predestination for our end of union with Him from providence which concerns means proportionate to our end.[6] The Creator providentially endows many philosophers with gifts of intelligence and will, strong passions of desire and love for truth, and, hopefully, with a good education, and being placed in situations where persons and texts could be encountered to open the world of philosophy. Then a person may experience, as Heidegger so poignantly stated, "The question 'What calls on us to think?' [which] strikes us directly, like a lightning bolt."[7]

St. Edith Stein, Sister Teresa Benedicta of the Cross, O.C.D., suggests that the Christian experiences a deep and, hopefully, more integrated call:

> Everything that penetrates into the interiority of the soul is an appeal of a call to the *person*, an appeal to the person's *intellect*, i.e., to that power which "understands" what is happening; an appeal also to *reflection*, i.e., to that power which searches for the *meaning* of that which approaches the soul; and an appeal to

[5] *The Holy Bible*, Revised Standard Version, Catholic Edition (San Francisco: Ignatius, 1966). This text is used for quotations from Scripture unless otherwise indicated.

[6] Thomas Aquinas, *Summa Theologica*, trans. Fathers of the English Dominican Province (Westminster, Maryland: Christian Classics, 1981), 5 vols., I, 23.1.

[7] Martin Heidegger, *What is Called Thinking?* (New York: Harper and Row, 1968), 116.

> *freedom*, since even the intellectual search for meaning is already free activity. However, beyond this the soul is required to behave and act in accordance with the meaning for which it searches.[8]

If we are Baptized, then we are formed beyond human nature into the super-nature of Divine life; we are called into a rectitude of order by the justification which remits original sin.[9] Adrienne von Speyer adds that for a Christian: "A call is always from the Lord.... He continues to work redemption by calling persons to help Him in this task. That they should help, however, is not what first becomes apparent from the call."[10]

Considering this same challenge, Edith Stein directly refers to Maritain's observation that "grace purifies and strengthens the human intellect, making it less vulnerable to error (*though by no means safe from erring*) than it was in its fallen state."[11] While created grace is often placed in the philosopher's soul *accidentally* for the good of another (i.e., student or reader), uncreated grace is in the *essence* of the philosopher's soul through the indwelling of the Holy Spirit, prompting the person to become holy, i.e. glorified.

In the *Summa Theologiae*, St. Thomas observed that God gives to each person the grace needed to fulfill their vocation. Furthermore, he argued that Jesus Christ had "such a fullness of grace that it overflowed from Him into all.... Whereas the Blessed Virgin Mary received such a fullness of grace that she was nearest of all to the Author of grace." Thomas did not foresee Mary or contemporary women philosophers teaching others in the world: "[t]here is no doubt that the Blessed Virgin received in a high degree ... the gift of wisdom ... but she ... had

---

[8] Edith Stein, *Finite and Eternal Being: An Attempt at an Ascent To the Meaning of Being* (Washington D.C.: ICS Publications, 2002), 438-39.

[9] See Thomas Aquinas, *Summa Theologica*, "[J]ustification, 'implies a certain rectitude of order in the interior disposition of a man, in so far as what is highest in man is subject to God, and the inferior powers of the soul are subject to the superior, i.e., to reason; and this disposition the Philosopher [i.e., Aristotle] calls *justice metaphorically speaking* (*Ethic.* v. 11).'" I-II, 113.1.

[10] Adrienne von Speyr, *They Followed His Call: Vocation and Asceticism* (New York: Alba House, 1978), 3.

[11] Edith Stein, *Finite and Eternal Being*, 21; my emphasis.

not the use of wisdom as to teaching, since this befitted not the female sex...."[12] Yet, Thomas argued that Mary in her perfection in glory dispenses grace to all in union with her Son. Our analysis of the harmony between Mary and the vocation of true philosophy will consider how the encounter of philosophers with the glorified Mary, after her Assumption into heaven, has affected their self-understanding.

2. Mary as the "Table at which Faith Sits in Thought"

The poetic image in *Fides et Ratio* #108, from the Byzantine tradition of "Mary as the table at which faith sits in thought," will provide a continuity to our analysis. Pope John Paul II traces this image of table back to the Greek word *Trapeza* whose primary meaning is: altar.[13] He refers to Pseudo-Epiphanius' *Homily in Praise of Holy Mary, Mother of God*, where the literal translation of the text describes Mary as "the intellectual table of faith which furnished the bread of life to the world."[14] The Latin word *mensa*, used in the official text of *Fides et Ratio*, similarly includes the meaning of altar.[15]

---

[12] Thomas Aquinas, *Summa Theologica*, III, 27.5, ad 3. Note that the Latin *Theologiae* has been rendered in the published English translation as *Theologica.*

[13] John Paul II, *Fides et Ratio* footnote 132 to #108. According to the *Greek Patristic Dictionary* [PGL, 1399], *Trapeza* also includes: table of Last Supper, table of shewbread, manger at Bethlehem, the vessels laid upon the altar, Christ's tomb, Throne of God, place of Christ's death, burial, Resurrection, and Ascension, and womb of the Blessed Virgin Mary.

[14] John Paul II, *Fides et Ratio*, #108, note 132 referring to S.P.N. Epiphanii, *Opera, Patrologiae Graecae, Homilia V in Laudes Sanctae Mariae Deiparae*, vol. 43, 486-502, here 493. The phrase *"he noerà tés pisteos trápeza"* is translated by Marica Frank, PhD. The phrase comes from the following broader context: "You are the Mother of God who alone gave birth to the only-begotten Son of the one God. You did not bear God for the present time but God who is before you and before all, incarnate from you. The immaculate sheep who bore Christ the lamb. The heifer unyoked who bore a calf. The intellectual table of faith which furnished the bread of life to the world."

[15] *The Oxford Latin Dictionary* (L and S 1133): "A table for any purpose, as a dining-table; a market-stand for meat, vegetables, etc; a money-dealer's table or counter, a sacrificial table, etc." The Latin for this passage in *Fides et Ratio*

How can we think of Mary as the altar at which Catholic philosophers, who work through concepts, judgments, and arguments, sit in thought and as the intellectual table of faith which furnished the bread of life to the world? Jacques Maritain may have provided us a way in his essay "The Preconscious Life of the Intellect":

> Far beneath the sunlit surface thronged with explicit concepts and judgments, words and expressed resolutions or movements of the will, are the sources of knowledge and creativity, of love and supra-sensuous desires, hidden in the primordial translucid night of the intimate vitality of the soul. Thus it is that we must recognize the existence of [a] ... preconscious which pertains to the spiritual powers of the human soul and to the inner abyss of personal freedom, and of the personal thirst and striving for knowing and seeing, grasping and expressing...[16]

Following Maritain's analysis, can we hypothesize that Mary pre-exists in God as a type of philosopher and that there is a connaturality between Mary and a Christian philosopher? Also, if the type of table pre-exists in God as an altar, is there a connaturality between the tables at which we philosophers sit in thought and an altar of the Holy Eucharist?

Can we discover new ways to philosophize in Mary? Since John Paul II re-instituted the memorial of the Holy Name of Mary perhaps even just saying the name 'Mary' can elevate our minds and hearts.[17] It may also help us to find some concrete reminders of Mary as the 'table' at which our faith sits in thought. For some of us perhaps our desk, lectern, or seminar-table may call to mind this mystery. For others,

---

#108 is: "'...fidei mensa intellectualis' appellabatur. Ipsam congruentem verae philosophiae effigiem respiciebant sibique erant conscii se debere *cum Maria philosophari.*"

[16] Jacques Maritain, "The Preconscious Life of the Intellect," in *Creative Intuition in Art and Poetry* (New York: Meridian Books, 1955), 69.

[17] To be celebrated on September 12, 2005. Saint Bernard declared that the name of Mercy, Mother of God, should ever be on our lips and in our hearts. The feast of the Holy Name of Mary was first instituted in Spain in 1513. See *Magnificat* (September 2005), 148.

more distant analogies with a table-of-contents, chair of a department, or even an academic chair could serve as a reminder. All of us, however, when we attend to the Holy altar during Mass or other times of prayer, can be reminded of the harmony of the vocation to true philosophy with Mary as the 'intellectual table of faith which furnished the bread of life to the world.' To make these reminders more concrete, we will now turn to some selected aspects of Mary's vocation, whose meaning philosophers have pondered and articulated.

3. The Annunciation

At the Annunciation, Mary engaged in an interpersonal dialogue with the Archangel Gabriel, emissary of the Eternal Father, while sitting at the table of her own embodied being.[18] She revealed her gift of intellect by seeking insight, as Bernard Lonergan would say, by questioning: 'How can this be?'[19] David Meconi, S.J., observes that: "Mary exemplifies philosophy's initial task to receive reality and not manipulate it. Unlike some Baconian mastery or Cartesian orchestration of the world, Mary symbolizes the awe of standing before a reality wholly independent of the human mind."[20]

In addition to the exercise of her intellect, Mary exercised her gift of free will. Søren Kierkegaard reflected on this dynamic of Mary's vocation in his *Journal*: "Theme: that the angel made the right choice—for Mary made the right choice.... She could, then—yes, as Sarah did—she could have smiled [or] dismissed it. Or she could have said ... I am not up to it." Mary's vocation exemplifies Kierkegaard's argument that willing the good end of a vocation demands willing the good means and being willing to suffer all for the Good. For the rest of us, willing the

---

[18] See John Paul II, *Mulieris Dignitatem (On the Dignity and Vocation of Women)* (Boston: Pauline Books and Media, 1988), #5. See also *Redemptoris Mater (Mother of the Redeemer)* (Boston: Daughters of St. Paul, 1987), #13.

[19] Bernard Lonergan, "The Question," in *Insight: A Study of Human Understanding* (Toronto: University of Toronto, 1957/1992), 33-34.

[20] David Vincent Meconi, S.J., "*Philosophari in Maria*," in David Ruel Foster and Joseph W. Koterski, S.J. eds., *The Two Wings of Catholic Thought: Essays on Fides et Ratio* (Washington, D.C.: Catholic University of America, 2003), 69-90, here 71.

good must involve working to overcome all double-mindedness, self-deception, and evasion.[21]

In *Mulieris Dignitatem*, John Paul II described Mary's actions in the Annunciation: "through her response of faith Mary exercises her free will and thus fully shares with her personal and feminine 'I' in the event of the Incarnation [and] ... by responding with her "fiat" Mary conceived a man who was the Son of God, of one substance with the Father. Therefore, she is *truly the Mother of God, because motherhood concerns the whole person*, not just the body, nor even just the human 'nature.'"[22] This personalist description of Mary's vocation is very important because some feminists have incorrectly suggested (in a post-Cartesian age) that Mary's identity was primarily limited to her body. Joseph Cardinal Ratzinger also rejected a Cartesian dualism in understanding the integrated nature of Mary's response at the Annunciation:

> In her believing response to the call of God, Mary appears as the prototype of a creation which is likewise called to respond; she manifests the freedom of the creature, a freedom which is not dissolved, but comes to its fulfillment, in love. But it is precisely as a woman that she exemplifies saved and liberated mankind.... The 'biological' is inseparable from the human, just as the human is inseparable from the 'theological.'[23]

Pope John Paul II furthermore suggested in *Redemptoris Mater* that Simeon's words at the Presentation were "a second Annunciation to Mary," namely that Jesus "and his Mother with him, will experience [being] ... a sign that is spoken against ... in misunderstanding and sorrow."[24] The Annunciation accentuates the great dignity of human free will, and the great love of the Eternal Father who waited for the free decision of his beloved daughter of Zion. The late Holy Father has

---

[21] Søren Kierkegaard, *Purity of Heart is to Will One Thing* (New York: Harper and Row, 1948), especially 197ff. and 148ff.

[22] John Paul II, *Mulieris Dignitatem*, #4.

[23] Joseph Cardinal Ratzinger, "Mariology and Marian Spirituality," in *The Church and Women: A Compendium* (San Francisco: Ignatius, 1988): 67-79, here 76.

[24] John Paul II, *Redemptoris Mater*, #16.

emphasized that, "All of God's action in human history at all times respects the free will of the human 'I.' And such was the case with the Annunciation at Nazareth."[25]

Some philosophers have misunderstood or intentionally distorted the Annunciation dialogue. Consider, for example, a vulgar example of Mary Daly, who describes Mary at the Annunciation as undergoing an "unspeakable degradation."[26] Daly concludes falsely: "...as a consequence of her initial rape ('grace') [of the Immaculate Conception] Mary has been totaled, made totally unable to resist divine aggression/lust/rape. At "The Annunciation," then, the already raped Mary 'consents' to further rape."[27] The false nature of Daly's argument seems to fit a pattern of conflict between the forces of evil and woman's identity as summarized in *Mulieris Dignitatem*: "'...before the woman who is about to give birth' (cf. Rev. 12:4), there stands 'the great dragon ... that ancient serpent' (Rev. 12:9), already known from the Protoevangelium: The Evil One, the 'father of lies' and of sin (cf. Jn 8:44). The 'ancient serpent' wishes to devour 'the child.'"[28]

Pope John Paul II appeals in *Fides et Ratio* to Christian philosophers to accept the "grave duty" to diagnose the erroneous opinions of philosophers.[29] How we may begin through our vocation to respond to this appeal is captured by Adrienne van Speyr's words: "When God's call really sounds, however, all previous judgments and valuations are bracketed, the sober ones as well as the fantastic. The call is the absolute fact, the unvitiated objectivity. It is the voice of God that addresses itself to a particular person. Through this call the person, the addressee, becomes who he is, and he enters the only light that truly illumines him."[30]

---

[25] John Paul II, *Mulieris Dignitatem*, #4.

[26] Mary Daly, *Pure Lust: Elemental Feminist Philosophy* (Boston: Beacon Press, 1984), 74. See also the discussion of 'The Immaculate Perception,' in Friederick Nietzsche, *Thus Spake Zarathustra* (New York: Penguin Books, 1988), 122-23.

[27] Ibid.

[28] John Paul II, *Mulieris Dignitatem*, #30.

[29] John Paul II, *Fides et Ratio*, #54.

[30] Adrienne von Speyer, *They Followed His Call*, 11.

Another aspect of the Annunciation mystery may help us here. Thomas Aquinas says: "It was reasonable that it should be announced to the Blessed Virgin that she was to conceive Christ ... that she should be informed in mind concerning Him, before conceiving Him in the flesh. Thus, Augustine says (*De Sancta Virgin.* iii): *Mary is more blessed in receiving the faith of Christ, than in conceiving the flesh of Christ....*"[31] Ponder how analogously a priest at the liturgy of the Eucharist is the vehicle who expresses himself through specific words and gestures over the altar, its sacred vessels, and their contents during the consecration, and then the Son of God, one in substance with the Father, becomes flesh in the Eucharistic species.

Msgr. Robert Sokolowski observes that: "The Mass involves both words and actions. The liturgy of the word, in the reading of Scripture, calls to mind the past actions of God, while the liturgy of the Eucharist makes the past action of God present again: what has been reported in words can now be registered in its sacramental presence."[32] Catholic philosophers, who are priests in communion with lay and consecrated philosophers at the altar of the Eucharistic sacrifice, may find inspiration in reflecting on how Mary serves here as the altar-table at which faith thinks. Here, with Epiphanius we can say: "Mary, you are the Mother of God ... the intellectual table of faith which furnishes the bread of life to the world!"[33]

4. The Visitation

The communal dimension of Mary's vocation is emphasized by Father Norris Clarke, S.J.: "...to develop properly, philosophy needs a *community of persons*, and especially the experience of *trust between persons*, since so much of what we know and take as data for understanding must come from trust in what others tell us. This is especially true with respect to the philosophical understanding of the person and interpersonal relations...."[34] By analogy we can ponder that

---

[31] Thomas Aquinas, *Summa Theologica*, III, 30.1.

[32] Robert Sokolowski, *Eucharistic Presence: A Study in the Theology of Disclosure* (Washington, D.C.: The Catholic University of America, 1993), 212.

[33] See note 12 above.

[34] W. Norris Clarke, S.J., "The Complementarity of Faith and Philosophy," *Communio* 26 (1999): 562-63.

in the Visitation Mary "went in haste" to be with Elizabeth, to share her vocation with a companion. The *communio* of the vocation to be a Catholic philosopher is not necessarily shared in other traditions. For example, Kierkegaard emphasized the isolation of Mary as like that of Abraham: "To be sure, Mary bore the child wondrously, but she nevertheless did it 'after the manner of women,' and such a time is one of anxiety, distress, and paradox.... The angel went only to Mary, and no one could understand her."[35] Yet, Elizabeth was able to be with Mary in a communion of persons, even without perhaps understanding completely the mystery of her encounter with God, and Joseph entered into communion with Mary after he came to realize his own call.

Have we welcomed the shepherds [analogically guided by faith] and the wise men [analogically guided by observation of the senses and reason] as Mary and Joseph welcomed them to adore Jesus Christ, who is Truth, as he lay in a manger-table? Consider also Edith Stein's meditation on the mystery of the Epiphany: "Again we kneel with the three kings at the manger. The heartbeat of the Divine Child has guided the star that led us here. Its light, the reflection of the eternal light, is variously distributed around the heads of the saints whom the church shows us as the court of the new-born King of Kings. They allow something of the mystery of our vocation to flash before us ... Mary and Joseph are ... completely imbued with his heavenly light."[36] How do we allow the mystery of our vocation to flash before us? Whose radiant light do we seek to communicate in our speaking and writing? With the faith and writings of which shepherds are we in complement collaboration to give glory to the One who is Truth?

In *Fides et Ratio,* the Byzantine phrase for table, or *trapéza,* in the broad sense connotes a communal reality that draws people together through what is laid out on it and made available for others. True philosophy, like a good *trapéza*, or *mensa*, is foundational to the individual strength and well being of those persons sitting around it

---

[35] Søren Kierkegaard, *Fear and Trembling/Repetition* (Princeton, New Jersey: Princeton University, 1983), 65.

[36] Edith Stein, *The Hidden Life: Essays, Meditations, Spiritual Texts* (Washington, D.C.: ICS Publications, 1992), 113. I am making an analogous application with Stein's reflections on her religious vows of poverty, chastity, and obedience.

and gathered together by it and for the health of the community as a whole. True philosophy is thus both analogous with ordinary bread as the staff of life and with the bread of life, or Jesus Christ as Sacrament of the Holy Eucharist.

5. The Wedding Feast of Cana

Consider how Mary analogously represents both the banquet table and providing for the things served at the table for the Wedding Feast of Cana. St. Edith Stein describes her this way: "Mary at the wedding of Cana in her quiet, observing look surveys everything and discovers what is lacking. Before anything is noticed, even before embarrassment sets in, she has procured the remedy. She finds ways and means, she gives necessary directives, doing all quietly. She draws no attention to herself. Let her be the prototype of woman in professional life."[37] For Edith Stein, Mary is acting here according to what she calls the *ethos* of woman, which is an "inner form [and] constant spiritual attitude" towards other persons, which manifests itself in external action.[38] Stein also fills out some specific content of woman's *ethos*: i.e., "Woman naturally seeks to embrace that which is living, personal, and whole."[39]

Pope John Paul II seemed to follow much of Edith Stein's analysis of women's *ethos* when he came to formulate his own philosophy of women's genius. We know that Roman Ingarden, a close colleague of Stein's in graduate studies, became Karol Wojtyła's professor at Cracow. Furthermore, in *Rise, Let us Be on Our Way* (1997), Pope John Paul II told us directly: "I was interested in her [Edith Stein's] philosophy. I read her writings."[40] In *Mulieris Dignitatem* (1988) John Paul II referred to "that 'genius' which belongs to women, and which can ensure sensitivity for human beings in every circumstance...."[41] Then, in *Letter to Women* (1995), he linked women's genius to the vocation of Mary:

---

[37] Edith Stein, "Ethos of Women's Professions," in *Essays on Woman* (Washington, D.C.: ICS Publications, 1987), 49.

[38] Ibid.

[39] Ibid.

[40] John Paul II, *Rise, Let us Be On Our Way* (New York: Time Warner Books, 2004), 90.

[41] John Paul II, *Mulieris Dignitatem*, #30.

"The Church sees in Mary the highest expression of the "feminine genius" and she finds in her a source of constant inspiration.... Through obedience to the Word of God she accepted her lofty yet not easy vocation as wife and mother in the family of Nazareth. Putting herself at God's service, she also put herself at the service of others: a service of love."[42]

6. The Last Supper

In *Mulieris Dignitatem* Pope John Paul II examined how, during the Last Supper, Jesus Christ, the Divine self-gift of Love, "reveals the spousal love of God. Christ is the Bridegroom because 'he has given himself': his body has been 'given,' his blood has been 'poured out' (cf. Lk 22:19-20).... The Eucharist is the Sacrament of our Redemption. It is the Sacrament of the Bridegroom and of the Bride. The Eucharist makes present and realizes anew in a sacramental manner the redemptive act of Christ..."[43]

The Eucharist can only be understood through faith. *Fides et Ratio* #7 summarizes the movement: "This initiative is utterly gratuitous moving from God to men and women in order to bring them to salvation."[44] Furthermore, in #15, "the truth made known to us by revelation is neither the product nor the consummation of an argument devised by human reason. It appears instead as something gratuitous, which itself stirs thought and seeks acceptance as an expression of love."[45]

---

[42] John Paul II, *Letter to Women* in *The Genius of Women* (Washington, D.C.: United States Conference of Catholic Bishops, 1997), #10.

[43] John Paul II, *Mulieris Dignitatem*, #26.

[44] For a more detailed consideration the complementarity of faith/reason, philosophy/theology, and philosophers/theologians see Prudence Allen, R.S.M., "Person and Complementarity in *Fides et Ratio*," in David Foster and Joseph Koterski, S.J., eds., *The Two Wings of Catholic Thought*, 36-68.

[45] The passage continues: "...The ultimate purpose of personal existence, then, is the theme of philosophy and theology alike. For all their difference of method and content, both disciplines point to that 'path of life' (Ps 16.11) which, as faith tells us, leads in the end to the full and lasting joy of the contemplation of the Triune God."

Since we are considering how a vocation to true philosophy harmonizes with Mary's vocation, and since Mary expresses the fullness of a woman's genius, let us identify three main components of her identity and dignity: 1) she was created with intellect and will as a human being with the highest capacities for thought and free choice, 2) she acted with loving concern and self-gift of service towards those other persons entrusted to her, and 3) she was called into an eternal union of love with the Transcendent God, who sent His Beloved Son into the world through her free cooperation with the Divine initiative. Many secular philosophers, from Nietzsche to Mary Daly, deny the existence of a transcendent God. In contrast, Msgr. Robert Sokolowski describes how the altar of the Eucharist draws us into the mystery of the truly transcendent identity of God: "Only the God who is so independent of the world as the biblical God is revealed to be could become incarnate and sacramentally present in the Eucharist.... The Eucharist is a constant reminder of the transcendence of God."[46]

7. The Way of the Cross

In a letter, Francis of Assisi links the Cross to the pre-imminent type of table: "The father willed that his blessed and glorious Son, whom he gave to us and who was born for us, should through his own blood offer himself as a sacrificial victim on the *altar of the cross*. This was to be done ... for our sins."[47] Pondering how the Cross is analogous to Mary's intellectual table of faith which furnished the bread of life to the world, let us consider three categories of philosophers' sins which could be examined in relation to Jesus' falls. In so doing, we may discover concretely the truth of Pope John Paul II's observation in *Fides et Ratio*: how "that part [of what persons produce] that contains a special share of his [or her] genius and initiative—can radically turn against himself [or herself]."[48]

Jesus falls under the weight of the cross-bar the first time when human identity is reduced from its great dignity given to it by being created in the

---

[46] Sokolowski, *Eucharistic Presence*, 108.

[47] Francis of Assisi, *Opuscula* (edit. Zuaracchi 1949), 87-94. *The Liturgy of the Hours* (New York: Catholic Book Publishing Co., 1975), vol. iv, October 4, Memorial of St. Francis of Assisi, Second Reading.

[48] John Paul II, *Fides et Ratio*, #47.

image of God with intellect and will and by Jesus Christ assuming it in the Incarnation. An example of such a reduction of human identity can be found in Jean Paul Sartre's caricature of woman's identity near the conclusion of *Being and Nothingness*: "The obscenity of the feminine sex is that of everything which 'gapes open.' It is an appeal to being as all holes are...; woman senses her condition as an appeal precisely because she is 'in the form of a hole.'"[49] Simone de Beauvoir complained in *The Second Sex* that the male human being condemned woman to her biological nature, and added that: "Only the intervention of someone else can establish an individual as an *Other*."[50] Yet she also reduced the dignity of woman's identity herself when she argued that: "Woman has ovaries, a uterus; these peculiarities imprison her in her subjectivity, circumscribe her within the limits of her own nature."[51] Beauvoir stated further that women gave up their own transcendence by allowing themselves to be thus reduced.

In a well-known artistic exhibit called *The Dinner Party,* Judy Chicago ended up reducing woman's identity in a similar way.[52] In her discursive description of this extensive work, Chicago described how she changed the table of the Last Supper into the table of a witches' coven, and depicted the works of thirty-nine women geniuses not by their great achievements or acts of personal transcendence, but rather

---

[49] Jean Paul Sartre, *Being and Nothingness: An Essay on Phenomenological Ontology* (New York: Philosophical Library, 1956), 613-14. I am grateful to Terry Wright, PhD, for his suggestion that I emphasize the contrast between Sartre with Beauvoir and Jacques with Raïssa Maritain.

[50] Simone de Beauvoir, *The Second Sex* (New York: Alfred A. Knopf, 1957), 267.

[51] Ibid.

[52] Judy Chicago, *The Dinner Party: A Symbol of Our Heritage* (Garden City, New York: Anchor Press/Doubleday, 1979), 11. Judy Chicago's 39 guests at the dinner party table included the philosophers Hildegard of Bingen (1098-1179), Christine de Pizan (1363-1431), Anna van Schurmann (1607-1678), and Mary Wollstonecraft (1759-1797). The floor in the middle of the three triangular sides of the table lists the names of 999 guests, including the philosophers Lucrezia Marinelli (1571-1653), Maria le Jars de Gournay (1565-1645), Margaret Cavendish (1624-1674), Mary Astell (1666/68-1731), Emilie du Chatelet (1706-1749), Simone Weil (1909-1943), and Simone de Beauvoir (1908-1986).

by plates representing their vaginas, and tapestries representing what happened to them (such as dying in childbirth).[53] What Chicago achieved is what women have for years objected to: namely, being turned into an object and specifically into a sex object by the other. In the *Dinner Party*, women have ironically done this to themselves.[54]

Jesus falls under the weight of the cross-bar the second time, when the bond of love between two human beings is reduced to utilitarian or hedonistic purposes. Consider the utilitarian relation between Jean Paul Sartre and Simone de Beauvoir. On the one hand, they claimed that theirs was a necessary bond of love, while, on the other hand, for years they both entered into multiple sexual relations with other persons of both sexes. Their acts undermined the possibility of their full gift of self to one another; they emptied mutual trust, broke fidelity, and transcendentally annulled the very possibility of true love.[55] The emptiness of love and of friendship is evident in Beauvoir's question near the end of Sartre's life: "Many of your friendships have ended in estrangement.... Why were things like that?" and Sartre's answer that "Breaking off doesn't affect me in the least. A thing is dead—that's all..."[56]

Beauvoir and Sartre both were baptized in the Catholic Church, and they both later publically rejected this gift of faith.[57] Subsequently, they approved of killing innocent persons—Beauvoir by abortion and Sartre by saying that he would have carried suitcases with bombs for the

---

[53] Ibid.

[54] One could add as another example in transition to the second fall, Eve Ensler's recent vulgar drama "Vagina Monologues," which, according to Sister Renée Mirkes, OSF, PhD, "A Tale of Failed Feminism," *Fellowship of Catholic Scholars Quarterly* (Summer 2005): 7-9, "celebrates the basest of human instincts," 7.

[55] Simone de Beauvoir, *Adieux: A Farewell to Sartre* (Harmondsworth, England: Penguin, 1986), 284-332.

[56] Ibid.

[57] See Jean-Paul Sartre, *The Words* (Greenwich, Connecticut: Fawcett, 1969), "I have just related the story of a missed vocation: I needed God, He was given to me, I received Him without realizing that I was seeking Him. Failing to take root in my heart, He vegetated in me for a while, then He died," 64-65; See also, Beauvoir, *Adieux*, 432-45.

Algerian Front into a café.[58] During the final days of their lives together Beauvoir describes how, with their minds deadened by drugs and alcohol,[59] they avoided speaking together about the true situation of Sartre's impending death. After Sartre died, Beauvoir concluded: "His death does separate us. My death will not bring us together again. That is how things are."[60]

Jesus falls under the weight of the cross-bar the third time when the profound love between the transcendent God and His creature is reduced or simply rejected. Of course many philosophers, such as Nietzsche, Marx, Freud, Sartre, and Foucault, have contributed to the crushing weight of this fall. A more recent example, tied up with woman's identity, is Mary Daly, who deconstructs what she calls: "the reified images often lurking behind such terms as 'Creator,' [and] 'Lord'...."[61] Next, implying a false dichotomy or radical conflict between God's transcendence and immanence, Daly follows "Whitehead's God [who] is not a creator God, that is, not merely *before* all creation but *with* creation."[62]

In *Fides et Ratio*, Pope John Paul II offers an observation that would be applicable to Daly's thought: "Of itself, philosophy is ... with the assistance of faith ... capable of accepting the 'foolishness' of the cross

---

[58] In the 1970's, Beauvoir signed on to the Manifesto of 343, admitting to an illegal abortion, in a campaign for free contraception and greater access to abortion. See Deirdre Bair, *Simone de Beauvoir: a biography* (New York: Summit Books, 1990) and Philip Thody, *Jean-Paul Sartre: a Literary and Political Study* (New York: Macmillan, 1961).

[59] Beauvoir, *Adieux,* 105 and 118.

[60] Ibid., 127.

[61] Mary Daly, *Beyond God the Father: Toward a Philosophy of Women's Liberation* (Boston: Beacon Press, 1973), 34; her emphasis.

[62] Ibid., 88. She cites Alfred North Whitehead, *Process and Reality: An Essay in Cosmology* (New York: Macmillan, 1929), 519-33. For others who have followed Whitehead down this same path see Sheil Greeve Daveny, ed., *Feminism and Process Thought* (New York and Toronto: Edwin Mellen Press, 1981), and Rosemary Radford Ruether, "Mistress of Heaven: The Meaning of Mariology," in *New Woman New Earth: Sexist Ideologies and Human Liberation* (New York: Seabury Press, 1975), 36-62; see also *Conscience: The News Journal of Catholic Opinion*, sponsored by *Catholics For Free Choice*, for which Ruether is the Editorial Advisor.

as the authentic critique of those who delude themselves that they possess the truth, when in fact they run it aground on the shoals of a system of their own devising."[63] Mary Daly draws out the implications of the system of her own devising when she states her goals: "a male savior ... is precisely what is impossible. A patriarchal divinity or his son is exactly *not* in a position to save us from the horrors of a patriarchal world.... In its depth, because it contains a dynamic that drives beyond Christolatry, the women's movement *does* point to, seek, and constitute the primordial, always present, and future Antichrist."[64] To conclude her distorted logic, Daly follows a Nietzschean line of thought; namely, that the Antichrist is not evil but simply either beyond good and evil, or, transvalued as the good "that can bring us beyond Christolatry into a fuller stage of conscious participation in the *living* God."[65]

Raïssa Maritain reflected back on an interior despair that had pierced her own heart in 1901, when as young students at the Sorbonne she and Jacques confronted the face of evil in the Jardin des Plantes: "This metaphysical anguish, going down to the very roots of the desire for life, is capable of becoming a total despair and of ending in suicide. I believe that during these last dark years, in Austria, in Germany, in Italy, in France, thousands of suicides have been due to this despair, even more than to the overburdening of other sufferings of body and soul."[66] Her own despair was so acute that she and Jacques made the decision to commit suicide themselves "if it were impossible to live according to the truth."[67]

The painful three falls of Our Lord under the weight of sins against women's human dignity, against human love, and against the love between God and human persons may bring to mind some images from Mel Gibson's *The Passion of the Christ*. Gibson shared his thinking about certain aspects of the film with John Bartunek, L.C., who was present

---

[63] John Paul II, *Fides et Ratio*, #23.

[64] Mary Daly, *Beyond God*, 96. Her emphasis.

[65] Ibid., Her emphasis.

[66] Raïssa Maritain, *We Have Been Friends Together* and *Adventures in Grace* (Garden City, New York: Image Books, 1961), 65.

[67] Ibid., 68.

during much of the filming.[68] Many images of the film were taken from the personal meditations of Catherine Emmerich. Raïssa Maritain described how the "*Revelations* of Anne Catherine Emmerich ... gave us a picture of Catholicism that was crowded and vivid, moving and yet familiar.... In our ignorance we had the greatest need for the help of images...."[69] Some of these images well-up from the depths of the soul in that arena that Jacques Maritain previously described in his essay on "The Preconscious Life of the Intellect."

In one particular image from Gibson's film, walking in the crowds beside her Son along the Way of the Cross, Mary's glance met for a time the eyes of the figure of Satan or the Devil. According to Fr. Bartunek and Gibson, "The only person in the entire film who sees that evil presence is Mary."[70] The image of this encounter of Mary with the presence of evil, and the claim that there is the deepest harmony between the vocation of Mary and the vocation of a philosopher, may help us understand the passage in which Pope John Paul II described Pope Pius XII's mandate to the philosopher's vocation to defend the truth:

> Catholic theologians and philosophers, whose grave duty it is to defend natural and supernatural truth and instill it in human hearts, cannot afford to ignore these more or less erroneous opinions. Rather they must come to understand these theories well, not because diseases are properly treated only if rightly diagnosed and because even in these false theories some truth is found at times, but because in the end these theories provoke a more discriminating discussion and evaluation of philosophical and theological truths.[71]

Turning again to the Way of the Cross, Jesus, after gathering strength from his inter-personal encounters of love with Mary and others, relentlessly moved towards His *Crucifixion*. As He was lifted up

---

[68] John Bartunek, L.C., *Inside the Passion* (West Chester, Pennsylvania: Ascension Press, 2005).

[69] Raïssa Maritain, *We Have Been Friends Together*, 121.

[70] Bartunek, L.C., *Inside the Passion*, 114-115.

[71] John Paul II, *Fides et Ratio*, #54, citing Pope Pius XII, Encyclical Letter *Humani Generis* (1950), AAS 42, 563-64.

on the Cross, all the sins of philosophers were lifted with Him unto their consummation. Mary, in suffering union with her Son, *stood at the Foot of the Cross* until His mission was completed, and the sacramental life of the Church began to flow from the water and blood flowing from His pierced side. Edith Stein/Sister Benedicta reflected on the hidden mystery of Mary at the foot of the Cross: "She lives, she is wedded to the Lamb, but the hour of the solemn marriage supper will only arrive when the dragon has been completely conquered and the last of the redeemed have fought their battle to the end."[72] When Jesus' lifeless Body is taken down and given to Mary, Throne of Wisdom, her lap becomes another table which holds the mystery of death and life.[73]

8. The Resurrection, Ascension, and Sending of the Holy Spirit

Recall again the time in 1901, when despair drove Raïssa and Jacques Maritain to a form of suicide pact in the Jardin des Plantes. Within the year, they began to have an experience of personal resurrection from the despair into which they had been plunged. The Maritains entered into dialogue with friends like Léon Bloy, read Bergson, Pascal, and Teresa of Avila, and visited Holy sites like the Cathedral of Chartres. These experiences of good people, religious philosophers, saints, and sacred beauty contributed to a beginning of resurrection from despair.

Raïssa also described the poignant moment in 1902 when she and Jacques were sitting together, and a gesture and glance brought the mutual realization of an eternal source of their human and divine love: "The feeling flowed through me that always—for my happiness and my salvation ... that always my life would be bound up with Jacques. It was one of those tender and peaceful feelings, which are like a gift flowing from a region higher than ourselves, illuminating the future and deepening the present. From that moment our understanding was perfect and unchangeable."[74] The discovery of profound, eternal

---

[72] Edith Stein, *The Hidden Life*, 98-99. See also, 107.

[73] Rev. John Bartunek, *Inside the Passion*, quoting Elizabeth Lev, describes how in Gibson's *Passion of the Christ*: "Mary [holds] one hand cradling his [Jesus'] body and the other hand open toward the viewer ... Mary looks straight out at us ... provoking a full and conscious acknowledgment of whom this suffering has been for," 164.

[74] Raïssa Maritain, *We Have Been Friends Together*, 85.

human love, like a grace of truth flowing from above, also contributed to the overcoming of temptations towards a meaningless life and death. Raïssa and Jacques decided to become engaged; and they were married in 1904. Through the Resurrection and Ascension of Jesus Christ, and the sending of the Holy Spirit at Pentecost, Christians are called into a true *communio*, which transforms their interpersonal relationships. Responding to this call, in 1906, Jacques, Raïssa, and Vera, her sister, were Baptized and received their first communion.

Years after their conversion to Catholicism, Raïssa and Jacques Maritain described in their *Journals* and *Notebooks* how they worked together to help one another become Christian philosophers. In retrospect Jacques wrote: "I want justice to be done to Raïssa. If there is anything good in my philosophical work, and in my books, this has its deep source and light in her contemplative prayer and in the oblation of herself she made to God."[75] A little later in the same text, he gives a more detailed example of how Raïssa fostered his personal integrity:

> ...[S]he succeeded by a hard effort of will (and because the collaboration I had always asked of her was, for her, a sacred duty) in revising in manuscript everything I have written and published, both in French and English.... Physically shattered by [her sister] Vera's death, she wept, less over her bereavement, than over certain passages in my first draft [of *On Moral Philosophy*] where I had allowed subjectivity with its bitternesses and its anger to intrude. This she rightly judged unworthy of philosophy, and her mind, bless her, was not set at rest until philosophical objectivity had won the day...[76]

This collaboration of Jacques and Raïssa is also evident when they wrote about love and friendship. In the *Fourth Notebook* for April 20, 1924, Raïssa entered: "The essence of love is in the communication of oneself, with fullness of joy and delight in the possession of the beloved. The essence of friendship is in desire for the good of one's

---

[75] *Raïssa's Journal presented by Jacques Maritain* (Albany, N.Y.: Magi Books, 1974), 8.

[76] Ibid., 13.

friend, strong enough to sacrifice for him."[77] Jacques elaborated on her theory in *On Moral Philosophy,* in a section entitled "Love and Friendship: A Marginal note to the *Journal de Raïssa*": "I will comment on and develop certain things which Raïssa expressed very clearly but very briefly ... Raïssa had the wisdom of the Holy Spirit."[78] During one of her long periods of illness and incapacity to speak, Jacques summarized: "I feel Raïssa is *consubstantialised* to truth, so that all words become a lie and a hurt.... No other resource, I think, than Jesus himself, Jesus in his humanity, Jesus Saviour ... whose human glance understands and heals."[79] Jacques here is in the place of Mary, at the foot of the cross of Raïssa, who is suffering her agony with Jesus; both were living the mystery of the sequence 'foreknown, predestined, and called to be conformed to the image of the Son.'

This dialogue of love dwelled in Jacques long after Raïssa's death: "And right up to the last, she found help and comfort in the precious exchanges which delighted her, in conversation with her friends, and in those talks which she knew so well how to direct and animate from her corner of the blue sofa in the living-room at Princeton—that place where I always see her and which I cannot think without a stab of pain."[80] Raïssa, in the genius of her unique *ethos* as a Christian philosopher, was truly the table at which Jacques sat in thought.

Pope John Paul II reminds us in his final publication, *Memory and Identity,* that "Mary's memory is a source of singular importance for knowing Christ, an incomparable source ... Mary was present at his Ascension into heaven, she was with the Apostles in the Upper Room awaiting the descent of the Holy Spirit, and she was a witness to the birth of the Church on the day of Pentecost."[81] Adrienne von Speyr also

---

[77] Ibid., 162. She adds: "God loves us with friendship by providing for all our necessities and by dying for us on the Cross," 163.

[78] Jacques Maritain, *Untrammeled Approaches* (Notre Dame: University of Notre Dame, 1997), 165.

[79] *Raïssa's Journal,* 251 (Loose Leaves from one of my notebooks, J.); his emphasis.

[80] Ibid., 13.

[81] John Paul II, *Memory and Identity: Conversations at the Dawn of a Millennium* (Rome: Rizzoli, 2005), 148-49.

draws out an important implication of Pentecost: "...the Son is in heaven while the Mother is still on earth: this distance has to be bridged ... there exists for her an especially active relationship of exchange between heaven and earth."[82]

How Mary was well-prepared for this mission by her Son, was beautifully described by Cardinal Newman: "Mary for thirty continuous years saw and heard him, being all through that time face to face with him, and being able to ask him any question which she wished explained, and know that the answers she received were from the Eternal God, who neither deceives nor can be deceived."[83] Newman further amplifies Mary's active engagement in her intellectual formation in relation to the Truth:

> She does not think it enough to accept, she dwells upon it; not enough to possess, she uses it; not enough to assent, she develops it; not enough to submit the reason, she reasons upon it ... to investigate, and weigh, and define, as well as to profess the Gospel; to draw the line between truth and heresy; to anticipate or remedy the various aberrations of wrong reason; to combat price and recklessness with their own arms; and thus to triumph over the sophist and the innovator.[84]

9. The Assumption and Four Marian Apparitions

The dogma of the Assumption, proclaimed in 1950 and reaffirmed by the Second Vatican Council in 1964 (*Lumen Gentium* #59) says that Mary, "on the completion of her earthly sojourn was taken up body and soul into heavenly glory."[85] Recalling the sequence that began this study: foreknown, predestined, called, justified, and glorified, Mary fulfilled the end of her vocation by being taken into the heart of the Holy

---

[82] Adrienne von Speyr, *Mary in the Redemption* (San Francisco: Ignatius, 2003), 108-09.

[83] John Henry Newman, *The Mystical Rose: Thoughts on the Blessed Virgin from the Writings of John Henry Cardinal Newman* (Princeton: Scepter, 1996), 95.

[84] *Mary: The Virgin Mary in the Life and Writings of John Henry Newman*, Philip Boyce, ed. (Grand Rapids, Michigan: Eerdmans, 2001), 188-89.

[85] John Paul II, *Theotokos: Woman, Mother, Disciple: A Catechesis on Mary, Mother of God*, vol. 5 (Boston: Pauline Media, 2000), 203.

Trinity, as daughter of the Eternal Father, Mother of the Beloved Son, and Spouse of the Holy Spirit.

Since Mary's Assumption, body and soul, into heaven, she has from time to time visited the earth, as a pilgrim guide, to continue to teach us who are still on pilgrimage.[86] Hans Urs von Balthasar explains why we should be attentive to the meaning of Marian apparitions:

> Simply by the fact that she shows herself she already leads us into the mystery of what the Church is in her essential nature: a pure work of God's grace. Mary is able, precisely in a spirit of complete humility, to point to herself because she is thereby pointing to nothing other than what God's almighty grace is capable of and at the same time what we should strive after in order to become proper vessels for this grace, in order to play the real role of the Church (as the body and bride of Christ) correctly in her mission of salvation for the world.[87]

Let us consider some brief reflections of a few philosophers who wrote about their profound personal encounter with truth revealed in a particular Marian apparition. Mary's appearance at La Salette, France, in 1846, deeply touched the Maritains. Raïssa wrote after she and Jacques had made a pilgrimage to the site of the apparition: "We climbed the steep road, said to be very dangerous; it was still difficult in those days. Surely its narrowness was like that of the gate of heaven. An immense rock wall to the left, an abyss to the right.... We finally arrived ... where the children had seen Our Lady sitting and weeping, then standing to speak to them, then drawn up into the heavens. In this lofty retreat we prepared ourselves to receive the Sacrament of Confirmation."[88]

Léon Bloy, a close friend of the Maritains, drew out some of the implications of this apparition: "Thus she is stricken, even in the very bosom of Beatitude. Reason is lost in this thought. A beatitude that

---

[86] John Paul II, *Redemptoris Mater* (Boston: Daughters of St. Paul, 1987), Part II 'The Mother of God at the Center of the Pilgrim Church,' #25-49.

[87] Hans Urs von Balthasar, *Mary for Today* (San Francisco: Ignatius, 1988), 44.

[88] Ibid., 150.

'suffers' and weeps— is it possible to conceive such a thing?"[89] The conjunction of beatitude and suffering in Mary at La Salette helped the Maritains overcome their previous understanding of the limits of Aristotelian metaphysics and theology. Raïssa wrote:

> This conjunction of suffering and Beatitude is allowed neither by theology nor by Aristotle. Beatitude means absolute fullness, and suffering is the cry of that which is wounded. But our God is a crucified God: the Beatitude of which He cannot be deprived did not prevent Him from fearing or mourning ... or from passing through the throes of death on the Cross, or from feeling abandoned.... For a created being, to be capable of suffering is a real perfection; it is the lot of life and of the spirit, it is the greatness of man.[90]

In Guadalupe, Mexico, in 1531 and Lourdes, France, in 1858, Mary teaches about pregnancy and conception. Our Lady of Guadalupe gave a real imprint of herself as a young pregnant woman and, at Lourdes, she tells her name: "I am the Immaculate Conception."[91] In our present context of a culture of death, Mary revealed in these apparitions that she was foreknown, predestined, and called at the moment of her conception. This dogma of faith should stir the minds of philosophers who write about when human life begins.

Balthasar wrote about the transforming effect of a smile of love in interpersonal encounters: "Now man exists only in dialogue with his neighbor. The infant is brought to consciousness of himself only by love, by the smile of his mother."[92] Mary of Guadalupe's radiant smile, joined to the words with which she would help Juan Diego overcome

---

[89] Léon Bloy, quoted by Raïssa Maritain, *We Have Been Friends Together*, 148.

[90] Ibid., 48-49.

[91] For a history of the dogmatic bulls on the doctrine of the Immaculate Conception, see *Mother of Christ, Mother of the Church: Documents on the Blessed Virgin Mary* (Boston: Daughters of St. Paul, 2001).

[92] Hans Urs von Balthasar, *My Work: in Retrospect* (San Francisco: Ignatius, 1993), 114. See also Johann Roten, S.M., "The Two Halves of the Moon: Marian Anthropological Dimensions in the Common Mission of Adrienne von Speyr and Hans Urs von Balthasar," in David L. Schindler, ed. *Hans Urs von Balthasar: His Life and Work* (San Francisco: Ignatius, 1991): 65-86, especially 79-81.

the Bishop's lack of belief in her appearance, filled him with joy. Even today the image on Juan Diego's *tilma* left during the apparition portrays Mary's smile. At Lourdes, St. Bernadette also concluded that Mary was happy with her actions because of "the Beautiful Lady's smile."[93]

John Paul II said in *Crossing the Threshold of Hope* that there "is a certain continuity among La Salette, Lourdes, and Fátima (1916-1917)—and, in the distant past, our Polish Jasna Góra."[94] This continuity contains two dynamics: Mary had no fear after the Resurrection, and "Christ will conquer through her, because he wants the Church's victories now and in the future to be linked to her."[95]

Symbolically depicting this, the Crown of Our Lady of Fatima now contains the bullet, which wounded the late Holy Father on her feast day, May 13, 1981. In a chapter entitled "Someone must have guided that bullet," in his final publication *Memory and Identity* (2005), Pope John Paul II pondered: "Acga knew how to shoot, and he certainly shot to kill. Yet it was as if someone was guiding and deflecting that bullet."[96] Repeating a conversation with the late Holy Father, Archbishop Stanislaw Dziwicz shared his experience of how Mary's presence helped support the fulfillment of the Pope's vocation:

> Five months after the attack, the Holy Father returned to Saint Peter's Square to meet the faithful once again. He showed not a trace of fear, nor even of stress, although the doctors had warned that this was a possibility. He said on that occasion: "Again I have become indebted to the Blessed Virgin.... Could I forget that the event in Saint Peter's Square took place on the

---

[93] In another well-known example, Thérèse of Lisieux recounts how, after being gravely ill, she became instantly cured while looking at a statue of Mary in her room: "The Blessed Virgin had seemed very beautiful to me, and I had seen her smile at me." Hans Urs von Balthasar, *Two Sisters in the Spirit: Thérèse of Lisieux and Elizabeth of the Trinity* (San Francisco: Ignatius, 1992), 99-100.

[94] John Paul II, *Crossing the Threshold of Hope* (New York: Alfred A. Knopf, 1994), 221.

[95] Ibid., 200-21.

[96] John Paul II, *Memory and Identity*, 159.

day and at the hour when the first appearance of the Mother of Christ to the poor little peasants has been remembered for over sixty years at Fatima in Portugal? For in everything that happened to me on that very day, I felt that extraordinary motherly protection and care, which turned out to be stronger than the deadly bullet."[97]

10. Conclusion

The harmony between the vocation to true philosophy and Mary's vocation has many points of contact. Mary, as a type of philosopher, sitting in thought at the altar, which provided the bread of life to the world, gives us much to ponder. We have considered Mary's personal acts of intellect and will at the Annunciation, her communal sharing of vocation at the Visitation, her symbolic receptivity to faith and reason at the Epiphany, her generous and thoughtful acts of love at Cana, her consistent willingness to walk with and stand by the Transcendent God, her beloved Son, in the presence of the evils surrounding Him and whose weight were carried by His Cross, and her continued availability to teach us through the Holy Spirit after her glorious Assumption. May we be reminded whenever we are at an altar of the Eucharist, Cross, banquet, desk, podium, or seminar table, that God and Mary gently but persistently invite us into a deeper love and fidelity to our vocation to become Christian philosophers, foreknown and called to be conformed to the image of the Beloved Son.

[97] Ibid., 163.

PART II

The Vocation of Philosophy

Yves R. Simon: A Question of Calling

Ralph Nelson

Although he published some forty articles previously, it seems convenient to date the beginning of Yves R. Simon's academic career to the appearance of his two works in 1934, *An Introduction to Metaphysics of Knowledge* and *A Critique of Moral Knowledge*.[1] In the former, he addresses the relation between knowledge and activity or action. To these two lines of inquiry, he added political philosophy, understood as part of ethics in the Aristotelian sense, from the Aquinas Lecture of 1940 to his more complete account in *Philosophy of Democratic Government*.[2]

So while he is primarily known as a political philosopher, a very strong argument can be made that he was above all a metaphysician,[3]

---

[1] [From 1923-1933, Simon published a number of mostly short articles, in *Les Cahiers Catholiques*, *La Démocratie*, *La Vie Intellectuelle*, and *Revue de Philosophie*. He then published *Introduction à l'ontologie du connaître* (Paris, Desclée de Brouwer, 1934): English, *An Introduction to Metaphysics of Knowledge*, trans. Vukan Kuic and Richard J. Thompson (New York: Fordham University Press, 1990), and *Critique de la connaissance morale* (Paris: Desclée de Brouwer, 1934): English, *A Critique of Moral Knowledge*, trans. Ralph McInerny (New York: Fordham University Press, 2003). For reference to Simon's earliest articles, and also to more recent, and sometimes revised, editions of works cited herein, see Anthony O. Simon's "Definitive Yves R. Simon Bibliography," in *Acquaintance with the Absolute: The Philosophy of Yves R. Simon*, ed. Anthony O. Simon (New York: Fordham University Press, 1998), 189-293—ED.]

[2] Yves R. Simon, *Nature and Functions of Authority* (Milwaukee, Wisconsin: Marquette University Press, 1940), and *Philosophy of Democratic Government* (Chicago: University of Chicago Press, 1951). [For Simon's later reflections on authority, see the posthumously published *A General Theory of Authority*, intro. Vukan Kuic (Notre Dame, Indiana: University of Notre Dame Press, 1980)—ED.]

[3] Raymond L. Dennehy says that "metaphysics remains both pervasive in and key to his thinking" in "Yves R. Simon's Metaphysics of Action," in *Acquaintance with the Absolute*, 19.

especially in establishing the basis of his democratic philosophy using the Thomist theory of universals in dealing with issues of equality. Even before his first book, he had expressed praise of metaphysics in an essay on the philosopher Alain.[4] And then, after the *Metaphysics of Knowledge*, there was *Foresight and Knowledge*,[5] a treatise in the philosophy of science which, as Simon remarks, is construed as part of metaphysics, even as was *Trois leçons sur le travail*, in which he says: "Let us pursue then the metaphysical analysis of manual work."[6] And later he refers to the "metaphysical characteristics of contemplation,"[7] indicating at each stage of the analyses that it is metaphysical, as would be the forms of activity between these two principal poles.

We may add to this list the very important essay "On Order in Analogical Sets," stating that "the fundamental concepts of metaphysics are analogical."[8] In like manner, let us consider his treatment of practical knowledge in its various forms: from moral philosophy to prudential determination. In this respect, a rather long period was to pass until Simon reexamined a number of the basic issues contained in the collection entitled *Practical Knowledge*.[9] Of course he had written a treatise on free choice, *Traité du libre arbitre* (1951), revised later in the

---

[4] Yves R. Simon, "The Politics of Alain," trans. John M. Dunaway, *Interpretation*, vol. 13, no. 2 (1985): 231.

[5] Yves R. Simon, *Foresight and Knowledge*, eds. Ralph Nelson and Anthony O. Simon (New York: Fordham University Press, 1995), xxi. "We believe that the part of philosophy which takes scientific knowledge as its object is only metaphysics itself in the exercise of its critical function": "Philosophy of Science," *Revue de philosophie*, VI, no. I (1935): 62.

[6] Yves R. Simon, *Trois leçons sur le travail* (Paris: Pierre Téqui, 1938), 2. [For his most mature reflections on work, see *Work, Society, and Culture*, ed. Vukan Kuic (New York: Fordham University Press, 1971)—ED.]

[7] Ibid., 3.

[8] Yves R. Simon, *Philosopher at Work: Essays by Yves R. Simon*, ed. Anthony O. Simon (Lanham, Maryland: Rowman and Littlefield, 1999), 139.

[9] Yves R. Simon, *Practical Knowledge*, ed. Robert J. Mulvaney (New York: Fordham University Press, 1991).

English translation.[10] His lectures on *The Tradition of Natural Law* and *The Definition of Moral Virtue* were published posthumously.[11]

What is characteristic of Simon's writing on almost any subject is the tendency to return to earlier problems for reconsideration and emendation. The contrast between *A Critique of Moral Knowledge* (1934) and *Practical Knowledge* (with inclusions from 1953 to 1961) is instructive not only on a range of issues, but significantly on the task of moral philosophy itself. In the earlier work, in which the conception of a theoretically practical science was elaborated at length, the purpose of moral philosophy was stated to be "to direct action from a distance, doubtless, but even so efficaciously,"[12] and again he says, "moral philosophy has for its end to direct action, however remotely."[13] Or the purpose could be stated, "to guide action, though from a distance." The repetition of such expressions in the *Critique* suffices to inform us how important this aim was in the earlier case. It also brings to our attention how Simon's meditations had evolved in the following twenty-five years. For in *Practical Knowledge*, while the idea of a directive moral knowledge is not repudiated, there is clearly a different emphasis.

Using the important distinction between explanation and fulfillment, he describes a "discipline in which the features of scientific thought unite with the purpose of directing action."[14] Furthermore, "inasmuch as ethical science directs human action (albeit from a distance), it exercises a function that is entirely foreign to the theoretic sciences."[15] And Simon next wants to emphasize the theoretical side of theoretically practical knowledge: "the primary purpose of moral

---

[10] Yves R. Simon, *Traité du libre arbitre* (Liège: Sciences et lettres, 1951): revised English edition *Freedom of Choice*, ed. Peter Wolff (New York: Fordham University, 1969).

[11] Yves R. Simon, *The Tradition of Natural Law*, ed. Vukan Kuic (New York: Fordham University, 1965) and *The Definition of Moral Virtue*, ed. Vukan Kuic (New York: Fordham University, 1986).

[12] Yves R. Simon, *Critique de la connaissance morale*, 87.

[13] Yves R. Simon, *A Critique of Moral Knowledge*, 47.

[14] Yves R. Simon, *Practical Knowledge*, 42.

[15] Ibid., 46.

philosophy is to understand moral essences."[16] And a little further he adds, "the explanation of moral essences."[17] The reliance on explanation over fulfillment leads him to state "that moral philosophy is principally analytical,"[18] whereas earlier a rather clear cut distinction was made between the analytical aspects of philosophy and the moral synthesis.

Why does he now pay so much attention to the theoretical character of moral philosophy? I think he finds this concentration necessary at a time when tradition and traditional values are in decline, and when there is a general demand, not only in ethics, for reasons to be given and for explanations to be provided; and if that is indeed the situation, then moral philosophy's primary aim in these times is theoretical, analytical, and explanatory. Whatever guidance it can provide now plays a secondary role.

Simon raised questions about moral and social facts in the *Critique*, particularly the relationship between moral philosophy and the social sciences. In an essay that appeared in 1932, he takes up the issue of the role of 'facts' in philosophy generally. This is a topic that certainly shows the influence of Henri Bergson, particularly concerning the use of scientific facts in philosophical discourse. It is a principle of Aristotelian philosophy that the source of all our knowledge is sense experience. Even in metaphysics, which is purely rational, it is also empirical in that it incorporates facts. When it comes to the resolution of concepts, metaphysics is resolved in the intelligible, in being. Physics, on the other hand, resolves its concepts in the observable, the senses. There are also differences between the definitions of terms in the philosophical and empiriological spheres.[19]

In the conclusion of his analysis, Simon indicates "the empirical character of philosophy;" that is, it is based on facts.[20] However, there

---

[16] Ibid., 53.

[17] Ibid., 54.

[18] Ibid., 56. "To say that moral philosophy directs human action *from a distance* is to use a well-grounded metaphor. In fact, the distance is often great."

[19] Yves R. Simon, "Philosophers and Facts," *The Great Dialogue of Nature and Space*, ed. Gerard J. Dalcourt (Albany: Magi Books, 1973), 142.

[20] Ibid., 144.

are three kinds of fact: the vulgar, the scientific, and the philosophical. "In each case there is an absolute that determines the mind's attitude; in each case it is an experience that resolves the issue."[21] In a more technical formulation: "*To formulate a fact then is to make an existential judgment under the guarantee of a sensation.*"[22] In pursuit of his principal thesis that there are three different levels, so neither science nor philosophy can take a fact from the vulgar or common level without refinement or, let us say, 'transformation.' But more to the point, he rejects the notion of a philosophy based on scientific facts. "Philosophy ought to entrust to nothing but itself the task of establishing the facts which it uses."[23] He offers us a list of philosophical facts:

> Being exists; sensible being is multiple and subject to change; every sensible being presents a plurality of parts outside of each other; the things that fall under our sense admit of inequalities of perfection; there is order in the universe; all sensible beings are endowed with activity; there are some beings that are alive and others that are not; there are some beings that can know and some that cannot.[24]

He then adds that "these fundamental philosophical facts are at the same time facts of common experience."[25] However, some of the data of common experience require philosophical grounding: stated somewhat differently, "some philosophical facts can be established only through the technical elaboration of an experience."[26]

Simon uses the expression "*the empirical absolute*"[27] in this context. At the end of "An Essay on Sensation," he returns to this theme when he says:

---

[21] Ibid., 146.

[22] Ibid., 147.

[23] Ibid., 152.

[24] Ibid., 153.

[25] Ibid.

[26] Ibid.

[27] Ibid., 155.

> The experimental absolute, the fact, the thing by reason of which we make the difference between to be and not to be, is primarily delivered to us in an act that relativity and fluidity characterize. By going more deeply into the contrasted meanings of the experimental absolute and of the flux in which it is attained, much could be learned about sensation, and also about human nature, for the definition of man implies, among other things, that it is in the flux of a relation to sense qualities that he achieves his first acquaintance with the absolute.[28]

Simon maintains that "there are no metaphysical facts because we experience only physical beings."[29] He distinguishes moral facts from physical facts, and he argues that the former is "absolutely *sui generis.*"[30] So there will be facts appropriate to practical knowledge as there are to theoretical. And there are judgments of value just as there are judgments about states of affairs.

Now the previous remarks may give an idea of the range of Simon's interests, but what I shall try to explain is how Simon conceived the vocation of the philosopher, and I believe this can best be discussed by seeing how he approached four topics: common sense, ideology, current affairs, and theology. For my thesis is how the treatment of these topics reveals not only the task of the philosopher, but his vocation as well. Let us begin with the passage that introduces philosophy and common sense: "Common sense includes a rudimentary philosophy and this philosophy formulates facts which a technical philosophy will make its own while rendering their formulation more precise."[31]

No one was a more indefatigable champion of common sense in philosophy than Mortimer Adler. In a series of books spanning some twenty years, he has discussed common sense in philosophy generally, in moral philosophy (ethics and politics), and in regard to Aristotle. Sometimes he seemed to treat common sense as opinion rather than

---

[28] Yves R. Simon, "An Essay on Sensation," in *Philosopher at Work*, 111.

[29] Yves R. Simon, *The Great Dialogue of Nature and Space*, 161, n. 8.

[30] Ibid., 159.

[31] Ibid., 155.

knowledge. However, for the most part he represents it as a *kind* of knowledge, as in *The Conditions of Philosophy*.[32] When it concerns ethics, however, Adler seems to make common sense more than a starting point that philosophic reason adopts, but the whole itself. In other words, it seems that the ethics of common sense and philosophy are co-extensive. The ethics at stake is Aristotelian, for this is the conclusion one comes to when Adler states, "as Aristotle is uniquely the philosopher of common sense, so his moral philosophy is uniquely the ethics of common sense."[33]

The principal objection to Adler's use of the term, here and elsewhere, is that one never knows precisely what is the object and scope of common sense awareness. I mentioned Adler in order to situate Simon's reflections on common sense and philosophy in regard to a tendency to find a close connection between the two. What, then, are Simon's conclusions?

The most thorough account of common sense can be found in *Freedom of Choice*.[34] Lacking any functional unity, common sense "is an aggregate of propositions, none of which requires, in the mind that assents to it, the refinement of a special and technical training."[35] Not all these propositions are known to all, nor are they "equally clear to all."[36] There are three kinds of proposition: those of a "philosophic character which are the starting point of every philosophy and science, propositions dictated by the leanings of the imagination, and propositions expressing a practical vision of the physical world."[37] And this means that a certain purification is required to render them fit for intellectual inquiry. Simon notes that "science normally conflicts with the imagery of common sense according to which the earth is flat,

---

[32] Mortimer J. Adler, *The Conditions of Philosophy* (New York: Atheneum, 1965), 139.

[33] Mortimer J. Adler, *The Time of Our Lives: The Ethics of Common Sense* (New York: Holt, Rinehart, and Winston, 1970), 236. See also his *Six Great Ideas* (New York: Macmillan, 1981), 7.

[34] Yves R. Simon, *Freedom of Choice*, 83-94.

[35] Ibid., 84.

[36] Ibid.

[37] Ibid.

people at the antipodes have their heads hanging downwards, light bodies cannot fall as fast as heavy ones ... substance is something dense and hard like a desk made of oak, etc."[38]

Sometimes common sense is in conflict with physics, for which "the earth and the feather attract each other, whereas for common sense, the earth attracts the feather, though weakly, and the feather does not attract the earth at all."[39] But sometimes science adopts the common sense understanding of the world, so "the concept of chance occurence as an unpredictable event is a common sense notion accepted and modified by science."[40] In *Foresight and Knowledge*, this was explained at greater length. And the reason common sense accepts this notion of chance is attributed to its practical perspective, and so what is right in one context, the practical, "may hamper the perception of theoretical truth."[41] Simon counters this common sense (and scientific) proposition by a definition of chance as "*the manifest plurality of the causal process from which it results.*"[42] So the common sense notion of chance is influenced by practical interests. Consequently, since "common sense defines chance in relation to prediction, because it considers chance from the standpoint of action, we should not be surprised that philosophy has to correct common sense on a subject whose human significance never abates."[43]

Simon then turns to what he calls "the rudimentary"—sometimes elementary—"philosophy professed by common sense."[44] This is limited by the images it employs as well as by practical interests. We can say that this rudimentary system is philosophy in an imperfect state. It is the source of technical philosophy as common sense is a source of science. Firstly, it may contain the axioms of universal reason, although Simon says that these axioms are "antecedent to all philosophy and

---

[38] Ibid.

[39] Ibid., 85.

[40] Ibid.

[41] Yves R. Simon, *Foresight and Knowledge*, 8.

[42] Ibid., 9.

[43] Ibid., 10.

[44] Yves R. Simon, *Freedom of Choice*, 85.

placed above all philosophy —that of common sense included."[45] Secondly, a philosophy of common sense includes the statement of philosophical facts. Lastly, he asserts that common sense philosophy includes demonstrations, and he singles out those pertaining to God and to human freedom. But he recognizes that such propositions are in a state in which it is difficult to sort them out. He even refers to "the metaphysics of common sense," while admitting that "the metaphysical thoughts of common sense are living and active only within an atmosphere saturated with images."[46] All of this ends up convincing us that common sense philosophy is an imperfect state, immersed in imagery, and lacking adequate means of communicability.

As to the common sense notion of freedom, it may grasp the relation between reason and responsibility and freedom. It is sometimes believed that the deliverances of common sense are sufficient for philosophical demonstration and this is not supported by Simon. What he has tried to show is how rudimentary and inadequate such a common sense philosophy is, in order to make the case for a "technically elaborated apparatus."[47]

So in comparing Adler's position with that articulated by Simon, there is no doubt that common sense is a source for both of them, and there may be agreement between them concerning the common sense presuppositions of technical philosophy. However, the salient difference between the two is that Adler wanted to identify both his ethics and his political philosophy with common sense, while Simon never expressed, nor suggested, such an idea. He was intent on pointing out the contrast between them.

If philosophy, in Simon's estimation, is not the same as common sense as a system of thought, it is important for him to distinguish it from another system of thought more likely to be confused with it: ideology. The relevant texts on the comparison of the two are found in *The Tradition of Natural Law*, based on a course given at the University of Chicago in the winter quarter of 1958. "An ideology is a system of propositions which, though indistinguishable so far as expression goes

---

[45] Ibid., 86.

[46] Ibid., 89-90.

[47] Ibid., 94.

from statements about facts and essences, actually refers not so much to any real state of affairs as to the *aspirations* of a society at a certain *time* in its evolution."[48] Since a natural law theory may be either philosophical or ideological, we have to show in a more precise way what factors divide them. This is found in the definition of ideology and in its three major components. Its notion of truth is utilitarian, sociological, and evolutionistic.[49] This means that it is an instrument of change or preservation; the aspirations it expresses are those of a definite group, and "when that group expresses its timely aspirations in the language of everlasting truth."[50] As an instance of a writer who is noted for his slavery ideology, Simon mentions the political works of John C. Calhoun. He does not question the sincerity of such statements.

Philosophy, on the contrary, sees in its propositions an objective property, not founded on the "sociological weight of common belief."[51] To this extent an ideology is similar to folklore, superstition, and old wives' tales. "An ideology, precisely considered as such, is a system of propositions which carry a heavy sociological weight."[52] The philosopher's role is to examine an ideology for its truth-value and he can be called a critic of ideology. "Ideology imitates philosophy; it uses expressions principally relative to essential, intelligible, and everlasting necessities."[53] Thus one can contrast the two because ideology involves "an object of desire," while "the object of philosophy is a pure object."[54]

Simon does not want to exaggerate the degree to which philosophy and science are successful in turning out completely demonstrative arguments, nor does he believe that it is an easy task to keep philosophy from the contamination of ideology. Only a perfect philosophy could achieve this. He is of the opinion that the Greek

---

[48] Yves R. Simon, *The Tradition of Natural Law*, 16-17.

[49] Ibid., 17.

[50] Ibid.

[51] Ibid., 19.

[52] Ibid., 20.

[53] Ibid., 21.

[54] Ibid.

philosophers succeeded in transcending these social aspirations, though he thought that Aristotle, so exemplary in this regard, was not free from ideological influences when he deals with manual labor and slavery. This transcendence is clearly more difficult in moral matters. Natural law enters the picture here, and there have always been legal scholars like Hans Kelsen to argue that all natural law theories are ideological.[55]

Having shown ways in which philosophy and ideology are different, Simon admits that sometimes there is an identity between an ideology and a philosophy, and a society might consider itself blessed "when aspirations coincide with truth."[56] However, I think that his basic message is that there is an inevitable tension between the philosophical vocation and the ideological temptation; that is, there are contemporary instances of ideological contamination of the particular kind that leads philosophers to abandon or hide the truth. That is, he was concerned with the need to resist the siren songs of twentieth century ideologies.

There is a passage in which Simon raises the issue of the function of philosophers in society that provides a transition to our next theme, the philosopher and commentary on current events. "Are there circumstances in which philosophers are called to utter judgments about present events and trends and by public statement to try to influence history?"[57] Writing as he did in the last years of his life, Simon's question might seem merely rhetorical. Yet there were obviously problems in undertaking that task since a philosopher spends a good deal of time doing research in libraries, and he is mainly experienced in the treatment of abstract ideas. Moreover, "a philosopher is not equipped to handle contingent matters and he probably can never fully escape the ideological influence of the society in which he lives."[58] Yet, on the positive side, he knows what prudence

---

[55] Hans Kelsen, *Pure Theory of Law*, trans. Max Knight (Berkeley: University of California, 1967), 217-21.

[56] Yves R. Simon, *The Tradition of Natural Law*, 24.

[57] Ibid.

[58] Ibid., 25.

is, and as a student of theoretically practical science, he is qualified as a moral educator.

In *The March to Liberation*, Simon, speaking as a "man of science by profession,"[59] with a responsibility for serving humanity, will discuss specific issues that have arisen in the Second World War. In *Community of the Free*, a "reflection upon the concrete conditions of public morality in these days in which we live,"[60] he confronts the confusion of consciences and what he calls "mechanisms of illusion." "A philosopher has some chance of making himself useful by trying to understand the operation of these mechanisms and exposing them."[61] This work is particularly interesting for, in the course of dealing with the concrete conditions, the moral philosopher who as a theoretician examines the question of truth, defines the freedom of autonomy, argues for a universal ethics, invokes the principles of commutative justice, and remarks on what is wrong with the use of quotas.

So beginning with *La Compagne d'Ethiopie et la pensée politique française* (1936),[62] continuing with *The Road to Vichy: 1918-1938* (1942)[63] and the *March to Liberation* (1942) and finally with the original version of *Community of the Free* (1945), Simon addressed contemporary political issues. Did he succeed in avoiding ideological bias in these works? I think he did.

---

[59] Yves R. Simon, *La Marche à la délivrance* (New York: Editions de la maison française, 1942), 10: English, *The March to Liberation*, trans. Victor M. Hamm (Milwaukee, Wisconsin: The Tower Press, 1942), 102. I have used the French original because the English translation is inaccurate here.

[60] Yves R. Simon, *Community of the Free*, trans. Willard R. Trask (New York: Henry Holt and Company, 1947), ix.

[61] Ibid., x.

[62] Yves R. Simon, *La Compagne d'Ethiopie et la pensée politique française* (Lille: Société d'impressions littéraires, industrielles, et commerciales, 1936). [For a revised English edition, see *The Ethiopian Campaign and French Political Thought*, ed. Anthony O. Simon, trans. Robert Royal (Notre Dame, Indiana: University of Notre Dame Press, 2009)—ED.]

[63] Yves R. Simon, *The Road to Vichy: 1918-1938*, revised edition, trans. James A. Corbett and George J. McMorrow, new introduction by John Hellman (Lanham: University Press of America, 1988).

However, the reasons for the philosopher occupying himself—"making himself useful"—with such practical and contingent events was not brought out clearly until his lectures on the tradition of natural law in 1958. Simon first states the problem:

> When souls devastated by skepticism, desperation, and meaninglessness express their willingness to believe that the universe of morality is not merely a tale told by an idiot, philosophers would fail in their function if they requested these eager souls to wait until definitions are perfect, deductions strict, and axioms expressed in incontrovertible formulas.[64]

Accordingly, "the appropriate behavior may be described as a movement back and forth between the kind of thought and expression that the state of society and souls urgently require and the condition of theoretical purity and intelligible lucidity, which can be approached only very slowly and only through many trials and errors."[65] That explains what Simon hoped to achieve in his reflections on current affairs from 1936 to 1945.

Finally, let us examine the relationship between the philosopher and theology, supernatural theology. In a rare piece in which he directly deals with theology, Simon addressed the topic of "The Rationality of Christian Faith."[66] More precisely he analyzes faith, philosophy, and theology. This paper may be seen as a completion of his epistemological project since he compares philosophy and theology, in order to clearly mark their distinctive realms, their starting points, their demonstrations, and their conclusions. It is an extremely fine, rich account of theology, but it is not controversial.

On the other hand, he reported on Jacques Maritain's position that moral philosophy must be subalternated to theology if it is to be adequate to its object, as first expressed in *An Essay on Christian Philosophy*. Simon's remark in a footnote in *Critique* is noncommital: "The idea is quite new, open to discussion, and we do not mean to take

---

[64] Yves R. Simon, *The Tradition of Natural Law*, 39.

[65] Ibid.

[66] Yves R. Simon, "The Rationality of Christian Faith," *Philosopher at Work*, 41-55.

a stand on it now."[67] In fact, a considerable time was to pass before Simon took up the subject again, particularly in his extensive correspondence with Maritain. Concerning the question of moral philosophy, Simon says, "our own position is that a purely rational moral philosophy is essentially misleading."[68] He admits the possibility of a moral philosophy adequately taken. But he wonders if it is just "a duplicate of moral theology."[69] After reviewing the various factors in play, Simon states: "I merely raise this question without attempting to answer it, or even to formulate it properly."[70] Furthermore, he insists that "better judges will be able to say whether all this weighs in favor of a moral philosophy adequately taken, subalternated indeed to theology, but distinct from it."[71]

The exchange between Simon and Maritain, I believe, shows some misunderstanding, especially on the latter's part. Simon remarks that "my remaining doubts concerning the necessity of a moral philosophy adequately taken would vanish forever."[72] So to some extent Simon does not seem completely convinced. But I think Maritain overlooks Simon's tentativeness when he writes: "I am very happy with our agreement over the notion of moral philosophy adequately considered."[73] Now if those were all the indications we had, it might be impossible to discover where Simon comes down on this point.

In his last public appearance, speaking about Jacques Maritain, Simon pointed out the difference between Maritain and himself, particularly in regard to moral philosophy. From the very start Simon was hesitant to accept Maritain's idea of moral philosophy subalternated to theology. He then came to contrast the two positions:

> Whether it is desirable that philosophical issues be treated in a state of abstraction or in a concrete condition of association

---

[67] Yves R. Simon, *A Critique of Moral Knowledge*, 61, n. 4.

[68] Yves R. Simon, *Practical Knowledge*, 95.

[69] Ibid., 96.

[70] Ibid.

[71] Ibid., 98.

[72] Ibid., 106.

[73] Ibid., 108.

> with the problems of our supernatural destiny, I would not hesitate to say that it is, to a large extent, a question of calling. I am strongly attracted by the method of isolation because it furnishes special guarantees of epistemological purity and logical rigor.[74]

Philosophy is not the same as common sense; it should seek to avoid ideological contamination; it may have the responsibility in certain situations to comment on current affairs; and, if the method of isolation is accepted, would keep its distance from theology. Such are the conclusions to be drawn from this exercise.

Simon had often stressed the disagreements between philosophers, the solitariness of the philosophical life, and the virtues required to pursue this vocation:

> A philosopher who has ever succeeded in communicating his inspiration together with his demonstration, and who has experienced the joy of a friendship born of such communication, will always feel that if he had to choose again, philosophy would again be his calling.[75]

---

[74] Yves R. Simon, "Jacques Maritain: The Growth of a Christian Philosopher," in Joseph W. Evans (ed.), *Jacques Maritain: The Man and His Achievement* (New York: Sheed and Ward, 1963), 23.

[75] Yves R. Simon, "The Philosopher's Calling," *Philosopher at Work*, 6.

"Redeeming Modernism": Jacques Maritain and the Catholic Vocation

Cornelia A. Tsakiridou

In the winter of 1965, having been recognized by Pope Paul VI for inspiring the reforms of the Second Vatican Council, Jacques Maritain left a euphoric Rome and returned to his stark quarters in the community of the Little Brothers of Jesus on the Garonne River in Toulouse.[1] There, he started writing *The Peasant of the Garonne: An Old Layman Questions Himself about the Present Time*—his "last testament," as he called it. It was to be a "blunt" work and certain to create controversy.[2] It did.

In the book, Maritain describes himself as being "at one and the same time [as a] *person* and *member*" of the Church.[3] The distinction suggests two forms of communion: natural and supernatural. With its emphasis on renewal and on making the Church relevant to things human, the Council had given legitimacy to ideas that were troublesome on both counts: philosophically and spiritually. Maritain saw philosophy as a vocation. At its center, was a commitment to truth that saw in the principles of Thomism the only path to universal holiness. *The Peasant* is his critical and at times caustic response to theological, philosophical and cultural trends that threatened to undermine these principles. It also reflects Maritain's conviction that the authentic initiatives of the modern age could not be captured without first exposing the fallacies of modernist thought. This paper takes a closer look at his ideas on this subject and offers a brief outline of their key components.

---

[1] Julie Kernan, *Our Friend, Jacques Maritain* (New York: Doubleday, 1975), 165-66.

[2] Brooke Williams Smith, *Jacques Maritain: Antimodern or Ultramodern: An Historical Analysis of his Critics, his Thought and his Life* (New York: Elsevier, 1976), 21-22.

[3] Jacques Maritain, *The Peasant of the Garonne: An Old Layman Questions Himself about the Present Time*, trans. M. Cuddihy and E. Hughes (New York: Holt, Rinehart and Winston, 1968), 219.

The Peasant has been studied mainly for its biographical significance and particularly for Maritain's modernist (or anti-modernist) leanings. In my view, it becomes a more coherent and challenging work if it is read in the context of two movements.

The first is Maritain's life-long effort to use the realist philosophy of Thomas Aquinas as an instrument for constructive cultural criticism and renewal. In this regard, *The Peasant* attests to his unique interpretation of Thomism and his critique of modernism that dates back to the 1920 publication of *Art and Scholasticism*.[4] Modernism in this context is mostly an intellectual phenomenon affecting Catholic theology and philosophy.[5] Maritain uses the term in a more comprehensive way to include avant-garde developments in the arts where, as it is well-known, he had many friends and admirers. His observations in this area suggest that his approach to modernist art was often selective and unduly influenced by his interest in artistic creativity and intuition.

The second movement is more complex. It combines the Thomist concept of connaturality as a key (intuitive) source of knowledge in religious and artistic experience with the belief that supra-conscious prayer and contemplation, centered on love, are the *sine qua non* of Christian life.[6] Prayer and contemplation give rise to a variety of gifts and vocations. Without them, neither art nor philosophy can meet their true ends.

Maritain's discussion of contemplation in *The Peasant*—a work that is "more Raïssa's than mine"—focuses on what he sees as the most grave problem affecting the Church and his times: the reduction of the Christian vocation to social activism, of theology to anthropology. Faith that becomes too concerned with reflecting its times (and its thinkers)

---

[4] Jacques Maritain, *Art and Scholasticism and the Frontiers of Poetry*, trans. J.W. Evans (New York: Charles Scribner's Sons, 1962).

[5] For the meaning assigned to "modernism" in Catholic theology, its official condemnation in 1907, and the debate that ensued between its adherents and critics see Michael Kerlin, "Reginald Garrigou-Lagrange: Defending the Faith from *Pascendi dominici gregis to Humani generis*," *U.S. Catholic Historian*, 25 (1) (Winter 2007): 97-113.

[6] Maritain, *The Peasant*, 223.

ends up losing its proper object and form of activity.[7] The problem is not social activism as such but the pursuit of moral action without contemplation and without a deep identification with the objects of one's work.

Maritain elaborates on this relationship of "immediate connivance" between subject and world in his discussion of analogies between mystical and ethical experience in *Degrees of Knowledge* (1932).[8] A disposition toward virtue, acquired as a result of virtuous actions, generates spontaneous moral judgments. Despite the fact that it lacks certitude, this connatural form of practical knowledge "creates a certain affinity in the soul for the *spiritual order*, in the most indefinite sense of the term."[9] In prayer and contemplation, similar dispositions toward divine things are formed. Both should be at the center of Christian life. Overconfident and temporal in its aims, Christian activism overlooks this dimension of human experience that allows poet, philosopher, artist and layman to gain insights in action and (analogically) into mystical contemplation—the poet "connaturalized ... with the mystery that is scattered in things."[10] Its effect on the spiritual life is detrimental.

According to Maritain, *The Peasant* is inspired by a book that Raïssa always wanted to write, but never did: *La contemplation sur les chemins (Contemplation on the Roads)*. The reference to Raïssa in this context is significant, because it serves to underscore the spiritual nature of the work. Raïssa credited the idea for this book to *la petite voie* of St. Thérèse of Lisieux who saw the salvation of souls through prayer as a form of spiritual activism—and herself as a missionary of the cloister. While away from the world, Thérèse practiced contemplative love and surrender to God in all things. The idea had a powerful impact on Raïssa and Jacques who understood their intellectual mission in similar terms.[11] In a spiritual manual that they wrote together, they argued

---

[7] Ibid., 232-33.

[8] Jacques Maritain, *The Degrees of Knowledge (Distinguish to Unite)*, trans. Gerald B. Phelan trans. (Notre Dame: University of Notre Dame, 1995), 299.

[9] Ibid.

[10] Ibid., 300.

[11] Ibid., 233-35.

that prayer is indispensable to the intellectual life: it brings a peace of mind which clears the intellect and rids it of redundancies.[12]

The basic arguments of *The Peasant* date back to *Art and Scholasticism* (1920) and *Antimoderne* (1922), a collection of essays and lectures that is most often read in connection with Maritain's initial support of *Action Française* (until its condemnation in 1926 by Pope Piux XI).[13] In *Antimoderne*, Maritain set the foundations of his critique of the philosophical and spiritual underpinnings of modernism. These were to remain unchanged. *The Peasant* is a testament to the consistency of Maritain's views on the significance of the spiritual life in all aspects of human knowledge and action.

In *Art and Scholasticism*, Maritain made it clear that aesthetics would be an integral part of his philosophical mission. The reason was his belief that at the basis of Thomistic realism is "an inexhaustible center of intuitivity" that precedes and grounds discursive reasoning.[14] In 1927, he wrote in "The Frontiers of Poetry" that a true artist will access this center and discover "the secret rules of being."[15] Artists pursued unconsciously a hidden intimacy with Christ while living in the midst of the world.[16] Many were (unwitting) contemplatives. Contemplative artists, philosophers and poets can intuit in their own activities the signs of the divine presence "scattered throughout nature."[17] Like poetry, love has the same effect on its objects. It creates images of mystical realities in the natural world. In this respect, the one who loves senses metaphysically what the mystic experiences supernaturally. Maritain calls the relationship between metaphysics and

---

[12] Jacques and Raïssa Maritain, *Prayer and Intelligence* (London: Sheed and Ward, 1928), 5.

[13] Jacques Maritain, *Antimoderne* (Paris: Editions de la revue des jeunes, 1922).

[14] Maritain, *Art and Scholasticism*, 131. For a critical reading of Maritain on this point, see Umberto Eco, *The Aesthetics of Thomas Aquinas*, trans. Hugh Bredin (Cambridge, Massachusetts: Harvard University, 1988), 61-63.

[15] Ibid., 127.

[16] Maritain, *The Peasant*, 231-32.

[17] Maritain, *Degrees of Knowledge*, 300-01.

mysticism "vital."[18] It is this vitality that he tries to tap in modernist thought and art.

Criticized as anachronistic and reactionary, *The Peasant* made the eighty-three year old Maritain the target of ungracious attacks that questioned his moral and intellectual integrity.[19] The book's subtitle, *An Old Layman Questions Himself about the Present Time,* suggests a simple man, perhaps puzzled and weary of words, writing in reflective solitude somewhere in the countryside. By assuming the position of a layman and a peasant, Maritain makes it clear that he speaks from the margins rather than the center of ecclesiastical power. This stance is reminiscent of the contemplative who ponders in solitude the mystical life of the Church. But Maritain is ever eager to invite dialogue. A made-up Chinese proverb serves as an example of his intractable and self-deprecating humor. Appearing on the dedication page, it seems to admonish both the author and his readers: "Never take foolishness too seriously."

These moments of Socratic irony reflect Maritain's affection and admiration for the iconic philosopher and tenacious servant of truth. Early in the book, Maritain describes the Socratic mission in these terms: "But Socrates saved at once reason, the future of culture and the rights of Truth."[20] The mission of the Catholic philosopher was identical. It was more important than ever in times of crisis to speak the truth and speak it from the heart. This included going to the roots of the philosophical enterprise, to a view of philosophy for which integrity of intellect and integrity of life were indistinguishable. We are reminded of Jude Dougherty's observation that Maritain had a "Greek confidence in the human intellect and the intelligibility of nature," which made him discern in modernist theology and philosophy a "call to de-Hellenize Christianity."[21]

---

[18] Ibid., 301.

[19] Smith, *Jacques Maritain: Antimodern or Ultramodern*, 21-28.

[20] Maritain, *The Peasant*, 17.

[21] Jude P. Dougherty, *Jacques Maritain: An Intellectual Profile* (Washington, D.C.: The Catholic University of America, 2003), 38. The de-Hellenization of Catholic and Protestant theology is also a main theme in Pope Benedict XVI's 2006 Regensburg address. See http://www.vatican.va/holy_father/bene

As early as 1963, Maritain had been apprehensive about modernist trends in the Council.[22] Having observed its proceedings from a prominent position, he was now certain that the reforms it embraced ran the risk of being misinterpreted. There were dangerous visions of renewal that would undermine the very essence of Catholicism if left unchallenged: "When one is dealing with the great idols of the day, it is one's duty toward what is highest in the world to use the knife (and there is no point in being too gentle)."[23] Maritain's certainty was based on Church teaching. According to *Aeterni Patris* (1879), a Thomist revival was necessary if the Church were to counter the philosophical ideas that threatened its doctrine and the cultural values it had promulgated for centuries.[24] The encyclical was so important to Maritain that it was reprinted in its entirety in his biography of Saint Thomas, *The Angelic Doctor* (1931).

It was followed in 1907, under Pope Pius X, by *Pascendi Dominici Gregis*. Under the term "modernism," *Pascendi* condemned agnostic, immanentist, anti-intellectualist and fideist trends in philosophy, theology and other areas of intellectual and religious life.[25] Modernism was therefore associated with the assertion of secular humanistic values, the emphasis on the contribution of subjectivity and inter-subjectivity to human knowledge, and the marginalization of Church authority in the social realm.

Of special relevance to philosophy, and to Maritain's project in particular, was the significance attached by adherents of these ideas to the vital experience of dogmatic truths. It became the standard by which their validity was to be measured. Maritain, too, wanted a vital faith, but not at the expense of truth. As his writings on religious and

---

dict_xvi/speeches/2006/september/documents/hf_benxvi_spe_20060912_university-regensburg_en.html.

[22] Ralph McInerny, *The Very Rich Hours of Jacques Maritain: A Spiritual Life* (Notre Dame, Indiana: University of Notre Dame, 2003), 203.

[23] Maritain, *The Peasant*, 98.

[24] Jacques Maritain, *The Angelic Doctor: The Life and Thought of Saint Thomas Aquinas*, trans. J.F. Scanlan (New York: The Dial, 1931).

[25] Papal Encyclicals, "On the Doctrine of the Modernists," (September 8, 1907) http://www.papalencyclicals.net/Pius10/p10pasce.htm.

aesthetic experience show, he was fascinated by vitalism and shared the modernist emphasis on an activist, timely and engaging faith. But, for Maritain, the path to a vital faith is Thomism. Thomism is providentially equipped with openness to the particularities of different eras and cultures. It can reconcile any tensions that might arise between society and the Church. In fact, to be a Thomist is to seek in the cultural trends of the day a deeper, existential and spiritual significance. Philosophy, theology and art that are genuinely contemporary draw from the hidden ground of human culture, where the truths gifted to the Church by Christ live forever. Only a theology or an art that is informed supernaturally with grace can renew and restore the intellectual, moral and spiritual integrity of the human person and society. While faithful to *Aeterni Patris* and *Pascendi*, Maritain's Thomism was in essence creative and mystical. It sought to bring to Scholastic discourse unprecedented vivacity and energy, the kind of Platonic *mousike* that he associated with the very essence of poetry. According to *Creative Intuition in Art and Poetry* (1953), poetry is "the free creativity of the spirit, and the intuitive knowledge through emotion which transcends and permeate all arts."[26] Maritain's philosophy was a philosophical poetics.

Yves Simon said about Thomism before Maritain that it had evolved into "at best an academic and ecclesiastical affair." In his view, Maritain re-infused Thomas' work with the epistemic, poetic and existential vitality that it had lost in its long history as the official philosophy of the Catholic Church.[27] Simon's essay in *Jacques Maritain: Homage in Words and Pictures* is an eloquent and penetrating study of philosophical character. It reminds us that what makes Maritain unique is the fact that he brought to the Scholastic enterprise his extra-ordinary ability for "intuitive, poetic and thought-provoking expression."[28]

---

[26] Jacques Maritain, *Creative Intuition in Art and Poetry* (Princeton, New Jersey: Princeton University, 1953/1981), 393.

[27] John H. Griffin and Yves R. Simon, *Jacques Maritain: Homage in Words and Pictures* (Albany: Magi Books, 1974), 7.

[28] Griffin and Simon, *Jacques Maritain: Homage in Words and Pictures*, 5.

Simon writes characteristically: "Maritain was the first non-scholastic among the disciples of Saint Thomas."[29] And we might add: and the first (with the possible exception of Newman) to define modernism in Catholic terms, re-orientate its spiritual yearnings, and give them a home in Christian thought and culture. Intuition, contemplation and the mystical life are inextricable aspects of his philosophical activity. He shared all three with Raïssa. Maritain stood with one leg in art and poetry and the other in Thomist philosophy. He kept the dialogue with modernism open throughout his life.

Some examples from his early writings highlight the spirit of this dialogue and show a connection to the arguments of *The Peasant*. Maritain approached modernist ideas in the same manner that Thomas approached Greek antiquity and the Church Fathers. Fully aware of their errors and limitations and unrelenting in his criticism, he engaged them in order to integrate and advance the unity of truth. It was in some ways an inclusive approach, but not a relativist one. Essential in this project was the mystery of the human person. Characteristically, Maritain wrote in *Integral Humanism* (1936): "In the scheme of Christian humanism there is a place not for the *errors* of Luther and Voltaire, but *for* Voltaire and Luther, according as in spite of the errors they have contributed in the history of men to certain advances (which belong to Christ as does every good among us)."[30] The Church had the truth. Those outside who intuited or sensed it were already partaking of its life. It was important to make that known. Maritain characteristically wrote: "The saints who visibly belong to the Church enable us to recognize their far-off brethren who do not know Her and yet who belong to Her invisibly—St. John of the Cross enables us to do justice to Ramakrishna."[31]

There are many examples of Maritain's attempts to open Catholic philosophy, art and culture to the secular world. Bergsonian intuition, he observed in *Antimoderne*, may be "entirely unacceptable" when

---

[29] Ibid., 3-4.

[30] Jacques Maritain, *Integral Humanism: Temporal and Spiritual Problems of A New Christendom*, trans. Joseph E. Evans (New York: Charles Scribner's Sons, 1968), 92.

[31] Maritain, *Degrees of Knowledge*, 292.

applied to epistemology, but it can become "particularly interesting if we apply it to the domain of art, to practical intelligence, and to the dynamic vision with which the artist creates the work of art."[32] Another example comes from *Art and Scholasticism*. According to Thomas, beauty is a transcendental, whose qualities of integrity, clarity and proportion please the intelligence when perceived through the senses. Maritain gives the concept sufficient latitude to apply it to works of artists as different as Leonardo da Vinci and Georges Rouault.[33] He is not exact in his criticism when it comes to the plastic qualities of the works he considers, and there is also a tendency to wash over significant differences for the sake of a unitive approach. What is significant, however, is the (Aristotelian) emphasis on the uniqueness of the aesthetic object at hand.

Thus, what determines whether a work is beautiful or not is not a fixed universal standard, such as Hegel's Idea. It is, rather, how the dynamics of individual compositions reflect Thomistic principles. "Integrity and proportion," he wrote, "have no absolute signification, and must be understood solely in relation to the end of the work, which is to make a form shine on matter."[34] The principles are the same but the configurations in which they appear vary with each individual work. They have a distinct and specific form. Context matters.

Maritain did not hesitate to criticize modernist artists for intellectualizing art. In *Creative Intuition in Art and Poetry*, he uses the concept of "poetic intuition" to question modernism's claim for authenticity and truth. According to Maritain, poetic intuition is based on the natural sympathy between imagination and the *intellectus agens*. The artist's mind gets hold of things directly without the use of abstraction. Creative inspiration and action originate in the non-conceptual, spontaneous union of intelligence and being. Through poetic intuition, the artist's perceptions acquire a depth and density that will make the work of art existentially vital and meaningful. How

---

[32] Maritain, *Antimoderne*, 149.

[33] Maritain, *Art and Scholasticism*, 27.

[34] Ibid., 27-8.

exactly this happens is not clear, but it is certainly mediated by grace.[35] The finished work communicates objectively what the artist experienced subjectively. Without this transformation on the subject's side, the work is lifeless.

Aesthetic solutions based on theories are not acceptable. Wassily Kandinsky (1866-1896) and Kasimir Malevich (1878-1935) argued that "non-objectivity" can free the artist from servitude to reality and create an art of pure forms.[36] For Maritain, such efforts were doomed to fail. Objectless art hinders genuine creative expression. He calls it "the proper perversion of fine arts," a recipe for stagnation and academicism.[37] The judgment relies on generalization and seems not to observe the contextual application of concepts that he set as a standard. Avant-gardes said a lot of things about their art that their art did not reflect. It is the art rather than its theory that matters. But despite these problems, this and related statements give us a good idea of how eager Maritain was to part with art that was dominated by rationalist priorities. In *Creative Intuition*, he uses the term "academic" to describe works that use their plastic elements as conceptual devices. He is especially critical of Surrealism.[38]

Art's missteps are philosophical in origin. It is therefore the task of philosophy to elucidate them. There is a shade of Hegelianism in this position that gives thought a reflective and corrective function over art. Maritain's objective, however, is the reverse of Hegel's aesthetics. He wants to keep the work of art in touch with nature and the world of things and persons. With few exceptions, modernist art in his view is the sensuous analog of "ideosophy," philosophical thought that

---

[35] It remains controversial whether this is a direct contact between intellect and sensible that is unmediated by the senses and whether Maritain is interpreting Thomas loosely on this point. See Eco, *The Aesthetics of Thomas Aquinas*, 60-63.

[36] Maritain, *Creative Intuition in Art and Poetry*, 220-22.

[37] Ibid. For a discussion of the role of the object in photography based on Maritain's interpretation of connaturality see, Cornelia A. Tsakiridou, "The Connatural Eye: Photography without Representation," *Philosophical Inquiry: International Quarterly* 29, no. 3-4 (Summer-Fall 2007): 41-57.

[38] Ibid., 26-27, 63, 82-83.

discards extramental reality and is based on thought alone.[39] Husserl, for example, is an "ideosopher." [40] The phenomenological position that thought cannot carry its object except as phenomenon—as something thought rather than as something that *is*—has its parallel in modernism's fascination with formal abstraction. For Maritain, the rejection of realism begins in philosophy and extends from there to the entire realm of human activity. Deeper yet, it begins from the loss of spiritual life.

In 1922, Maritain had outlined his vision of Thomist renewal in *Antimoderne*. Chapter III of the book ("On Certain Conditions for a Thomist Renaissance"), reprints his address to the *Institut Supérieur de Philosophie*, in Louvain in January of 1920. Its basic thesis can be encapsulated in this statement: "a Christian renaissance...will be ephemeral and without vigor if it is not primarily a Thomist renaissance."[41] He makes the exact same argument while discussing Vatican II in chapter VI of *The Peasant*, titled "The True New Fire: The Requests and Renewals of Genuine Knowledge."

According to *Antimoderne*, a return to Thomism is needed to combat "the maladies of modern thought."[42] These include naturalism, subjectivism, individualism, scientism and egocentrism. They are the combined errors of Cartesian, Kantian and Comtian philosophies condemned in *Pascendi*.[43] Even though centuries old, Thomism is perenially relevant to human culture. This is why Maritain refused to add the prefix "neo" to the term. Ten years later, in *The Angelic Doctor*, he explained: "Thomism is a form of wisdom. Between it and the particular forms of culture *incessant vital exchanges* must be made, but it is rigorously independent in its essence of those particular forms."[44] It is an "indefinitely progressive" philosophy because it remains "in *vital*

---

[39] Maritain, *The Peasant*, 101-02.

[40] Ibid., 106.

[41] Maritain, *Antimoderne*, 124.

[42] Ibid., 123-24.

[43] Dougherty, *Jacques Maritain: An Intellectual Profile*, 57-58.

[44] Maritain, *The Angelic Doctor*, vi, xiii; my emphasis.

communication with the superior wisdom of theology and contemplation."[45]

Modern ideas and conditions can be met creatively only when they are not met exclusively through the consciousness and thought of their times. For Maritain, the sources of intellectual and artistic vitality are transtemporal, the forms they take contemporary, and their significance perennial. Without this kind of origination, ideas and works of art are only temporal constructs, relative and transient.

Antimoderne's goal was to prove that Thomist philosophy is the "natural philosophy of the human spirit," a spirit that errs but also plows creatively into the circumstances of its time, unafraid to engage the world.[46] According to Maritain, modernism's intellectual errors can be traced to the demise of Scholastic thought.[47] A reformed, dynamic Thomism will cut through the history of Western thought like a "knife" to reveal its "partial truths and good intentions" and remove all else.[48] This analogy reflects its supernatural, charismatic character. Thomism is the intellective life of the Church condensed in what appears to be a philosophical system. In essence, it is much more. Its "principles are truly *comprehensive*" and its "discriminating light superior" to any other system of thought. It is uniquely equipped to "understand in depth

---

[45] Ibid., xvi; my emphasis.

[46] Maritain, *Antimoderne*, 144.

[47] Maritain considered modern philosophy to have grown out of the gradual decadence of Scholasticism that begins with Duns Scotus (c. 1266-1308) and William of Ockham (c. 1280-c.1239). Scotus introduced the supremacy of the will over the intellect; Ockham excluded reality and the truths of faith from conceptual knowledge. Renaissance individualism disrupted the organic unity of thought that linked Aristotle and Thomas. The worship of physical nature through a combination of occultism, myth and science prepared the ground for the union of fideism and rationalism that followed the Reformation and the Enlightenment. Scholasticism failed to clear Aristotelian and Thomist philosophy from the outdated scientific material that it used to demonstrate its metaphysical principles. As a result, its ability to respond critically to the challenges of scientific inquiry and discovery was seriously undermined. See Maritain, *Antimoderne*, 123-24.

[48] Ibid.

modern philosophy better than the moderns themselves."[49] Without Thomism, the Church cannot have a genuine renewal. In fact, Thomism is not an instrument. It is *in* it rather than through it that the Church can encounter and inform contemporary culture.

Maritain's critical openness to his times and his enthusiasm about Thomism's modernity is echoed in the remarks of Pope John Paul II at the centenary (1979) of *Aeterni Patris*: "This realistic and historic method, fundamentally optimistic and open, makes St. Thomas not only the *Doctor Communis Ecclesiae* ... but the *Doctor Humanitatis*, because he is always ready and available to receive the human values of all cultures."[50] In an address given on the same occasion at the Angelicum, John Paul II remembered Maritain "as one of the best interpreters of Thomistic thought" who introduced Thomism into the most challenging intellectual, moral and cultural debates of his generation.[51] In this opinion he was preceded by Pope Paul VI. In the winter of 1965, Maritain was convinced that elements in the Church were straying away from its tradition.

At the same time, he remained committed to the idea of transforming modernist ideas into opportunities for genuine renewal and dialogue with secular culture. The task of preserving and assimilating what he poetically called "all the riches being accumulated in modern times" was very important to him. It was in this spirit that he declared himself in *Antimoderne* to be "ultramodern."[52] And it was in the same spirit that in the winter of 1966 he took on the "pseudo-renewal" that was threatening the achievements of the Council.

The Peasant warns that the creative energies underlying the modernist quest for an intellectual and cultural renaissance will be squandered if Thomism is abandoned, and renewal becomes synonymous with "chronolatry," the worship of ephemeral rather than perennial truths.[53] He terms this tendency "neo-modernism."[54] Neo-

---

[49] Ibid., 147-49.

[50] John Paul II, *Two Lectures on St. Thomas Aquinas* (Niagara Falls, New York: Jacques & Raïssa Maritain Institute, 1991), 269.

[51] Ibid., 216-17.

[52] Maritain, *Antimoderne*, 21.

[53] Maritain, *The Peasant*, 12-14.

modernism is a mutation of modernist thought. What makes it more subversive than the set of ideas confronted by Pius X (and *Antimoderne*), is the fact that it is not as direct and upfront about its objectives. Having usurped the spirit of the Council, it hides behind the clichés of change and relevance.

Maritain notes with apprehension the popularity of theological trends influenced by form criticism and phenomenology that interpret the sacramental and historical truths of Christianity in mythical and symbolic terms, consistent with anthropological and psychological theories.[55] Their objective, as he puts it, is "to empty the faith of any content."[56] He remembers Socrates, who also opposed "verisimilitude," and he calls "Grand Sophistry" the claim that "we know Being on condition that it is put in parenthesis and abstracted out of sight."[57] Putting faith and spiritual life in a parentheses is not different from denying to art an intimate contact with the world. We can see here why (with what rationale) Maritain objected to certain types of avant-garde art. He was, of course, principally criticizing how artists expressed themselves about their work rather than the works themselves. Still, the fundamental idea remains that Catholic philosophy (and life) is committed to the radical love of all beings. The Catholic artist also begins from this premise.

The incompatibility of neo-modernist ideas with Catholicism is defended in philosophical and theological terms that repeat the theses of *Antimoderne*. But Maritain is most compelling when he reaches into the existential, poetic and mystical aspects of this problem. What he has to say on the subject resonates with the words and presence of Raïssa (she had died in 1960), his spiritual muse: "For to love is to give what one is, his very being, in the most absolute, the most brazenly metaphysical, the least phenomenalizable sense of this word."[58] The existential, realist conception of love is unmistakable, as are its sacramental underpinnings. If love becomes a metaphor, so will life, so

---

[54] Ibid., 5, #6.

[55] Ibid., 6.

[56] Ibid., 8.

[57] Ibid., 7-8.

[58] Ibid., 9.

will Christ (and the Church). The philosopher, like the artist, gives himself Eucharistically to being. Being, in turn, reciprocates. Maritain saw this movement in the thought of Thomas and pursued it in his work.

With a mixture of sadness and sarcasm, he goes on to ask: "But we must put all this [love] in parentheses, too, mustn't we, if we are to follow the new golden rule?"[59] Next to the demise of extra-mental reality and truth, what troubled Maritain the most about neo-modernism was its reduction of love to sentiment. He saw with great concern the emergence of a "truly visceral Christianity," marked by a superficially charitable anthropocentrism, a parody of Christ and humanity.[60] He recalls Pilate's indifference to truth. The question "*Quid est Veritas*?" was asked (tragically and ironically) in the presence of Christ. Like Pilate, some advocates of renewal "have simply ceased to believe in Truth, and believe only in verisimilitudes pinned to *some* truths..."[61]

In the 1920s, Maritain had written to artist and playwright Jean Cocteau that art arises from the convergence of supernatural truth and love. Their union is so pure in form that, like the saint, the artist has a deep sense of truth.[62] Creation is spontaneous rather than self-conscious. When art arises from this unitive moment, it lacks artifice. It springs from the depths of human experience rather than from its surface. In *The Peasant*, he borrows from Raïssa and Father Victorino Osende the notion of "prayer-love" or "prayer of the heart."[63]

The term describes the ongoing unconscious and unformulated act of love in the contemplative soul. Osende compares it to Bergson's image of a mother watching over her child even when she is asleep. It is love that has been existentially incorporated or incarnated and must be

---

[59] Ibid.

[60] Ibid., 7, 9, 17.

[61] Ibid.

[62] Jacques Maritain, *Art and Faith: Letters between Jacques Maritain and Jean Cocteau*, trans. J. Coleman (New York: The Philosophical Library, 1948), 108-09.

[63] This is not the Orthodox ascetical prayer associated with theophany. See Maritain, *The Peasant*, 228-29.

met concretely, in its act of existence. There is nothing phenomenological or mythical about it. Maritain's focus is principally on the subjective side of this experience. There is a psychological emphasis that is hard to miss. But we can also see what he has in mind. What differentiates love from sentiment is its concrete interaction and inherence in its objects.

This inherence runs deeper than reflection or thought. Maritain quotes Osende: "We cannot continue to think always, whereas we can love always."[64] According to Osende, the maternal act of loving centers on the one loved rather than on the action undertaken to that end. This is an important distinction. A spirituality that is centered on action (intention) and ultimately on the self—a false, egoistic love—cannot really center on the other. Or, if it does, it can only do so superficially. Lacking a metaphysical ground and an intuition of the mystical life, this type of love is easily satisfied with facile precepts expressed in spiritual clichés (e.g., the need "to see Jesus in our brothers").[65] The inner life of the heart and its intimacy with the mystical Christ have no place in it. In this regard, there is an obvious resemblance between certain modernist artists and neo-modernist theologians.

The key theme of *The Peasant* is that a Church driven by intellectualist and historicist ideas will suffer in its capacity to love. Or, it will love in a superficial way only. The exchange of the profound realities of spiritual life with intellectual constructs will deplete thought and devastate the soul. Maritain's question, "*Quid est veritas?*," is principally aimed at Catholic intellectuals. For those caught in their own versions of renewal, unfounded in the Catholic spiritual and intellectual tradition, *The Peasant* has a simple message. Thought uninformed by spiritual life loses its objects and itself. Being in this way loveless toward being, it is also loveless toward the One who brings all things to life.

---

[64] Ibid.

[65] Ibid., 237.

To Philosophize *for* the Faith: Jacques Maritain's Intellectual Vocation

Michael D. Torre

The title of this paper indicates a conclusion my researches have forced on me: I do not think that Jacques entirely understood himself. Unquestionably, he presents his vocation as that of a Christian *philosopher*. I believe his vocation was rather that of a lay *theologian* engaged as a Catholic apologist with the culture of his day, pre-eminently with its philosophical ideas. I will try here to make the case for this interpretation.[1]

If that is where I am headed, it is not where I must begin. In seeking to fulfill my announced topic, I find myself having to go back: back to the early years of Maritain's time at the Sorbonne, of his marriage and his conversion; and back to my own first American Maritain

[1] That Maritain was a theologian is not a novel idea. See Charles Journet's "Jacques Maritain Theologian," *The New Scholasticism* 46 (1972): 32-50. Rightly, I believe, Journet notes that his theology is more "intuitive" than "scholastic" (49)—a theology not "burdened with the heavy equipment" (of one scholastically trained in theology). Ralph Nelson also notes Maritain's tendency towards theology (in contradistinction to Simon's) in his "A Controversy Reconsidered": see *Maritain and America*, eds. Joseph Allan Clair and Chris Cullen, S.J. (American Maritain Association: Washington, D.C., 2009), 114-28. In truth, Maritain had always been a "research worker" for theology. Now, a "research worker" in a field is someone whose work is achieved according to its norms and lights, even if subject to higher authority (as Maritain no doubt saw those more highly, and "scholastically," trained than he as being): thus, a role analogous to the one a para-legal possesses relative to attorneys. Nevertheless, all theologians are subject to a higher authority: namely, the working of the Spirit in the Church and her Magisterium. Thus, however humble may be a research worker's own work in the field, it is a work of theology, and its greater "subservience" to higher authority is only one of degree, not of kind. When Maritain denies he is a theologian, he is thinking of one "scholastically trained" or he is thinking of "exegetical" or "dogmatic" theology; but theology is wider and freer than that!

Association meeting 20 years ago. For, if we are to understand the meaning and significance of Jacques Maritain's intellectual vocation and its present challenge, we must understand its context and empathize with how it came about.[2]

Truth to tell, it is not easy to get a handle on Maritain's early years. Despite the many things Raïssa (and Jacques himself) has shared with us concerning their lives, there is much left unsaid about which we would like to know. Nor, as far as I have been able to discern, have his biographers been of much aid. Let me cite several instances. Jacques was baptized. What was his Christian upbringing? From what we would gather from his *Notebooks* and from Raïssa, it would seem to have been

---

[2] Before beginning, I wish to acknowledge those who have written before on his person and work. I have read with profit and enjoyment and been helped in my reflections by the following: Gerald Phelan, *Jacques Maritain* (New York: Sheed and Ward, 1937); Charles A. Fecher, *The Philosophy of Jacques Maritain* (Westminster, Maryland: Newman, 1953); Henry Bars, *Maritain en Notre Temps* (Paris: Grasset, 1959); Donald and Idella Gallagher's introduction to *The Achievement of Jacques and Raïssa Maritain* (Garden City: Doubleday, 1962); Yves R. Simon, "Jacques Maritain: The Growth of a Christian Philosopher," in *Jacques Maritain*, ed. Joseph Evans (New York: Sheed and Ward, 1963), 3-24; Julie Kernan, *Our Friend, Jacques Maritain* (New York: Doubleday, 1975); John Dunaway, *Jacques Maritain* (Boston: Twayne, 1978); Olivier Lacombe, "L'itinerario spirituale di Jacques Maritain," in *Jacques Maritain E La Societá Contemporanea*, ed. Roberto Papini (Milan: Massimo, 1978), 26-40; Bernard Doering, *Jacques Maritain and the French Catholic Intellectuals* (Notre Dame, Indiana: University of Notre Dame, 1983); Judith Suther, *Raïssa Maritain: Pilgrim, Poet, Exile* (New York: Fordham, 1990); James Schall, *Jacques Maritain: The Philosopher in Society* (Lanham, Maryland: Rowman & Littlefield, 1998); Jude Dougherty, *Jacques Maritain: An Intellectual Profile* (Washington, D.C.: Catholic University of America, 2003); Ralph McInerny, *The Very Rich Hours of Jacques Maritain: A Spiritual Life* (Notre Dame, Indiana: University of Notre Dame, 2003); but especially Jean-Luc Barré, *Jacques et Raïssa Maritain: Les Mendiants du Ciel* (Paris: Stock, 1995), for the wealth of information he provides. Nevertheless, it seems to me that an intellectual biography of Maritain adequate to the science of history remains to be written. (None of these authors, or any other, appears ready or willing to defend the thesis of this paper: that Maritain should best be seen as a Catholic lay theologian and apologist, and not as a Christian philosopher [but see Dougherty, op. cit., 42].)

non-existent, rather like that of his friend Ernest Psichari. We are told *his* "introduction to religion stopped short with his baptism"[3] and that his family "did not fight Christianity," believing instead that one had "assimilated it and outgrown it" (*WHBFT*, 52). Yet this seems to be said by way of contrast to *his* own case. Jacques certainly seemed much more ready to "fight" Christianity,[4] regarding it as "Bourgeois:" unjust to the working class and on the side of unjust and entrenched interests in the Dreyfus affair. These views of his adolescence are clear enough; but his earlier exposure to Christian things is not. His mother, described by Raïssa as possessing a "*religious* loyalty to the passionate ideal which animated the republican opposition under the Empire... [and] a fervent hope for the *spiritual* future of mankind" (*WHBFT*, 49: my italicizations), had given over her son's early education to a liberal Protestant, Jean Réville. What kind of Christian faith or intellectual formation did he seek to impart? We would like to know more about this than we do.[5]

---

[3] Raïssa Maritain, *We Have Been Friends Together* (New York: Longman, Green and Co., 1942), 50. This work is hereafter abbreviated WHBFT and placed within the text.

[4] He writes the following to Ernest Psichari on September 26, 1899: "Pour établir la Religion nouvelle, pour supprimer ce qu'il y a de mauvais dans le catholicisme, pour détruire le pape, il faudra attaquer, détruire tout le catholicisme (avec ce qu'il a de bien et ce qu'il a de mal):" see Barré, op. cit., 61.

[5] Maritain is hostile to Protestantism even before his conversion (albeit under the influence of Bloy): see his *Notebooks* (Notre Dame, Indiana: University of Notre Dame, 1984), 26-27. He comes to see Luther, and German Protestant thought in general, as the chief cause of modern Europe's intellectual and spiritual malaise, and World War I as more or less a holy war to save Christian civilization: see his "Le Rôle de L'Allemagne dans la Philosophie Moderne," *Oeuvres Complètes*, I (Paris: Éditions Saint-Paul, 1986), 891-1043. Raïssa even describes these lectures as "combat duty, a sort of intellectual contribution to the war" (*Adventures in Grace* [New York: Longman, Green and Co., 1945], 213: this work is hereafter abbreviated AIG and references to it are placed within the text). To the best of my knowledge, Maritain never visited Germany after 1908, save for a week's passage through it in 1931, and he remained relatively uninvolved in its philosophical trends after both of the World Wars, e.g. Husserl, Heidegger, Habermas. (An interesting exception to this was an offer he made to Heidegger after World War II to use his office as

More directly to my purpose, what was Jacques's early intellectual background or his philosophical "formation"? For example, I have tried (but so far in vain) to ascertain just what he studied to obtain his Sorbonne *agrégation* in philosophy. Just what were his courses? What was he reading? Barré tells us of his plan to read modern philosophers in his first year at the Sorbonne (1900-1901), a program that included Bergson.[6] Yet Raïssa informs us that he had *not* read Bergson's works before attending his lectures, over a year later (1902), and that neither of them were to do so until "a little later" (*WHBFT*, 83). One has the impression of them attending a weekly lecture, with many another

---

Ambassador to the Holy See to help locate his sons, who were still being held prisoner in Russia at the time: see Maria Pia Benini, "Maritain ambasciatore a Roma," in *Jacques Maritain E La Societá Contemporanea*, 50-59, p. 57, #15, quoting from E. Castelli's *Il tempo invertebrato* [Padua: CEDAM, 1969], 51, #4.) In any case, it is somewhat curious that he never seemed interested in Protestantism prior to his conversion, and (as far as I can tell) he had very few Protestant friends prior to his coming to the United States. His mention of the minister Paul Vergara (*Notebooks*, 189) is the only one I know of. (Indeed, during the Meudon period, Gabriel Marcel found Raïssa, in particular, to be hostile to his own Protestant wife, and described her religious attitude as that of a "fanatic": see *En Chemin, Vers Quel Eveil* [Paris: Gallimard, 1971], 156. While it is hard not to believe that he may be exaggerating here, his judgment is nonetheless striking.) By contrast, while Maritain appears not even to have considered Orthodoxy prior to his conversion, he came to have various Orthodox friends (especially via Nicolas Berdyaev) and to feel much closer to Orthodoxy. (After all, the greatest friend of his youth, Ernest Psichari, had been baptized as an Orthodox.) In relation to Orthodoxy, he says, "Greek and Russian piety, which differs apparently from Catholic piety not so much in divergences of dogma as in certain characteristics of spirituality, is much less hostile, in my opinion, to the philosophy of St. Thomas then might at first be supposed. It approaches the problems from another angle and the scholastic presentation as a rule irritates and offends it. These are merely questions of modality; and I am convinced that a proper understanding of the Thomist system would dispel innumerable misunderstandings and facilitate unexpected encounters" (*St. Thomas Aquinas* [London: Sheed and Ward, 1931], 40-41). Again, while Orthodoxy tended to remain "within herself" as a result of the schism, this was "not so completely as is commonly thought" (42). He speaks of "our Orthodox friends" in *Notebooks*, 160.

[6] Barré, op. cit., 65.

interested Frenchman. They must, after all, have been rather busy with Péguy and his *Cahiers*. They followed Bergson more closely in his course on Plotinus, but Raïssa tells us that she read Plato only *after* this (*WHBFT*, 98), and that seems likely for Jacques too. (From what we can tell, it appears that neither of them read Aristotle at the Sorbonne.)

Raïssa tells us that Jacques's "*artistic* cultivation had already reached a *very high* level" (*WHBFT*, 42), but perhaps this statement owes much to her ability to enter vividly into her memory of 40 years previously. She is, after all, referring only to a young 18-year-old, and the only evidence she gives for her judgment is that he knew the Louvre better than she.[7]

When we think of Jacques at the Sorbonne in 1905, obtaining his *agrégation*, we should not think of him as at a level equivalent to an American ABD; rather, we should think of his intellectual training as closer to that of a fine, but ambivalent, American student earning a BA in Philosophy.[8] Nor did he *ever* receive a formal philosophical

---

[7] The difficulty faced by any biographer is how to treat Raïssa's memoirs (and also Jacques') as a source of their life. Given how important these are, this question deserves to be faced squarely and treated in depth. To the best of my knowledge, this task has yet to be accomplished. For myself, I am reluctant to contradict their *considered* judgment, but I am ready to query one where little evidence is supplied or to correct an idea that could lead to a misimpression (see my next footnote). McInerny goes further than this, I believe, when he argues that Maritain's commitment to *Action Française* was greater than he affirms (cf. *The Very Rich Hours*, 60-65). Maybe. Certainly Henri Massis thought so (see Barré, op. cit., 212), but he was deeply involved in this matter and is not an impartial witness. If one is to argue otherwise, it seems to me one needs to supply convincing evidence. The speculation that Villard would not have bequeathed his legacy to Maritain except that he was deeply involved in *Action Française* is just that: mere speculation. (One could just as well argue that he saw something importantly different in Maritain from Maurras...or otherwise why not just bequeath everything to Maurras?) To my mind, this is not sufficient evidence to question his account, which seems basically credible, given the evidence presently at hand.

[8] Raïssa says that he already had a "master's degree" in philosophy before he entered the Sorbonne, at 18 (*WHBFT*, 41); this must refer to his degree from the lycée. No doubt the Lycée Henri IV was more advanced than an American high school, but we should not think of it as equivalent to an American MA.

formation. By his own admission, the six years following his conversion had very little to do with philosophy.[9] And his later doctorate from the Angelicum was purely honorary. The truth is that he was entirely an autodidact when it came to his formation in Thomistic Philosophy, one decisively directed by Father Clérissac (and then by Father Dehau and Father Garrigou-Lagrange). Notably, he was directed and informed in his personal studies by Dominicans, and he would remain faithful to

---

[9] He, Raïssa, and Vera entered the Church on June 11, 1906. When he showed his first article to Fr. Clérissac on April 13, 1910, he did not yet know scholastic philosophy (*Notebooks*, 62). He first reads the *Summa* only four and a half years after his entrance into the Church (September 15, 1910), and it is notable that his only further reference to it throughout the reminder of that journal (to October, 1911) refers to *Raïssa's* reading of it (August 9, 1911) and *not* his. (We may thus well wonder whether his remark of 1954 on his first reading—"an inundation of light. The intellect finds its home" [*Notebooks*, 65]—does not slightly exaggerate its impact. Even if true, there is no evidence that he then began a systematic study of Thomas. It seems quite likely that the "violent temptations against the faith" he experienced sometime in 1911 or 1912 [*Notebooks*, 73] preceded his full attention to Thomas, and the "inundation of light" of which he speaks.) His "profoundly discouraging" work for Hachette's *Dictionary of Practical Life* (*Notebooks*, 72) will preoccupy him for another two years. It is again Raïssa, not he, who first begins the philosophical article on Bergson, to which he only seems to turn his full attention in September, 1911, and which is largely expository, rather than critical (even if his preference for Thomas and difficulty with Bergson is evident). His article for the *Thomist* a year later evinces a knowledge of Thomas (and the work of Garrigou-Lagrange), but it is very brief. He began to teach at the Collège Stanislas in October, 1912, and it is from *then* (which is also the date of his becoming an oblate of St. Benedict and taking his vow of celibacy) that we should date the true beginning of his formation in Thomistic philosophy: a date confirmed both by Raïssa's account—he then ceased his work for Hachette and began a full-scale study of Thomas (AIG, 199-201)—and by his own statement in his *Notebooks* (68) that his "spiritual childhood" lasted "for six or seven years:" thus up to 1912-13, just when he first begins teaching Thomistic philosophy. (His in-depth course on Bergson at the Institut Catholique was only given in the Spring of 1913. Even after it, and before "their" book on Bergson, Raïssa will describe herself as "still under ... [his] influence" [AIG, 209].)

their perspective all his life;[10] yet, even more notably, his philosophical studies were directed not by Dominicans with a *philosophical* degree, but rather by priests renowned chiefly as spiritual directors and by a theologian.

In noting his absence of philosophical formation, I do not wish in any way to minimize the depth of his intellectual struggle. If we ask ourselves what generated the sense of meaninglessness that was clearly present when he and Raïssa made their famous vow in the *Jardin des Plantes*, I believe we should answer: a conflict between his heart and his head, between *praxis* and *theoria*.[11] From his mother, his youth, and his connection with Péguy, he inherited a deep and abiding commitment to rectify social injustice. He was deeply committed to the laboring poor. Nor was he ever to lose this commitment, in that way showing himself to be his mother's son (and no doubt maintaining an important bond between them). His political passion was all the stronger for his absence of religious passion; something of what properly belongs to our commitment to God was no doubt displaced upon politics. Yet that commitment was undermined at root by the theoretical philosophy he was encountering "in full flower" at the Sorbonne. For, if we were no more than the accidental product of blind forces, what could ground a commitment to justice? And, if we were determined by physical forces, how could one reasonably be outraged at iniquity or inequity? After all, our action was ultimately outside our control.

---

[10] It is interesting that, as one of the first Catholics favorably to welcome Étienne Gilson's thesis (1913), he nevertheless criticizes his account of the *de auxiliis* controversy: see "L'Ésprit de la Philosophie Moderne: La Réforme Cartésienne," in *Oeuvres Complètes*, I, 823-52, p. 832, n. 8. (This article was first published in June, 1914, in the *Revue de Philosophie* XXIV, no. 6: 601-25.) Significantly, from the very beginning of their work, Maritain defends the great Dominican interpreters of Aquinas, whereas Gilson does not or with greater qualification.

[11] He himself was aware of this; on March 19, 1899, at least six months before attending the Sorbonne, he wrote this passage to Psichari: "J'ai comme toi une sort de religion du progress humain. Mais ... je pretends bâtir ma foi sur la raison et ... je sais que la Raison est chancelante et que la Science ne me donne pas encore de suffisantes certitudes:" See Barré, op. cit., 57.

Maritain himself was later to describe his fundamental dilemma in eloquent words:

> A man is bound to die for justice. That means that he stakes *his all* on the moral order of justice. To stake all, to give my life, I need to know the intrinsic value of justice and the obligation of justice are unconditional or absolute ... a thing which no mere statement of fact, as are all statements of phenomena, and no possible consideration born out of Empiricism, can ever establish.[12]

The greater our moral outrage at injustice and our desire to rectify it, the greater the importance of explaining to ourselves how our stand is not simply a "relative opinion," no more defensible than the next. Nor will it find itself satisfied in front of any species of naturalism that is inevitably driven towards subjectivism and relativism, however much its sophisticated defenders might desire otherwise. When we imagine Jacques at 16 hurling himself on the rug in despair because "there was no answer" (*WHBFT*, 67), I believe that we should see the question he faced as being of this nature: what account can I give myself that justifies the course of my life's action?

This question is, we might say, a theoretical one. It points towards the Absolute and towards theism, as providing an *intellectual* answer to an intellectual problem. Perhaps finding such a philosophy might have satisfied Jacques, at least for a while. It would not by itself, however, have satisfied Raïssa;[13] for *hers* was not simply a theoretical problem. To understand this, we must recall one who is without name in her

---

[12] Jacques Maritain, "The Cultural Impact of Empiricism," in *From An Abundant Spring: The Walter Farrell Volume of the Thomist* (New York: Kenedy and Sons, 1952), 448-66, p. 465.

[13] Jacques' mother, Geneviève Favre, with a mother's instinct, senses that he has been very much changed by his relation to Raïssa, that he is now "hard to penetrate" (as she wrote to Psichari [Barré, op. cit., 88-89]). This change occurs before Bloy. Is it not because he has come under the influence of Raïssa's search?

memoirs: her maternal grandfather.[14] She describes him in these moving words:

> Concerning my maternal grandfather I have preserved memories of a great goodness, and of a gentleness which even to my childish eyes seemed extraordinary... [these] came from his great piety, the piety of the *Hasidim*.... My grandfather's religion was one altogether of love and confidence, of joy and charity.... The hospitality of my grandparents was proverbial, and often belated travelers knocked on their door in the middle of the night. My grandfather would then get up in great haste and awaken his wife as joyfully as if God Himself had come to visit them, and the unknown guest would be received as well as their modest means allowed.... When the guest was refreshed and rested and wished to leave, my grandfather himself always went with him to see that he took the right road, no matter how late the hour (*WHBFT*, 2-4).

A combination of Tevye and the sweet and holy *Rebbe* of Anatevka,[15] this man imparted to Raïssa's mother a deep sense of the mystery and holiness of God, a sense which she maintained in her household, faithfully keeping *Shabat* and celebrating the great feast of *Pesach* with all the mystery and solemnity proper to it. Raïssa's childhood was that of Chagall's paintings: the mystery of God was deeply present in her life. It was just this presence she had lost, and that the "learned of the Sorbonne" told her was an illusion.

---

[14] Another important person, a contemporary of her grandfather, is unmentioned by her and unnamed by Jacques: the mother of Léon Bloy. This remarkable woman offered her health to God that her wayward son be protected by the Virgin's care, an offer apparently accepted: see "Homage to our Dear Godfather Léon Bloy," in *Untrammeled Approaches* (Notre Dame, Indiana: University of Notre Dame, 1997), 26-45, p. 28. This was in 1866, when Raïssa's mother was newly born. Another unnamed person of the same generation, the deeply religious, Orthodox, grandmother of Ernest Psichari, had seen to his being baptized (*WHBFT*, 50). How truly we do not see with God's eyes nor understand the secret workings of His Providence!

[15] The comparison is more than evocative, for both the time and the place of *Fiddler on the Roof* was his.

Should her reaction to Plotinus surprise us, then, that she should find herself on her knees kissing the book of the *Enneads* (*WHBFT*, 97). For, as she says, his philosophy is "as much in the character of a mystic as in that of a metaphysician" (*WHBFT*, 97). I rather imagine her as reading a passage such as this one, on the vision of Absolute Beauty:

> Seeing, with what love and desire for union one is seized—what wondrous delight! If a person who has never seen this hungers for it as for his all, one that has seen it must love and reverence it as authentic beauty, must be flooded with an awesome happiness, stricken by a salutary terror. Such a one loves with a true love, with desires that flame. All other loves than this he must despise and all that once seemed fair he must disdain.[16]

If Bergson had brought her to Plotinus, she could not be satisfied with the fare his own philosophy offered; for he had awakened in her a desire to find again the *divine presence* that had so filled the heart of her childhood. She wanted to *experience* the living God.

Léon Bloy comes as an answer to the desire of her heart and it is again difficult not to see her "taking the lead" in wanting to see him and in being caught by him. With Bill Bush, we should recall the importance of Maritain's tombstone, the degree to which he owed *everything* to Raïssa, perhaps indeed his faith above all else.[17] In entering Bloy's house, in which "all values were dislocated... [and] one guessed that only one sorrow existed... —not to be of the saints" (*WHBFT*, 119), *she* was "returning home:" to the presence of God in her childhood and to one who would talk as intimately to St. Barnabas as Teyve (and no doubt her grandfather) would talk to God about his hardships. Let us also recall the image that Erasmo Leiva also has given us of Bloy: "a Hasid dancing for joyful woe at the foot of the cross."[18]

---

[16] Plotinus, "Beauty," in *The Essential Plotinus* (Indianapolis: Hackett, 1984), 41.

[17] See William Bush, "RAÏSSA MARITAIN ... et Jacques," in *Understanding Maritain: Philosopher and Friend*, eds. Deal W. Hudson and Matthew Mancini (Macon, Georgia: Mercer University, 1987), 57-70. (This book is based on essays given in the first AMA conference that I attended, in Atlanta, in 1985.)

[18] Erasmo Leiva, "Léon Bloy and Jacques Maritain: *Fratres in Eremo*," in *Understanding*, 71-90, p. 78.

Here was a man heaven-sent for them as a couple: someone whose love of the poor and whose anger at bourgeois Catholics was as great or greater than Jacques'; and whose love of Israel, and his appreciation that God's promises to her remained irrevocable, revealed a love for Raïssa's people as deep as her own. Yet, in both cases, a man whose judgments and inner life were founded upon his burning love of The Poor Jew—Israel's and mankind's dispossessed and crucified Savior—and upon his filial devotion to His mother, who gave Him to the world, and to His Holy Catholic Church: that Jewish Mother who continued to offer Him to us, nowhere more deeply and personally than in the Holy Eucharist, the partaking of which, each morning, fortified him to face the penury of his prophetic life.

What they both came to want, then, was not simply the surety that God existed, but to discover the Word He had *spoken*, that they might be guided surely back to Him. They found themselves having to "test this out," to discover whether the Church's claim was credible. This is philosophy at its limit: looking at the claims of religion "from the outside," to see if they are believable. They found them so, being unable to resist the imperious witness of their godfather,[19] and soon crossed Her threshold, thereby leaving behind forever the light of philosophy alone. From the Spring of 1906, they will walk by the light of Catholic faith and be a devoted son and daughter of the Holy Roman Church.

Raïssa herself emphasizes their mutual love of the Church, and its importance in their conversion: speaking of their experience at baptism, she writes that "the Church kept her promises. And it is *she whom we first loved*. It is through her that we have known Christ" (*WHBFT*, 178, my italics). Their spiritual itinerary followed a classic path: in the

---

[19] Raïssa quotes the following passage from one of Bloy's first letters to her: "The importance, the DIGNITY of souls is beyond utterance, and your souls, Jacques and Raïssa, are so precious that it took no less than the Incarnation and the agony of God to ransom them—exactly as my own...*Empti estis pretio magno*, you have been bought at a great price. That, my friends, is the key to everything, in the Absolute. We have been ransomed, like most precious slaves, by the ignominy and the willing torture of Him Who made heaven and earth. When we know this, when we see and feel it, we are like Gods, and we do not cease from weeping" (*WHBFT*, 139). This excerpt gives us the power of his prose; but they believed his truth because he lived it.

Spirit, through the Son, to the Father. As Jacques later told Jean Cocteau, like many a convert, he was "a man God had turned inside out like a glove."[20] From an 18-year-old who had written his friend Psichari that they had to "destroy the pope and all of Catholicism" (see n. 3), he became the Church's ardent champion.[21] In Her he had found his Saviour; from Her hands he daily received Him. His love for Her was irrepressible.[22]

If we ask what his first, deepest, and most important intellectual and spiritual formation was, the answer lies in the title of their last book: liturgy and contemplation. This altogether remarkable "little flock" of three souls, all three consecrated to Mary, was formed first on the liturgy, and soon the habit of daily communion. Later, Father Clérissac's greatest witness, and greatest gift to Jacques, was the recollected and holy way he celebrated the Eucharist. Through Fr. Pègues (another Dominican), their house would soon even have its own chapel. Daily reading of the Missal and *lectio divina* became a staple of their life. And their life was formed in the second place on the saints, upon contemplative mystics and spiritual writers. As Jacques said, "for

---

[20] Jacques Maritain, *Art and Faith* (New York: Philosophical Library, 1948), 73.

[21] Raïssa says that "It was as a man of the Church and with the weapons of the Church militant that this layman confronted the public of the universities" (AIG, 215). Even earlier, in his teaching at the Collège Stanislas, she remarks that "there was something worse than his Thomism: from the first day of class Jacques undertook to begin his classes with prayer—an Ave Maria, followed by an invocation to St. Thomas" (AIG, 200). One thus cannot help but wonder how he would regard today's Catholic universities!

[22] Raïssa writes: "Jacques has not feared her [the Church], he has loved her and given himself to her with complete trust" (AIG, 215). Psichari relates his journeying towards "the Catholic apostolic and Holy Roman Church" as a "dwelling of peace and joy... one could desire nothing more than to live eternally in its shadows," and Raïssa comments: "All those who with a sincere heart cross the threshold of the Church have this vision at one time or another" (AIG, 131). And, commenting on his vision of the Church as the mystical Jerusalem, she writes, "[although] this inspired, real, and mystical vision might later pale ... we shall never lose—unless by mortal faults of infidelity—the knowledge of the essential goodness of this protecting mother of souls, of this city 'shining with the glory of God'" (AIG, 132). They never did.

six or seven years, we *devoured* the lives of the saints, books of spirituality and the works of the mystics."[23] Tellingly, Maritain says of them:

> [T]he most profound and the most lasting—*definitive*—impressions are those of the years during which the child accomplishes this prodigious task: to conquer the visible world. It is the same for the years of spiritual childhood which follow conversion, when the intelligence throws itself on the world of divine truth.[24]

We would do well to take him seriously here. He was shaped first and definitively not by philosophy, but by Holy Tradition, by the liturgy and the mystical witness of the saints.[25] Nor, of course, should we forget the constant and deep influence of his godfather, as well as his spiritual interests, such as in Anne Catherine Emmerich or Our Lady of La Salette.

I come now to my promised thesis. I have heard it said that Maritain the philosopher turned to matters theological only at the end of his life, when he came to the Little Brothers. This won't do. It is important that we recognize the constancy of his theological reflection. I trust there will be no argument that one who reflects upon the mysteries of the

---

[23] Jacques Maritain, *Notebooks*, 68. Here are some that he had mentioned: St. Ignatius's *Exercises*, St. Francis de Sales's *Treatise on the Love of God*, Denis the Carthusian's commentary on John, the *Imitation of Christ*, the *Little Flowers of St. Francis*, Ruysbroeck, Angela of Foligno, the *Dialogue* of St. Catherine of Siena, and various saints' lives: St. Francis Xavier, St. Catherine of Genoa, [St.] Catherine Labouré, St. Frances of Rome, St. Catherine of Bologna, St. Mary Magdalen of Pazzi, St. Lydwine (Ibid., 39-53).

[24] Ibid, 68; my emphasis.

[25] In fact, because of the bequest of Pierre Villard, their spiritual life displayed a union and balance between the active and contemplative life. Their life's work was to share the fruits of contemplation with others. This is obvious in the case of Jacques, but it is no less for Raïssa as well, who not only was busy hosting the *Cercles Thomistes*, but whose literary output was considerable. (Indeed, if we are to believe Jacques—and why should we not?—she was involved in *all* his own work.) Likewise, as Jacques is careful to note, Vera's obviously more active apostolate was balanced by an interior life that was deeply contemplative.

Trinity, the Incarnation, or the Church's sacramental and mystical life is properly engaged in a work of sacred theology, is one seeking to understand and/or to defend truths of faith that transcend philosophy. Using such a standard, then, here is only a partial list of his theological works: his manuscript on La Salette (to which he devoted two years); his 23-page Preface to Fr. Clérissac's *The Mystery of the Church*, the third and fourth essays in *Théonas*, articles such as "À Propos de la Question Juive," "Sainte Gertrude," and "Pascal Apologiste," *Prayer and Intelligence*, much of the *Three Reformers* (especially its chapter on Luther), all of his writings on the *Action Française* affair (such as *The Things That Are Not Caesar's*), *St. Thomas Aquinas*, *Religion and Culture*, the second part of *The Degrees of Knowledge* (over one third of the main text), the second essay of *Du Régime Temporal et de la Liberté*, *Questions de Conscience*, *The Thought of St. Paul*, much of *The Philosophy of History*, *The Mystery of Israel*, *Liturgy and Contemplation*, *Notebooks*, *The Peasant of the Garonne*, *On the Grace and Humanity of Jesus*, *The Church of Christ*, and most of *Untrammeled Approaches*. Regarding that last, it is worth noting that a commentary on Genesis, an essay on love and friendship—two-thirds of which is devoted to the mystical state and to Christian marriage—and a commentary on Vatican II's *Gaudium et Spes* are listed as being of a "primarily philosophical order."[26] One should, I think, argue otherwise.

---

[26] See Jacques Maritain, *Untrammeled Approaches*, II (47). He describes (151) his method of reading *Genesis* as of "*any Christian in search of intelligibility*" (thus "faith seeking understanding" or theology); he describes his method in his essay on love and friendship as neither that of a theologian nor a philosopher (165), yet he there interweaves reflections on human love with ones on divine charity, the Trinity, and even the Latin sub-diaconate; there is a similar interweaving in his reflections on *Gaudium et Spes*, as is not surprising in a commentary on a Church document. It is of course possible for truths of faith to provide matter fit for philosophical work: that the doctrine of the Trinity furthered philosophical reflection on the category of relation and that of the Incarnation on the idea of subsistence or personality is well attested. Yet Maritain's reflections in many of the above-mentioned works are not confined to such investigations; rather, they not only suppose truths of faith, they also seek to understand them and relate them to human culture. Perhaps an analogy might help make my point here clearer. There are "high" and "low" Christologies, ones that approach the mystery of the Incarnation from the Divine Word, made flesh, or from the human child of Mary guarded by Joseph, a man who was initially identified by those who

You will note that the above list deliberately avoids works such as *Integral Humanism* or *Christian Philosophy*, although these works arguably depend upon a commitment to truths of faith,[27] nor does it include works of moral philosophy "adequately considered."[28] Even so, it is clear that Maritain not only is engaged in theological reflection, but is actively publishing works of theology, from the beginning to the end of his career. Nor should we forget his constant preoccupation with the Cercles Thomists. As he indicates, many of the themes he chose for its Sunday discussions were theological: The Trinity, the divine Persons, the state of the first man, Original Sin, The Incarnation, the motive of the Incarnation, the human nature and the human faculties of Christ, On love and the Holy Spirit.[29] Maritain obviously was called to be a teacher, and he obviously was engaged in teaching theology at all of these meetings.

I am hardly suggesting that Maritain did not engage in philosophical writing or lacked the *habitus* proper to philosophy! But then, presumably, no one will dispute that Aquinas had the same. His series of commentaries on Aristotle, to which he devoted the labors of his maturity, are notorious for remaining at the level of philosophy; but no

---

knew him as a rabbi, or a miracle worker, or a prophet, and yet who also revealed by His words and actions that He was "more" than these human titles could capture. Maritain's theological reflection is, as it were, a "low" Theology, coming at the truths he reflects on very much from the human side: the human culture they impact. Yet it is still theological reflection, just as a "low" Christology is still a Christology.

[27] *Integral Humanism* proposes a *Christocentric*, rather than a *Theocentric* ideal. Maritain never explains why the second would not be adequate. Presumably, it is because a theocentric humanism, absent any *de facto* revelation (even if open to this), would not supply the forces sufficient to leaven the secular order. This indicates that a Christocentric humanism is itself insufficiently specific. Maritain would seem, in fact, to be committed to a *Catholic* humanism of the Incarnation. In any case, he appeals here to matters of faith.

[28] As the tenor of this paper suggests, it seems to me that *any* reflection based upon the truth and light of faith is properly *theological*, not philosophical. Philosophy as such (and however qualified) remains an inadequate guide to morals.

[29] Jacques Maritain, *Notebooks*, 133-85.

one that I know of thinks that Aquinas was anything other than a Catholic theologian doing philosophy.[30] I think that, considering his intellectual labor in its entirety, Maritain succeeded in following his intellectual master better than he realized.

Several reasons help explain Maritain's failure to grasp the degree to which his work as a whole is that of a Catholic lay theologian. First, what precedent or role model did he have? He would have had to go back to Boethius: a rather long stretch of time![31] Second, he recognized that he had not devoted himself to the exegesis of Scripture or to the Fathers as Aquinas had (even though he often comments on the first and devotes a chapter of the *Degrees of Knowledge* to "Augustinian wisdom"): since he did not systematically study theology's sources, no doubt he did not think of himself as having its *habitus*.[32] But this is to think chiefly in terms of dogmatic and moral theology, of the *Summa Theologiae*. It is to overlook that Aquinas's most personal work, the *Summa Contra Gentiles*, is also a work of theology. Aquinas is concerned

---

[30] Here is Maritain's own testimony: "There is a Thomist philosophy based upon the sole evidence of reason. Saint Thomas achieved a great philosophical work; he had an extraordinary metaphysical genius. But he is not simply, or primarily, a philosopher, he is essentially a theologian. It is as a theologian, from the summit of knowledge which is architectonic *par excellence*, that he definitively establishes the order of Christian economy" (*St. Thomas Aquinas*, 19). The same could be said of Maritain, and precisely in relation to his most famous work: *The Degrees of Knowledge*.

[31] Boethius, like Maritain, is chiefly known as a philosopher, and the title of his most famous work fits Maritain's own spirit: *The Consolation of Philosophy*. Likewise, Boethius's project was to translate for his time the treasures of classical philosophy. Yet, despite this philosophical work, he also was a theologian, and a defender of the Catholic faith against Arianism. Indeed, he was likely a martyr for the faith. Of course, there were earlier lay antecedents: Pascal, More, Dante. Yet none of these—mathematician, statesman, or poet—however intelligent and "theologically aware" that they were, possessed a philosophical *habitus*.

[32] This is surely behind his later self-description as a "research worker" for theology: as a para-legal does not have all the technical training of a lawyer, so he felt he lacked all that was necessary to be a scholastic theologian. For some "critical" comments on the implications of this self-characterization, see my n. 1.

in this work first and foremost with distinguishing which truths of faith are accessible to reason and which transcend it; in another words, he is interested in a matter to which Maritain constantly devoted considerable energy: the relation of reason to faith, and of philosophy to theology.[33] Aquinas is concerned in the second place to engage in strictly philosophical arguments that demonstrate those truths of faith accessible to reason. This occupies three quarters of the work, just as (we might say) this task likewise occupied three quarters of Maritain's work.[34] Aquinas is further interested in showing that the truths of faith that transcend reason are not opposed to it, but even consonant with it: again, a fundamental preoccupation of Maritain. Finally, Aquinas' overarching purpose in this work is to show to his contemporaries that the Catholic faith need not fear all that reason, rightly used, demonstrates: the conclusions of the rational science then being propagated, at the Sorbonne of his day. And this is likewise the overarching purpose for all of Maritain's work.

I take his philosophical work to be preoccupied with three projects. In the realm of Beauty, to articulate a Thomistic aesthetics and—in applying it to art (chiefly painting and poetry)—to show its affinity for what was best in contemporary art. In the realm of Truth, to articulate a Thomistic theory of science and—by integrating contemporary empirical science with Aristotelian principles of natural philosophy and metaphysics—to demonstrate its assimilative capacity and contemporary relevance. Finally, in the realm of the Good, to articulate

---

[33] It is insufficiently remarked that you cannot decide what truths of faith are accessible to reason on the basis of faith alone, any more than you could decide whether or not modern science can prove the existence of God on the basis of faith alone. In the second case, you need to know science—its methods, limits, and conclusions—to answer the question, and in the first you need to know the same for philosophy. To answer properly the first matter posed by Thomas in the *SCG*, a theologian must also be a philosopher. Nor have Catholic theologians attended well to what Thomas says there (cf. *SCG* III, 147-163). Had they, arguably they would not have become embroiled the way they did in the 20th century debate on the right relation between nature and grace.

[34] Unquestionably, Maritain engaged in strictly philosophical work and had a philosophical *habitus*. My point is that this was part of a larger intellectual project: bringing Catholic faith to bear on modern culture.

a contemporary politics—by unifying Thomistic principles of natural law and the demands of the common good with a commitment to democracy, pluralism, and personal rights—to demonstrate the relevance of Thomism for today's social order.[35] Now, as with Aquinas's work in the *Summa Contra Gentiles*, all of these projects have an apologetic purpose: to show that Catholic faith, and the philosophical wisdom it had traditionally used as a tool, need have nothing to fear from the truth, whatever its secular or non-Catholic provenance may have been. He was seeking to do for his day what Aquinas had sought to do for his own.

Finally, if we ask "who was the audience to whom Aquinas addressed the *Summa Contra Gentiles*?" I believe the answer is this: principally, to his fellow Catholics, and secondarily to all reasonable men of good will. Aquinas well understood that the advent of Aristotle had posed and continued to pose problems for his fellow Catholics:

---

[35] Speaking of contemporary Thomism, Maritain writes that "the task which lies before it is to disengage from the enormous contributions which the experimental sciences have accumulated in the past four centuries a genuine philosophy of nature—as, in quite another sphere, to integrate the artistic treasure of modern times in a philosophy of art and beauty which shall be universal and at the same time comprehend the efforts being made at the present moment" (*St. Thomas Aquinas*, xi). Regarding the second task, he refers the reader to *Art and Scholasticism* (n. 1). He then immediately goes on also to speak of "the great principles of Christian politics (xi)." This is in 1930. He is about to produce *The Degrees of Knowledge*, and *Integral Humanism* is also not far off. If these three books represent his central work, it is clear from this text and from his entire life that he gave priority to the first task; for it was his conviction from his first to his last book that the central crisis of the contemporary world was a crisis of truth, and that this was brought about because modern science had supposedly replaced the Aristotelian philosophy of nature. Since he held that philosophy began with the concrete sensible—that "meta-" physics was "after" physics, supposed it, and then went "beyond" it—to undermine Aristotle's philosophy of nature was to undermine philosophical wisdom at its root. He believed the first task of contemporary Thomism was to assimilate and integrate modern empirical findings and science with the enduring and still true philosophical principles of nature found in Aristotle. Only if the realm of the true could first be defended could its principles then be applied to the realms of beauty and goodness (his other great enterprises).

first, to understand the proper relation between philosophy and the Faith; second, to recognize that the latter had nothing to fear from the former, properly pursued. As a consequence of addressing these fundamental needs, this work likewise could be used to speak to non-Catholics, showing them the degree to which Catholic faith defended truths accessible to reason and—by showing that where it went beyond reason it did not contradict it—inviting them to embrace that realm of truth as well, through faith. One could hardly summarize better, it seems to me, the project of Maritain's whole life.[36]

Let us recall that the reasons Maritain embraced Thomism were mainly apologetic, as a defense of the faith. No doubt, he thought this philosophy to be true. Yet his deeper reasons, and his deeper passion, derive from his faith. In the first place, it was hard for him to evade the clear call of the Catholic Magisterium to defend Thomas as an antidote to the errors of modern times.[37] Second, he saw that divine grace and faith were received by human nature and the vital truths of common sense, and that Thomism, in supporting these truths, gave the faith its necessary support.[38] Third, and specifically, he saw the need to defend conceptual knowledge, because he saw that to undermine it would be to undermine Catholic dogma, which relied upon human concepts to state its truths. (This was the reason he felt obliged to abandon Bergson.)[39] Lastly, he saw the degree to which modern philosophy had

---

[36] At the Fall of France, Raïssa movingly speaks of having "almost lost the hope which sustained us in our work and in the trials of our life: the hope that Christian love could pervade and transform the world" (WHBFT, vii). This summarizes the goal of their intellectual life and labors. Equally, in the Preface to *St. Thomas Aquinas* (p. ix), he says "it is for the *love of their souls* that I thomistize"; my emphasis.

[37] He makes this very plain in *St.Thomas Aquinas*, chapter 4.

[38] As he argued: "Destroy the force of reason and you destroy also the natural foundations themselves by which grace *takes* on the human being, you erect a divine building, exceedingly weighty, on ground already undermined.... What is necessarily required is the mind in its natural vigour, that spontaneous and naturally direct use of the mind which is called common sense" (*St. Thomas Aquinas*, 112-13).

[39] Here is his testimony: "It was in 1908—while I was deliberating, in the country around Heidelberg, whether I could reconcile the Bergsonian critique of the concept and the formulas of revealed dogma—that the

undermined confidence in common sense, reason, and objectivity, and consequently the adherence due Catholic doctrine. Thus, even were the Magisterium to have taken a more "ample" view, speaking well of other philosophies, and even though other philosophies supported the patrimony of common sense,[40] it remained his view that only a philosophy as "high-powered" and technical as Thomism possessed the "philosophical where-with-all" to confront the subjectivism of modern culture. It was this conviction that led to his readiness to defend the "barbarisms" of scholastic terminology involved in Thomism. Now, all of these reasons are basically apologetic: he defended Thomism above all because it was needed to defend the faith.

This leads me to my final point. For whom did Maritain principally write? The answer seems rather obvious: his fellow Frenchmen. France had remained Catholic during the Reformation, yet had compromised

---

irreducible conflict between the "conceptual" pronouncements of the religious faith which had recently opened my eyes, and the philosophical doctrine for which I had conceived such a passion during my years as a student and to which I was indebted for being freed from materialistic idols, appeared to me as one of those only too certain facts which the soul, once it has begun to admit them, knows immediately it will never escape" (*Bergsonian Philosophy and Thomism* [New York: Philosophical Library, 1955], 16).

[40] He characterizes that patrimony in the following terms: "Does not common sense firmly believe that what is *is*, that the same thing cannot at the same time be predicated as existent and non-existent, that in affirmation or denial, if we speak truly, we are dealing with what is, that whatever happens has a cause, that the sensible world exists, that man has a substantial self, that our wills are free, that the primordial laws of morality are universal, lastly, that the world did not make itself and that its Author is intelligent?" (*St. Thomas Aquinas*, 114). It is important to Catholic Faith that philosophy defend this patrimony, but Thomism is not alone in doing so, for it is defended by both Platonism and Aristotelianism, and their various schools. Thus, he will also say "I am not preaching here for any particular philosophy. I am preaching for any philosophy capable of restoring in man the sense of being and the sense of reason, and the sense of the unconditional value and unshakeable truth of the things which are the treasures of civilized consciousness" ("The Cultural Impact of Empiricism," p. 465). Thus, as a Catholic, he could remain friendly to forms of Augustinianism (as Thomas was to Bonaventure's views), while still preferring Thomism.

her commitment to her Catholic Tradition through adherence to some modern trends of thought (first of the Enlightenment and then of scientistic positivism) that undermined it. He was calling Frenchmen back to their true, Catholic, soul. His thought addressed chiefly Catholics. If practicing, it was to remind them of the weapons in the Church's intellectual armory, and to urge them to take them up. He was constantly showing them how they could appropriate the riches of modern culture while adhering to their own tradition. If Catholics "manqué," or those purely secular, it was to build bridges towards them: to show them that a Catholic could embrace what was best in their truth, while offering a deeper and truer vision of faith that surpassed what reason alone could reach, and which it needed.[41] He did not merely philosophize *in* the faith; rather, he was constantly philosophizing *for* the faith.

Much might be said concerning the *significance* of Maritain's vocation for us.[42] Allow me to conclude with just these two thoughts. First, I think that those who would follow his spirit should be seeking to address their own fellow countrymen, trying to get them in touch with their "better soul:" the religious foundations of the great institutions of their country and the need to recognize this fact, if its patrimony is not to be imperiled. Second, and more importantly, I think he would remind us that our first duty is to our fellow Catholics and to Catholic

---

[41] I can bear witness to his success in both endeavors, for I read Maritain as I was on my way to becoming a Catholic and repaired to him frequently thereafter. His work was a bridge for me, to move from my own secular standpoint, across the troubled and anxious waters of modern culture, to the Church. And then I found myself returning to him to understand what was the right perspective to take on so many of the questions posed by that culture and that I continued to take seriously, even while adhering to the Faith.

[42] Among the many other points that could be made, this one seems pertinent: Maritain shows us best what is involved in apologetics. If its reputation has waned, it is because it has been identified with some kind of "manual apologetics," rather than with the lived and vital apologetics to which he gave his life. If contemporary Catholics are again to be ready to "make a defense... of the hope that is in [them]" (1 *Peter* 3.15), they could hardly do better than to return to Maritain and take his spirit and judgment as their guide.

institutions. The forces in today's culture that lead towards meaninglessness and despair work as powerfully on undergraduates today as they did on those in the Sorbonne a century ago. And the absence of an intellectual tradition firmly opposing them is as palpable on many Catholic campuses today as it was at the Collège Stanislas and the Institut Catholique before his own call for a renewal of Thomism. I think he would again be ready "to break some windows." I think he would call us to that task: to get Catholic institutions of higher learning to recommit themselves seriously to the riches of their Catholic intellectual patrimony and especially to those of Aquinas. After all, who better than *we* should be called to that task? Ever-faithful godson of Léon Bloy that he was, I think his message to us here today would be a call to arms.

Gatekeeper of Small Mistakes: An Example of the Philosopher's "Other" Vocation

John G. Trapani, Jr.

Aristotle and Aquinas rightly identified the philosopher's vocation as one that seeks and acquires wisdom. This wisdom is found in the knowledge of first principles and causes, with the result that the philosopher is one who puts things in order—who puts things in their proper place.[1] Over the course of intellectual history, however, there have been many changes concerning this classical understanding of the philosopher's vocation. This is true not only for philosophy's own self-understanding, but also for the way that other disciplines and the general public perceive philosophers as well. In addition, recent developments in science and technology and the serious significance of many current ethical controversies have also contributed to these changes.

From a certain perspective, Descartes' endeavor to make philosophy and the philosophic method more like science and the scientific method may well be the origin of the most recent changes. Decades later, the many noteworthy truths and successes of Newton's work served to ratify and reinforce Descartes' ideal. In the process, the ancient and medieval kinship between science and philosophy, where science and philosophy shared a common search for "explanatory knowledge through causes," was replaced by the modern idea that only useful knowledge, as a consequence of the method of the natural or experimental sciences, has any real value. Indeed, over the past two centuries, we have witnessed a steady ascendancy of the influence of the experimental, natural sciences and, in the twentieth century, of the social sciences as well. However, over this same period of time, we have witnessed the steady decline of the cultural influence of philosophy. In general, many people today see philosophy as some form of esoteric scholarly game that is of use and delight only to the players of the

---

[1] St. Thomas Aquinas, *Commentary on the Nichomachean Ethics* (Chicago: Henry Regnery Company, 1964), 6.

game themselves. As a result, philosophy and philosophers today are notable for their general absence from the many various forums of public discourse. Philosophers have not been intentionally excluded; rather, since the public thinks philosophy is not "scientific," philosophers generally have been consigned to the dustbin of cultural irrelevance. One pertinent example of this form of disregard should suffice.

In 2000, ABC produced a TV Special on "Happiness," hosted by John Stossel. This entire 90-minute program considered only the psychological (as opposed to the ethical) notion of happiness; it consulted and interviewed no less than ten scientists (including seven psychologists). Not one philosopher appeared during the entire show! When a program on happiness entirely excludes any discussion about the concept of *eudaimonia*, it is a sure sign that the psychological idea of happiness has replaced the philosophical, ethical notion of happiness: the scientific study of "feeling good" has replaced the ethical study of "being good" or living a good life. Moreover, the content of this TV program underscores the presumption that only the sciences provide any validly useful knowledge.

The significance of this shifted focus also appears in the many serious contemporary ethical debates, especially those that have grave consequences for ordinary human life. Today, it is the social and biological scientists, joined by legal scholars and political pundits, who are the acknowledged public sources of authority in ethics, while philosophers are politely but rather conspicuously ignored. Our culture's bewitchment with the sciences might be considered a somewhat predictable and banal reflection of society's love for the pragmatic benefits of technology were it not for the fact that the dizzying proliferation and complexity of scientific achievement has led to so many serious ethical issues. The biological sciences in particular raise a host of ethical controversies that go beyond the strict subject matter of biology proper. Accordingly, since no science can be the judge of its own first principles, the time is long overdue for philosophers, especially realist philosophers, to reassert the "other" responsibility of their once nobly regarded profession; they need to become the gatekeepers of those proverbial "small mistakes in the beginning that lead to large errors in the end."[2] This is especially true concerning those first principles about human nature which serve as the starting points for the biological and social sciences; if these principles are mistaken, they become perfect examples of those initial small mistakes that lead to very serious ethical consequences in the end.

A specific example of this call for philosophical vigilance concerning the principles of human nature can be found within the discipline of philosophy itself. In ethicist Peter Singer's 2002 book, *Unsanctifying Human Life*,[3] the author argues forcefully against the idea that humans possess any unique, inherent dignity and sanctity. Singer's position accepts the scientific claim that human nature has an entirely materialist explanation. In the process, he fuels the idea that the human species has no real intrinsic value that transcends the "inherent" value that he sees all species possessing. Indeed, for the front cover of his book, Singer makes an amusingly oxymoronic but mocking use of Michelangelo's "Creation of Adam" from the Sistine Chapel—talk about poking God's finger in your eye![4]

1. Ideas That Need "A Good Scrubbing"

In an essay from Singer's book, one that shares the book's title, "Unsanctifying Human Life," the author remarks that the "doctrine of the sanctity of human life is a legacy of attitudes and beliefs that were once widespread, but which few people would now try to defend."[5] For Singer, the idea that human nature has any unique, inherent dignity and sanctity that transcends nonhuman animals is nothing more than a historical myth that no longer has any relevance in academic, scholarly, or scientific circles—it is, he says, "the historically conditioned product of doctrines...which hardly anyone now accepts;

---

[2] "A slight initial error eventually grows to vast proportions." St. Thomas Aquinas, *On Being And Essence*, trans. Armand Maurer, C.S.B. (Toronto, Canada: Pontifical Institute Of Medieval Studies, 1968), 28.

[3] Peter Singer, *Unsanctifying Human Life* (Malden, Massachusetts: Blackwell., 2002).

[4] Jacques Maritain, *The Peasant of the Garonne* (New York: Macmillan, 1969), 78.

[5] Singer, *Unsanctifying Human Life*, 228.

doctrines so obnoxious, in fact, that if anyone did accept them, we would be inclined to discount any other moral views he held."[6] Ouch! For Singer, there is no, nor can there be any, valid rational argument for a spiritual/intellectual dimension of human nature. Singer accepts as so scientifically certain the Darwinian claim that the human species differs only in degree from nonhuman primates that he does not consider as a respectable intellectual possibility any challenge to this assertion. Singer's conclusion in this regard is emphatic: "Although advocates of the doctrine of the sanctity of human life now frequently try to give their position some secular justification, there can be no possible justification for making the boundary of sanctity run parallel with the boundary of our own species, unless we invoke some *belief* about immortal souls."[7]

Ironically, it is precisely such a rational argument for the existence of a spiritual intellect that Mortimer Adler, following Aquinas, does provide in his 1967 book, *The Difference of Man and the Difference It Makes*. There is a summarized version of this purely rational argument in the text,[8] and a lengthy and highly technical version (i.e., seven single-spaced pages!) in his endnotes.[9] Sadly, as his a priori dismissal necessitates, Singer now pokes his fingers in his ears! The sad truth is that the substance and logic of Adler's argument, with all of the subtleties of its realist, Thomist vocabulary, is generally so far removed from contemporary philosophical discourse that it quite understandably falls on deaf ears.

And so the conclusion goes: since Singer's position conforms to the a priori assumption about the truth of the entirely materialist hypothesis of science, Singer is to be taken seriously; by contrast, since Adler's position does not conform to the a priori assumption about the truth of the exclusively materialist hypothesis of science, Adler is not to be taken seriously. The problem with this line of reasoning, obviously, is that Adler's position is not rationally rebutted or refuted; it is simply

---

[6] Singer, *Unsanctifying Human Life*, 230.

[7] Ibid.; my emphasis.

[8] Mortimer J. Adler, *The Difference of Man and the Difference it Makes* (New York: Holt, Reinhart and Winston, 1967), 220-22.

[9] Ibid., 340-47.

ignored. Those materialists, who incline toward this line of reasoning and who hold that there can be no spiritual dimension of human nature because it goes beyond the experimental limits of empirical science, will quite naturally conclude that to reach a contrary conclusion, Adler must be invoking some form of belief or faith-claim, which he, of course, does not do.

Not surprisingly, being dismissed in this way is not unique to the writings and ideas of Mortimer Adler alone. Jacques Maritain too received his share of intellectual disregard. Maritain's intuitions concerning the myriad modern metaphysical mistakes, with their linguistic tower of philosophical babble, was decades ahead of its time. In his 1969 book, *The Peasant of the Garonne,* Maritain remarks that he is fed up with sociological or descriptive portraits of the times. What concerns him, he says, is not the "value of the times," but rather the "values which have an impact on them." He writes, "It is not our era that worries me, but the ideas one runs into at every street corner, some of which could certainly stand a good scrubbing."[10] Since theoretical ideas do have practical consequences, they represent the first principles of values on which we depend...and which characterize and define our times. Perhaps even more importantly than our loss of specific philosophic truths, Maritain also lamented the more basic loss of what he called the knowledge of "pre-philosophy," that fundamental, inherent common sense of human intelligence. In the absence of this, many modern and contemporary philosophers find themselves caught in an intellectual Catch-22 of their own making—they need common sense intelligence to see the error of their "small mistakes," all the while that they doubt the very veracity of this common sense intelligence itself! "Bring on the fables!" Maritain says, "... as disoriented as we are, we must go on thinking anyway."[11]

One such fable concerns the human effort to understand the truth about human nature. Without a rational demonstration of the spiritual dimension of human nature, there is no rational defense of any *intrinsic* dignity and sanctity of the human person. When those, like Singer, who dismiss a priori the explanation of a spiritual dimension of human

---

[10] Maritain, *The Peasant*, 20.

[11] Ibid., 25.

nature as nothing more than a matter of religious belief, their entirely materialist assumption lays the foundation for those serious value-problems that result whenever the dignity and sanctity of human life is not intrinsic. From abortion, euthanasia, and capital punishment, to all of the forms of economic, social, racial, and gender inequality and injustice, the "consistent ethic of life" that the Catholic Church champions depends upon the rational affirmation of the inherent dignity and sanctity of human nature. And this, of course, can only be found in the spiritual reality of human nature, the very concept that Singer denies. And so we ask: how did it come to this? How did humans come to think so poorly about themselves as a natural species? Perhaps the answer to this question is to be found in philosophy after all; as Woodrow Wilson famously remarked: "Men [and women] die, ideas live." And so it is that, over the past few centuries, several philosophical errors, as the ideas that have served as the starting points for subsequent ethical consequences, have contributed to this lamentable state of affairs. Descartes may be dead, but the influence of his (and subsequent enlightenment thinkers') ideas lives on.

2. *Unsinging* Singer's Song of Unsanctity

Darwin's great scientific achievements get the question-begging ball rolling. Today, Darwin's materialist claim that the human animal differs only in degree from the rest of the primates from whom humans have evolved is perhaps more precisely explained as a "superficial difference in kind," i.e., an observable difference in kind (evidenced by the human ability to think conceptually) that is *explained by* an underlying difference in the degree of complexity of the human central nervous system involving a critical threshold. This explanation, of course, is still fundamentally a materialist explanation. And so, while immaterialists may dismiss Darwinian materialism *a prior* as incompatible with the Christian claim that humans are "spirit-incarnate" (and as such are "made in the image and likeness of God"), materialists for their part dismiss the idea that humans possess a spiritual dimension, as not rationally defensible. Remarkable as this may seem, Maritain suggested the possibility of reconciling these two positions—the materialist claim about evolution with the immaterialist claim about a spiritual dimension of human nature that occurs through divine intervention in history—in a seminar that he delivered in the late sixties, "Toward a Thomist Idea of Evolution;"[12] Pope John Paul II announced a similar position of compatibility in the nineties. But never mind; historically, Darwin's materialist hypothesis continued to be ratified through the contributions of paleo-anthropology in the latter part of the nineteenth century, then by comparative psychology at the turn of the twentieth century, followed by cybernetics in mid-century and, in the last half of the twentieth century, by the advancing work of neurology and brain research.[13] With the materialist hypothesis so scientifically persuasive and pervasive, the materialists completely ignored the rational argument that rescues the moderate immaterialist position:[14] the position that argues in favor of the claim that human beings do possess a spiritual dimension which not only alone accounts for their abilities to understand and to love in ways that are unique to the human species, but which also establishes their intrinsic dignity and sanctity.

With all of this in mind, it should come as no real surprise that all ten of the errors identified by Mortimer Adler in his book, *Ten Philosophical Mistakes,*[15] concern some relation to the first principles of human nature. Understand human nature incorrectly, and all ten of these mistakes result. The origin of the first five errors, all of which concern epistemology and ethics, are enlightenment errors that pre-date Darwin's scientific achievements. They are the subtle mistakes that set the stage for the more attention-getting ethical errors that would follow. Although they are primarily philosophical errors, they lay a foundation of compatibility with the future claims of scientific materialism.

Specifically, in chapter one, Adler corrects the most subtle and difficult of epistemological errors concerning human consciousness and its object by distinguishing between private, subjective experience

---

[12] Cf. Jacques Maritain, *Untrammeled Approaches,* trans. Bernard Doering (Notre Dame, Indiana: University of Notre Dame, 1997), Chap. VI, "Toward A Thomist Idea Of Evolution," 85-131.

[13] Cf. Adler, *The Difference of Man*, 41ff.

[14] Ibid., 223.

[15] Mortimer J. Adler, *Ten Philosophical Mistakes* (New York: Macmillan, 1985).

and public, objective experience. This in turn involves the realist/idealist disagreement concerning the function of ideas for consciousness—for realism, ideas are "that by which" the mind apprehends things (ideas are a *quo*), while for idealism, ideas are "that which," those "things" that the mind apprehends directly (ideas are a *quod*).[16] Chapters two through five correct the mistakes that follow from this first error and include distinguishing (1) sense powers and sense knowledge from the intellect and intellectual knowledge (chapter 2); (2) the difference in kind between perceptual and conceptual thought (chapter 3); (3) the true meaning of *episteme* (as distinguished from *doxa*) (chapter 4); and (4) the contrast between descriptive and prescriptive judgments (chapter 5).[17]

These distinctions themselves ultimately depend upon the metaphysics of the spiritual dimension of human intelligence and, consequently, human nature. The failure to understand the correct explanation of human nature leads to the failure to make these distinctions; the failure to make these distinctions leads to significant though subtle errors in thinking which are those small mistakes in the beginning that result in serious ethical consequences in the end.

Specifically, if one blurs the distinction between "that by which" and "that which," one ends up denying the common sense foundation of realism, that the mind truly knows reality. Make this mistake and the track leading to Humean and Kantian skepticism (a result of the split between noumenal and phenomenal reality) is assured and only the "likely truths" of science will be thought to provide any real and useful knowledge. Truth, as the conformity of the mind with reality, is gone, and in its place is the post-modern conclusion that truth and reality are only a matter of perspective.

Next, should one blur the distinction between sense powers and sense knowledge and the intellect and intellectual knowledge, one ends up ratifying Descartes' error of equating the mind with soul. Make this mistake and the materialist hypothesis (in the explanation of human nature) quite logically concludes that "soul" (and hence any spiritual dimension of our nature) is but an unnecessary hypothesis, a

---

[16] See also Adler, *The Difference of Man*, 341.

[17] Adler, *Mistakes*, 5-127.

multiplication of terms. As a result, this thinking leads to the conclusion that "soul" is nothing more than a "Ghost in the Machine," an unreal and unnecessary term that violates the logical principle of parsimony.

The next mistake conflates the distinction between perceptual and conceptual knowledge and, when combined with the previous error, falsely confirms the idea that these kinds of knowing—and hence human nature itself—differ only in degree, not kind, from other nonhuman animals. Make this mistake and Singer's song is complete: according to him, the sin of speciesism is grounded in what he holds to be the erroneous claim that the human animal has any spiritual uniqueness and, as a consequence, that it would have an *inherent* dignity and sanctity that gives it a superiority over other life forms.

What might we say in reply? The truth is that intrinsic dignity and sanctity can only come from the human possession of a spiritual dimension that is given through a causal participation with the Divine Creator; only in this way is the human species different in kind from, and transcendent over, nonhuman animals.[18] Such a conclusion makes clear the importance of Adler's (and St. Thomas's!) articulation of the rational argument for the spiritual dimension of human nature. Without the truth of this rational argument, all and any attempts to assign to humans some measure of dignity and sanctity must, by definition, be *extrinsically* bestowed. The consistent ethics of life can only be defended and affirmed through a rational argument for the human difference in kind from other animals. In this way, only, is Singer's song of unsanctity unsung.

This rational argument for the spiritual dimension of human nature provides but one example of a gate-keeping rational defense of the preambles of faith that ought to be the vocation of all Catholic, realist philosophers of common sense. In this regard, Jacques Maritain, our beloved "peasant of the Garonne," along with his friend, Mortimer

---

[18] Another matter of equal importance, though one that goes beyond the scope of this paper, concerns the idea that, even though we are transcendent over other life forms, we are nonetheless called to be caretakers of God's creation, and not dominating exploiters. This position is fully compatible with the idea of responsibility that accompanies human transcendence.

Adler, may rightly be regarded as model gatekeepers of small mistakes. They defended the truth of those rational first principles that, if uncorrected, lead to large errors in the end, errors that endanger the ethical values of not just the present age but future ages as well.

PART III

Pope John Paul II's *Fides et Ratio*

FIDES ET RATIO'S CALL FOR A RENEWAL OF METAPHYSICS AND ST. THOMAS AQUINAS

Msgr. John F. Wippel

While Pope John Paul II had some very positive things to say about Aquinas's philosophy in general and his metaphysics in particular in *Fides et Ratio*, he also made it clear that it is not the place of the Church's magisterium to endorse any particular philosophy or any particular metaphysics to the exclusion of all others. Rather, he wanted to indicate the characteristics of the kind of metaphysics which might be pursued by philosophers who are also believing Christians.

Although the Pope did not want to say that the magisterium was imposing Aquinas's philosophy and his metaphysics, one gets the impression that he judged Aquinas's philosophical thought and especially his metaphysics to be particularly well qualified to help meet the need he had in mind. In this paper, therefore, I propose to develop some of these desired characteristics as they are described by Pope John Paul II, and then to turn to the metaphysics of Aquinas in each case for the sake of comparison.

1. A Metaphysics in Harmony with Christian and Catholic Religious Belief

It is hardly surprising that in seeking for a philosophy and a metaphysics that will be of value to Christian thinkers, the Pope would insist that it should not be opposed to orthodox religious belief. As he notes in his introductory remarks, the Church sees in philosophy "the way to come to know fundamental truths about human life" (#5).[1] While recognizing that there have been many different schools of

[1] Unless otherwise indicated I will use this translation: *Encyclical Letter Fides et Ratio of the Supreme Pontiff John Paul II* (Vatican Translation: Daughters of St. Paul, 1998). I will use the Latin text contained in *Restoring Faith in Reason: A New Translation of the Encyclical Letter 'Faith and Reason' of Pope John Paul II together with a commentary and discussion*, ed. by L.P. Hemming and S. F. Parsons (Notre Dame, Indiana: University of Notre Dame, 2003).

philosophy, he also insists that there is a distinctive "core" of philosophical thinking which may be discerned within the history of human thought including principles such as noncontradiction, causality, finality, the concept of a person as free and intelligent with a capacity to know God, truth, and goodness (#4).

It is his conviction about the ultimate unity of truth that undergirds his defense of the harmony between reason and revelation:

> This truth, which God reveals to us in Jesus Christ, is not opposed to the truths which philosophy perceives.... The unity of truth is a fundamental premise of human reasoning, as the principle of non-contradiction makes clear. Revelation renders this unity certain, showing that the God of creation is also the God of salvation history (#34).

Readers of Aquinas can hardly fail to notice the similarity between the Pope's remarks on this point, and the thinking of Thomas Aquinas himself. Indeed, somewhat farther on, after briefly sketching the developing thought of earlier Christian thinkers on the relationship between faith and reason, John Paul II speaks in glowing terms about the originality and the contributions of Thomas Aquinas:

> Thomas had the great merit of giving pride of place to the harmony which exists between faith and reason. Both the light of reason and the light of faith come from God, he argued; hence there can be no contradiction between them (#43).

Here he cites *Summa Contra Gentiles*, 1.7 in support, and goes on to remark: "Just as grace builds on nature and brings it to fulfillment, so faith builds upon and perfects reason." For this he cites *Summa Theologiae* I, 1.8, ad 2.

With reference to this I would note that in a text from his somewhat earlier *Expositio super Boetium De Trinitate*, 2.3, Aquinas brings out both of these points and several others in what I regard as his best discussion of the harmony between faith and reason. This article is explicitly directed to answering this question: "Whether in the science of faith which treats of God it is permissible to use philosophical arguments and authorities." Thomas begins his response by commenting that the gifts of grace are added to nature in such fashion that they do not destroy nature but rather perfect it. Therefore, he continues, the light of faith which is infused into us as a grace (*gratis*) does not destroy the light of natural reason, which is also divinely instilled in us.[2]

He observes that while the natural light of the human intellect is insufficient to discover those things which are manifested to us (solely) through faith, it is nonetheless impossible for those things which are divinely revealed to us through faith to be opposed to those which are instilled in us by nature. Otherwise one or the other would be false. Here, of course, Thomas is appealing to the principle of non-contradiction and hence to the unity of truth. Two contradictory propositions cannot both be true at one and the same time. And so, he continues, both that which is divinely revealed to us and that which we discover by using our naturally given powers and principles ("that which is instilled in us by nature") come to us from one and the same source, God himself. Hence, to admit that they could really contradict one another would make God himself the author of falsity. This, of course, Thomas rejects as impossible.[3]

Here, then, we find the ultimate foundation both for Thomas's and for John Paul II's defense of the harmony between reason and revelation. As a religious believer, Thomas is convinced that revealed truth has God as its source. As a philosopher, he is convinced that every finite being, including human beings and their divinely given cognitive powers, is efficiently caused by God. This follows from his view that, in all finite beings, their act of being (*esse*) is efficiently caused (see *De ente et essentia*, c. 4; *ST* I, 3.4; *De pot.*, 3.5). But if faith when rightly interpreted could contradict reason when rightly exercised, one or the other would have to be false according to the principle of noncontradiction.[4]

---

[2] Ed. Leonina, vol. 50, p. 98, ll. 114-18=Leon. 50.98:114-18: "Responsio. Dicendum, quod dona gratiarum hoc modo naturae adduntur, quod eam non tollunt sed magis perficiunt; unde et lumen fidei, quod nobis gratis infunditur, non destruit lumen naturalis rationis divinitus nobis inditum."

[3] Leon. 50.98:118-99:126.

[4] Thomas then goes on to note in passing that because in imperfect things there is found some imitation of things that are perfect, in those things

Up until this point in this text, Thomas has concentrated on the relationship between faith and reason. Next he turns to the relationship between theology (*sacra doctrina*) and philosophy. Just as theology is based on the light of faith, so philosophy is based on the natural light of reason. Therefore, Thomas now concludes, it is likewise impossible for those things which are proper to philosophy to be contrary to those which pertain to faith, although the former fall short of the latter.[5]

Having concluded that there can be no real conflict between those things which are proper to philosophy and those which are proper to revealed truth, Thomas identifies two ways in which philosophy can be of assistance to someone who is attempting to understand his faith. Those things which are proper to philosophy contain (1) certain similitudes or likenesses that may be used to illustrate mysteries of faith; and (2) they contain certain preambles for faith (*praeambula fidei*), just as nature itself is a preamble for grace.[6]

But before explaining in more detail what he has in mind by each of these, Thomas introduces a third consideration. He is well aware that, over the course of time, certain conclusions proposed by some philosophers have been contrary to faith. He now explains that in such cases, when something is found in the sayings of a philosopher that is contrary to faith, this is not really something that is proper to philosophy as such. Rather, it is an abuse of philosophy following from a deficiency on the side of reason. In such cases, it is possible by using the principles of philosophy to refute an error of this kind in one of two ways, either by showing that the alleged philosophical claim is absolutely false (*omnino esse impossibile*), or else by showing that it is not necessarily demonstrated. He introduces the last-mentioned point to allow for the case of revealed mysteries. While truths which can be held solely on the grounds of faith cannot be demonstrated to be true, so too, certain alleged philosophical conclusions which are opposed to

---

which are known by means of natural reason certain likenesses (*similitudines*) are found of those things which we hold on faith (Leon. 50.99:126-30).

[5] Leon. 50.99:131-35.

[6] Leon. 50.99:135-37: "continent tamen aliquas eorum similitudines et quaedam ad ea praeambula, sicut natura praeambula est ad gratiam."

them cannot be demonstrated to be false. Otherwise, one would in effect demonstrate the truth of the revealed mystery. But, says Thomas, even in such cases it can be shown by reasoning philosophically that such claims which are opposed to faith have not themselves been demonstrated (shown to be necessary).[7]

In summing this up, Thomas now concludes that within theology it is permissible for one to use philosophy in three ways. The first way is most important for our purposes here today; namely, that philosophy may be used to demonstrate those truths which Thomas calls *praeambula fidei*, and which he says:

> it is necessary to know in one's faith, such as truths which are proved by natural arguments about God, such as the fact that God exists, that God is one, and other things of this kind concerning God or concerning creatures which are proved in philosophy and which faith presupposes.[8]

In this text we can see how closely the teaching in *Fides et Ratio* noted above concerning the harmony between faith and reason corresponds to and depends upon Thomas's position. Thomas calls for a philosophy, and hence a metaphysics, that is not only in harmony with revealed truth, but which can demonstrate preambles for faith, such as God's existence and his unity.

2. Philosophy as a Search for Truth

We are all familiar with the opening words of Aristotle's *Metaphysics*: "By nature all human beings desire to know" (980a 21). In *Fides et Ratio* Pope John Paul II also cites these very words from Aristotle's *Metaphysics* and turns to every day experience to illustrate how concerned we all are to "discover for ourselves, beyond mere opinions, how things really are" (#25). He also remarks that within "visible creation, man is the only creature who not only is capable of knowing

---

[7] Leon. 50.99:137-47.

[8] Leon. 50.99:148-54: "Sic ergo in sacra doctrina philosophia possumus tripliciter uti: primo ad demonstrandum ea quae sunt praeambula fidei, quae necesse est in fide scire, ut ea quae naturalibus rationibus de Deo probantur, ut Deum esse, Deum esse unum, et alia huiusmodi vel de Deo vel de creaturis in philosophia probata, quae fides supponit. . ."

but who knows that he knows, and is therefore interested in the real truth of what he perceives" (ibid). I would note here how this insight was anticipated by Aquinas's insistence that truth, when taken as an adequation between the intellect and reality, not only requires this *adaequatio* but also requires that the thinking person in whose intellect such truth resides be aware of this adequation through judgment (*ST* I, 16.2).[9]

The Pope comments that it is this desire to understand that has driven so many inquiries in the field of theoretical science, as well as much research in the practical arena which looks to the good which ought to be done. And in the practical area, when it comes to ultimate questions concerning the meaning of life and the issue of life after death (immortality), human beings are not satisfied with mere questioning but want to reach an ultimate answer. But, the Pope writes: "The high (*suprema*) point of this investigation will depend upon the answer given to this question: Whether or not we think it possible to attain universal and absolute truth" (#27).[10] He insists that people seek something absolute, something ultimate, a final explanation to give meaning and an answer to their searching, and which refers to nothing beyond itself (ibid). And so, down through the centuries "philosophers have sought to discover and articulate such a truth, giving rise to various systems and schools of thought." It goes without saying that Aquinas's entire career was dedicated to reaching such truth (see, for instance *SCG* I, 1 where Thomas cites Aristotle as holding that first philosophy, i.e., metaphysics, is the science of truth, not any truth whatsoever, but that truth which is the origin of all truth).

3. The Magisterium and Philosophy: Negative Role

In Chapter V Pope John Paul II takes up the issue of the Magisterium's interventions in philosophical matters. Here he makes the point

---

[9] For an excellent discussion of Aquinas's view that by nature all men desire to know, see Jan Aertsen, "Thomas von Aquin. Alle Menschen verlangen von Natur nach Wissen," in *Philosophen des Mittelalters. Eine Einführung*, ed. T. Kobusch (Darmstadt: Wissenschaftliche Buchgesellschaft, 2000), 186-201.

[10] Translation mine. "Ex responsis quae iisdem dantur suprema pendet investigationis pars: utrum fieri possit ut perveniatur necne ad veritatem universalem et absolutum" (#27, p. 46).

already noted above. "The Church has no philosophy of her own nor does she canonize any one particular philosophy in preference to others (#49)." His major reason for saying this is to protect the integrity and the legitimate autonomy of philosophy itself. Philosophy, even when engaged within theology, must remain true to its own principles and methods and proceed according to the light of reason (#49). Even so, and here again, as Aquinas had already noted, the Pope observes that history reveals that philosophy—especially modern philosophy, he adds—has "taken wrong turns and fallen into error." The Pope insists that it is the duty of the magisterium to respond clearly and strongly when particular philosophical views threaten or contradict a correct understanding of revealed truth (see #'s 49, 50).

Pope John Paul II remarks that it was not only in recent times that the Magisterium has spoken out about erroneous philosophical theories, but he acknowledges that since the mid-nineteenth century such pronouncements have become more frequent. During this period some Catholic thinkers judged it necessary to develop their own forms of philosophy in order to counter certain currents of modern philosophical thought. The Magisterium then found it necessary to be on guard lest some of these philosophies themselves promote erroneous views. Censures were directed on the one side against *fideism* and against radical *traditionalism* because both of these positions minimized the capacity of natural reason. On the other side, censures were also directed against *rationalism* and *ontologism* because these views assigned to reason knowledge which revelation alone can give. The Pope explains that the valid and the positive points resulting from these interventions were incorporated by Vatican I into its Dogmatic Constitution *Dei Filius*, wherein for the first time a general Council solemnly pronounced on the faith-reason relationship (#52).

Thereby the Council showed "how inseparable and at the same time how distinct were natural knowledge of God and revelation, reason and faith" (#53, trans. mine). The Pope states that the Council began "with the basic premise (*ex praecipua postulatione*) which Revelation itself presupposes, that [the fact] that God exists, as the beginning and the end of all things, can be known naturally" and concluded with the solemn pronouncement "that there are two orders of knowledge, distinct not only in their origin but also in their object" (ibid).[11]

As for the contemporary situation, John Paul II observes that certain problems of former times have returned today. He mentions a "deep-seated mistrust of reason which has surfaced in the most recent developments of much of philosophical research, to the point that there is talk at times of the end of metaphysics" (#55). In theology, a certain *rationalism* has appeared wherein certain unproven philosophical positions are uncritically accepted by some theologians who are not well versed in philosophy. Finally, he sees signs of a resurgent *fideism* which does not recognize the importance of rational knowledge and of philosophy for understanding faith and even for the possibility of having the capacity to believe in God. Against another kind of latent fideism evident in the small attention given to speculative theology, he recalls that both the understanding of faith and dogmatic formulae have taken their terminology from the concepts (*notiones*) of classical philosophy (#55). He urges philosophers, whether Christian or not, to "trust in the power of human reason and not to set themselves goals that are too modest in their philosophizing." And he concludes this section by observing that faith thus becomes the "convinced and convincing advocate of reason" (#56).

4. Philosophy and the Magisterium's Positive Role

Under the heading *Ecclesia philosophiae studiosa* the Pope then turns to a more positive role exercised by the Magisterium with respect to philosophy, noting that it "has sought to stress the basic principles for a genuine renewal of philosophical enquiry" (#57). He refers to Leo XIII's Encyclical Letter *Aeterni Patris*, noting that in it Pope Leo recalled and developed the teaching of Vatican Council I on the faith-reason relationship and indicated how philosophy contributes to faith and to theology. More than a century later, he continues, many of Pope Leo's insights retain their interest, and especially "his insistence upon the

---

[11] "Concilium ex praecipua postulatione sumpsit initium, quam ipsa Revelatio praesumebat, Deum scilicet esse naturaliter cognosci posse, rerum omnium principium et finem, atque sollemni illa iam memorata enuntiatione desiit: 'Duplicem esse ordinem cognitionis, non solum principio, sed obiecto etiam distinctum'." See *Restoring Faith in Reason*, 86, #53.

incomparable value of the philosophy of St. Thomas." Leo had judged that the best way to recover "the practice of a philosophy consonant with the demands of faith" was to reemphasize Aquinas's thought (#57). After summarizing the many positive results that followed from "the Thomistic and Neo-Thomistic revival," John Paul II notes that this was not the only indication of a renewal of philosophical thinking within Christian culture. Prior to and then parallel with Pope Leo's intervention, certain other Catholic thinkers drew upon other philosophical approaches to produce important works (#59).

Pope John Paul II then refers back to the teaching of Vatican II concerning philosophy, especially one chapter in *Gaudium et Spes* which, he comments, "amounts to a virtual compendium of the biblical anthropology from which philosophy too can draw inspiration." In particular he notes its emphasis on the value of the human person created in the image of God, human beings' superiority over the rest of creation, and human reason's ability to grasp the transcendent (#60). He cites from the Councils's recommendations concerning the study of philosophy required of candidates for the priesthood, along with a number of similar later interventions by the Magisterium concerning the need for a solid philosophical formation for such candidates.[12] John Paul II comments that he himself has found it necessary to repeat on several occasions the value of Aquinas's insights and to insist that his thought be studied because the Magisterium's directives concerning this have not always been carried out as fully as one might expect. He laments the fact that since Vatican II many Catholic faculties have been impoverished by a lessened awareness of the importance not only of Scholastic philosophy, but of philosophy as such (#61). Against such trends Pope John Paul II recalls once more that the study of philosophy is "fundamental and indispensable to the structure of theological studies and to the formation" of future priests (#62). And so he sees it as his task in this Encyclical to "state principles and criteria, which ... are necessary in order to restore a harmonious and creative relationship between theology and philosophy" (#63).

[12] See footnote #84 for a listing of these.

5. Philosophy and Theology

This leads him in Chapter VI to a more detailed examination of the interaction between philosophy and theology. He recalls certain specific tasks of theology which require having recourse to philosophy and distinguishes between two methodological tasks for theology, the "hearing of faith" (*auditus fidei*) and the "understanding of faith" (*intellectus fidei*). Philosophy assists theology in preparing for the "hearing of faith" by its consideration of the structure of human knowledge, of interpersonal communication, and of the forms and functions of speech (*loquelae*). In addition, philosophy also makes an important contribution by enabling the Church's tradition, pronouncements of the Magisterium, and the views of eminent theologians to be understood more accurately, and especially so since the last-mentioned often use ideas and forms of thought taken from a particular philosophical tradition (#65).

As for the "understanding of faith," he recalls that the divine Truth "proposed to us in the Sacred Scriptures understood according to the teaching of the Church" as Thomas puts it in *ST* IIa-IIae, 5.3, ad 2, enjoys an intrinsic intelligibility which is so logically coherent that it may be proposed as a true wisdom.[13] Hence dogmatic theology should have the ability to arrive at the universal meaning of the one and triune God and of the economy of salvation both as considered under the aspect of narrative and especially through sound reasoning. It must do this by using concepts which themselves are expressed through critical judgment which can be communicated to all.[14] Indeed, states the Pope, without the assistance of philosophy, major theological issues cannot be clarified, such as appropriate speech about God, the personal relations in the Trinity, the action of a creative God in the world, the relationship between God and man, or Christ's identity as true God and true man. Therefore, the Pope concludes:

---

[13] See #66: "Si vero intellectus fidei ponderatur, animadvertendum est apprime divinam Veritatem 'propositam nobis in Scripturis Sacris secundum doctrinam Ecclesiae intellectis' [*ST* II-II, 5.3, ad 2] propria fruere intellegibilitate tam logice congruenti ut proponatur veluti germana sapientia."

[14] #66: "Id efficere debet, profecto, intellectivis adhibitis notionibus quae critico iudicio effinguntur cum omnibus communicabili."

> It is therefore necessary that believing reason have a natural, true and consistent knowledge of created realities, of the world and of man, about which things divine revelation also treats. Moreover it should have the ability to control this knowledge by using understanding and argumentation. Consequently speculative dogmatic theology presupposes and embraces a philosophy of man and of the world, and more profoundly, a philosophy of *esse* itself, which philosophy is based on objective truth (#66).[15]

The Pope's reference to a philosophy of *esse*—that is, a metaphysics of *esse*—makes one think of both the language and thought of Thomas Aquinas and his special emphasis on the role of the *actus essendi* in accounting for the ontological structure and the actual existence of any particular being. This point, which is blurred by the translation of *esse* as "being" in the two English translations I have consulted and cited here, will recur below.[16]

In turning to fundamental theology (#67), the Pope assigns to it the role of justifying and expounding "the relationship between faith and philosophical thought." He harks back to the teaching of Vatican I, itself based on Romans 1.19-20, to the effect that there are some "truths which can be known naturally, and therefore, philosophically. Knowledge of these is necessarily presupposed for accepting God's revelation."[17] Here one is reminded of Aquinas's remarks in his *In De Trinitate* 2.3 about certain *praeambula fidei* which are presupposed for faith, even though the Pope does not here use the expression

---

[15] Translation mine (#66): "Necesse est ideo ut fidelis ratio naturalem habeat, veram congruentemque cognitionem de rebus creatis, de mundo et de homine, quas res etiam revelatio divina tractat; magis etiam, ipsa facultatem habere debet moderandi hanc cognitionem per modum intellectionis et argumentationis. Quapropter theologia dogmatica speculativa praesumit et complectitur philosophiam hominis, mundi atque, altius, ipsius 'esse', quae quidem in obiectiva veritate innititur."

[16] See Pauline translation, 85, #66; *Restoring Faith in Reason*, 107, #66.

[17] Translation mine (#67): "Concilium iam Vaticanum I, doctrinam resumens Pauli (cfr Rom 1.19-20), in id iam animos converterat, quasdam scilicet exstare veritates quae naturaliter, ideoque philosophice, cognosci possunt. Earum cognitio necessario anteponitur ad Dei revelationem suscipiendam."

praeambula fidei. Like Thomas, the Pope first mentions a natural knowledge of God (#67). Thomas himself frequently cites Romans 1.20 in support of his view.[18]

The Pope then quotes from his 1995 *Letter to Participants in the International Congress of Fundamental Theology on the 125th Anniversary of "Dei Filius:"* "'Although faith, a gift of God, is not based on reason, it can certainly not dispense with it. At the same time, it becomes apparent that reason needs to be reinforced by faith in order to discover horizons it cannot reach on its own'" (#67). Somewhat farther on the Pope comments that the relationship between theology and philosophy is best "construed as a circle." Theology begins with the word of God revealed in history, and its goal is to understand that word. Philosophy, when pursued according to its own principles, can help one better understand God's word. And reason is moved by revealed truth to explore "new and unsuspected horizons" (#73).

The Pope's presentation of the benefits resulting from this close interrelationship between philosophy and theology might raise some concerns about the autonomy of philosophy when it is involved in such a relationship. Perhaps with this concern in mind, the Pope next distinguishes three different stances (*status)* philosophy may take with respect to Christian faith. The first is that of philosophy viewed as completely independent of revelation. This is the position taken by philosophy as it first existed before the coming of Christ and even later in regions not yet reached by the Gospel. The Pope takes a positive attitude toward this stance on the part of philosophy, and recognizes in it a realization of philosophy's legitimate desire to be an autonomous discipline operating according to its own principles and natural powers. He also recognizes the limitations of human reason that follow from human weakness but observes that insofar as the pursuit of philosophy leads to the discovery of truth in the natural order, it is at least implicitly open to the supernatural (#75).

---

[18] For Thomas's text see n. 7 above. For other references to this see In *De Trin.*, 1.2, sed contra (Leon. 50.84:36-37), which merely quotes the text's opening words; 1.3 (Leon. 50.88:145-47); 5.4 (Leon. 50.154:154-57); 6.2, obj. 4 (Leon. 50:164:23-24); 6.3, sed contra (Leon. 50.166:32-35). Also see *ST* I, 2.2, sed contra, and the full discussion in *Super Epistolam ad Romanos Lectura, in Super Epistolas S. Pauli Lectura*, vol. 1 (Marietti, 1953), nn. 114-22.

A second possible stance for philosophy is often referred to as "Christian Philosophy." The Pope views this terminology as acceptable provided that it is freed from ambiguity. It must not be taken to imply that the Church has its own official (*publicam*) philosophy since the faith as such is not a philosophy. Rather, the Pope understands by this the "art of philosophizing in a Christian way, namely, a philosophical reflection which is vitally conjoined with faith."[19] Therefore it does not refer simply to those who are Christians who philosophize and who merely want to say nothing in their philosophizing that is contrary to faith. More than this, the Pope has in mind those advances within the field of philosophy which would never have occurred without the direct or indirect assistance of Christian revelation.[20]

The Pope distinguishes two forms (*species*) of "Christian Philosophy," one subjective and one objective. In its subjective form, faith as a theological virtue liberates reason from excessive self-confidence. The virtue of humility in turn may give a philosopher the courage to take up issues which are difficult to resolve unless the data of Revelation are taken into account: issues such as the problem of evil, the personal nature of God, the question of the meaning of life, or the radical metaphysical question: "Why is there anything at all?" (#76).

In its objective form "Christian Philosophy" has to do with content. Revelation manifests clearly certain truths which reason can discover in principle, but in fact might never have done so if it were left to its own devices.[21] As examples, the Pope mentions the notion of a personal God who is free and a Creator, (a notion which he remarks, has contributed much to the development of philosophical thinking especially with respect to the philosophy of *esse*), as well as the reality of sin, the notion of a person considered as a spiritual being, the

---

[19] Translation mine: "Hac locutione ars designatur christiane philosophandi, meditatio scilicet philosophica quae vitaliter cum fide coniungitur" (122, #76).

[20] "Cum de philosphia christiana sermo fit, omnes comprehendi debent praestantes illi progressus philosophicae disciplinae, qui numquam contigissent nisi opem directe vel oblique christiana fides attulisset" (122, #76).

[21] "Lucide quasdam exhibet veritates Revelatio, quas tametsi attingere potest ratio, nunquam tamen easdem repperisset si suis unis viribus innixa esset" (122, #76).

Christian proclamation of human dignity, equality and freedom, and the recognition of the importance for philosophy of history as event (#76).

The Pope points out that in exploring such questions philosophers have not become theologians since they have not tried to understand the truths of faith by relying on revelation. They have remained within their own field and worked with reason alone, even though they have extended their investigations into new areas. Here, I would note, he is attempting to maintain a delicate balance and draw a very fine line between his repeated defense of philosophy's autonomy, and the legitimacy of its being moved by revealed truth to take up new issues for investigation.

In order to assist us in maintaining this difficult balance, I would mention in passing a distinction I have developed elsewhere when considering the much disputed issue of "Christian Philosophy," even though this distinction is not original with me. I have found it helpful to apply to this discussion the distinction between the moment of discovery and the moment of proof in one's recognition of a particular truth. In the moment of discovery, it may well be that a believing person who is also a philosopher first came to recognize a particular truth such as God's existence or God's unity solely on the grounds of his or her religious belief. But if such a person is also a philosopher or perhaps later becomes one, that person may be encouraged by the fact that he or she already believes in such a truth to examine it now from the standpoint of reason by asking whether natural reason can demonstrate this truth as well. If subsequent investigation shows that it can, one will then be engaged in philosophy in the moment of proof. But because one initially discovered such a truth as a result of one's religious faith and only subsequently examined the philosophical evidence for it, one may refer to this as "Christian Philosophy" in the moment of discovery, although not in the moment of proof.[22]

A third possible stance arises for philosophy when theology calls upon it. As the Pope has already explained and as he repeats in this context, theology has always needed the assistance of philosophy and

[22] See Wippel, "The Possibility of a Christian Philosophy: A Christian Perspective," *Faith and Philosophy* 1 (1984): 272-90.

continues to do so. He comments that it was not by accident that the Fathers of the Church and the medieval theologians turned to non-Christian philosophies in their theologizing. And this historical fact, the Pope observes, in turn points to and confirms the autonomy of philosophy which it preserves even in this third situation. However, he also acknowledges that when philosophy is so employed, it then undergoes certain necessary and important changes and, together with theology, falls under the authority of the Magisterium (#77).

In light of these reflections the Pope returns to Aquinas and explains why the Magisterium has always praised his philosophy and has regarded him as a guide and exemplar for theological study. This was not and is not done in order to canonize any particular philosophical positions nor to impose them, the Pope points out, but to show how St. Thomas is an authentic model for those who seek after truth. As Pope John Paul II puts it:

> In his thinking, the demands of reason and the power of faith found the most elevated synthesis ever attained by human thought, for he could fully defend the distinctiveness of revelation without ever demeaning the venture proper to reason.[23]

The Pope indicates that in the final section of his Encyclical he will identify certain requirements which theology—and even more fundamentally the word of God itself—makes today on philosophical thinking and on today's philosophers. His remarks there cast more light on his views about metaphysics.

6. Metaphysics

Accordingly, in Chapter VII he refers to a current "crisis of meaning." "Perspectives on life and the world, often of a scientific nature," have multiplied to such an extent that we are faced with a fragmentation of knowledge. This in its turn renders the search for

---

[23] Translation slightly modified: "Eius enim in meditatione rationis postulata et fidei vis altissimam invenerunt summam ex iis quae humana cogitatio unquam attigit, quippe qui Revelationis proprietatem radicitus tuitus sit, proprium rationis cursum numquam deprimendo (#78)."

meaning even more difficult and leads to doubt, skepticism, indifference, or even to different forms of nihilism (#81).

In light of this situation the Pope counters that, as a first requirement for a philosophy to be "consonant with the word of God," it must recover its "*sapiential dimension as a search for the ultimate and overarching meaning of human life.*" This is especially needed today because the great advances in technology require a renewed appreciation of ultimate values, lest technology be pursued solely for utilitarian purposes, and, he adds, perhaps finally lead to the destruction of the human race (#81).

This in turn leads to a second requirement for such a philosophy, the Pope continues, and one which he has already mentioned, namely that it support the human intellect's ability *to know the truth* of things themselves, that is, to arrive at objective truth or, as the Pope also puts it, at the very essence of objects of knowledge (*ad essentiam ipsam obiectorum cognitionis*) "by means of that *adaequatio rei et intellectus* to which Scholastic Doctors referred" (#82). In a note, the Pope explicitly refers to Thomas's *ST* I, 16.1, and to Bonaventure's *Collationes in Hexaemeron*, Collatio III.[24] Here, therefore, the Pope is calling for a robust philosophical realism.

These first two requirements imply still a third, the need for a philosophy of a "genuinely metaphysical nature,"[25] which can go beyond empirical data in order to reach something absolute, ultimate and foundational (#83). He notes that here he is not speaking of metaphysics as that of some particular school or historical tradition. He simply wants to emphasize that both reality and truth transcend particular facts and empirical data and to defend human beings' ability to grasp "this transcendent and metaphysical dimension in a way that

---

[24] In *Restoring Faith in Reason*, 133, #99, reference is given to Bonaventure's text as found in Rega Wood, "A Transcription of the Collatio III of the Hexameron," *Franciscan Studies* 53 (1993), Collatio III, q. 8, a. 1.

[25] Translation mine. Note the unfortunate mistranslation of this in *Restoring Faith in Reason*, 135, #83, of the Latin "opus est philosophia naturae vere metaphysicae as "need of a truly metaphysical philosophy of nature," which would obliterate Aquinas's carefully worked out distinction between metaphysics and the philosophy of nature.

is true and certain, albeit imperfect and analogical" (*refert etiam defendere hominis potestatem cuius vi hanc rationem transcendentem ac metaphysicam percipiat modo vero certoque, licet imperfecto et analogico*).[26] The Pope adds that metaphysics should not be seen as opposed to (philosophical) anthropology since it is metaphysics itself which can solidly establish the dignity of the person by reasoning from the person's spiritual nature. The person itself serves as the special place for an encounter with the *actus essendi* and hence with metaphysical thinking itself.[27]

Continuing to emphasize the importance of metaphysics, the Pope writes that "[w]herever men and women discover a call to the absolute and transcendent, the metaphysical dimension of reality opens up before them: in truth, in beauty, in moral values, in other persons, in being itself (*esse*), and in God." He stresses the great challenge facing us today to move from phenomenon to foundation (*a phaenomeno ad fundamentum*). He comments that any philosophy which rejects any place for metaphysics (*omne metaphysicum spatium*) thereby renders itself radically unsuited for the task of mediating in the understanding of Revelation. And so, too, a theology without a metaphysical perspective (*prospectus*) would be woefully inadequate. It could not go beyond investigating religious experience nor reach a real *intellectus fidei* (#83).

The Pope explains that if he is insisting so much on the importance of metaphysics, this is because it is the path that must be taken in order to move beyond the crisis pervading various areas of philosophy today (#83-86). He maintains that philosophers who want to respond to "the demands which the word of God makes on human thinking" should do so along the lines he has mentioned and in continuity with the great tradition which began with the ancient Greeks, passed down through

---

[26] For the Latin see *Restoring Faith in Reason*, 134, #83.

[27] "Persona, nominatim, locum constituit praecipuum ut quis congrediatur cum actu essendi ac, propterea, cum meditatione metaphysica" (ibid., 134-36, #83). Note the unfortunate translations of *actus essendi* both in *Restoring Faith in Reason*, p. 135 ("the very activity of being") and in the Pauline Books version, p. 105 ("being"). On the special role of the understanding of *esse* as *actus essendi* in the metaphysics of Aquinas, which is simply missed by these two translations, see below.

the Fathers and the medieval Scholastics, and includes positive contributions made by more recent and contemporary thought (#85).

In the next section of this Chapter, while setting forth a number of "current tasks for theology," John Paul II returns to the "understanding of revealed truth"—the *intellectus fidei.* He recalls that he has already noted that this requires the contribution of a *philosophia essendi*, which enables dogmatic theology to perform its functions properly. So too, if the "understanding of faith" wishes to include the treasures of the theological tradition, again it must have recourse to a *philosophia essendi* which should be able to raise once again the question of being in accord with the demands of the entire philosophical tradition. When placed within the Christian metaphysical tradition, he comments that the *philosophia essendi* is an active and dynamic philosophy "which ... finds its impetus and enduring force in the fact that it is grounded on the "act of being itself:" "*actu ipso 'essendi' sustentatur*" (#97).[28]

If I may conclude by returning to the three requirements for a philosophy consonant with revelation which the Pope has just singled out, I would first recall that he has not identified them with the metaphysics of any one figure, not even with that of Thomas Aquinas. But when we compare these requirements with Thomas's own metaphysics, we find therein all three of them strongly emphasized.

First of all, according to the Pope, for a philosophy to be consonant with revelation and to perform the kind of service to it which he has in mind, it should have a sapiential dimension. It should be interested in ultimate questions and aim at developing a general or universal view of reality. For Aquinas, of course, metaphysics is indeed a form of wisdom; i.e., philosophical wisdom. It has as its subject being as being, or being in general (*ens commune*), and is directed at arriving at a knowledge of things, of beings, in terms of their first principles and ultimate causes. Knowledge of God, the First Principle and Ultimate Cause of all other being, is proposed by Thomas as the very goal of metaphysics.[29] And

---

[28] "Impetum suum ac perennem impulsum in eo reperit quod actu ipso 'essendi' sustentatur" (*Restoring Faith in Reason*, 156).

[29] See In *duodecim libros Metaphysicorum Aristotelis expositio, Prooemium* (Marietti ed., 1950), 2: "Nam cognitio causarum alicuius generis, est finis ad quem consideratio scientiae pertingit." Cf. *Expositio Super Boetium De Trinitate*, 5.4

this is the nature of wisdom, to investigate things in terms of first principles and ultimate causes. This sapiential dimension of philosophy is not original with or unique to Aquinas, of course, but is deeply indebted to the ancient Greeks, and especially to Plato and to Aristotle. But it certainly applies to Aquinas's metaphysics.

Second, this sapiential dimension presupposes that the philosophy or metaphysics in question will defend the intellect's ability to arrive at objective truth, at a knowledge of things as they really are. Again, while not original with Aquinas, and while also shared by most of his contemporaries, it is well known that he defended such a theory of truth. Indeed, Pope John Paul II has explicitly commended him for this, along with St. Bonaventure.

Third, the Pope also strongly emphasizes the importance of the metaphysical dimension. This we have just seen. Obviously metaphysics is of central importance to the philosophical thought of Aquinas himself, and 20th century research has pointed out just how original many of his contributions were to this discipline. If the Pope has not restricted his remarks about the indispensable role of metaphysics to Aquinas's thought, he has frequently referred to it as dealing with *esse*, and has emphasized the importance of *esse* in the metaphysician's understanding and explanation of reality. Indeed, he has, near the end of this discussion, explicitly twice referred to the *actus essendi*. Students of Aquinas's metaphysics can hardly fail to recognize how central this notion is to his metaphysics and how original in the thirteenth-century was his understanding of the *actus essendi* as the actuality of all acts and the perfection of all perfections (*De potentia*, 7.2, ad 9).[30] And so I would submit that while there were indeed many, and still are, other philosophies of being or metaphysics which might meet John Paul II's call for a return to this discipline, none

---

(Leon. 50.153:82-86): "Sciendum siquidem est quod quaecumque scientia considerat aliquod genus subiectum, oportet quod consideret principia illius generis, cum scientia non perficiatur nisi per cognitionem principiorum. . ."

[30] On this see my work, *The Metaphysical Thought of Thomas Aquinas: From Finite Being to Uncreated Being* (Washington, D.C.: The Catholic University of America, 2000), 173-75, and the references given there to C. Fabro and F. O'Rourke.

of them has so heavily emphasized the importance of the *actus essendi* as has that of Aquinas.

I would also note that the Pope does not mention in *Fides et Ratio* Aquinas's view that every finite being is composed of an essence principle and a distinct *actus essendi.* But this is absolutely central to Aquinas's metaphysics and must be retained by anyone who would put his particular metaphysics at the service of theology. And, in light of major discoveries made in the mid-twentieth century and subsequently, I would say the same about his metaphysics of participation according to which every finite being participates in *esse*, whether in *esse subsistens,* or in *esse commune,* or in its own intrinsic *actus essendi*, since Thomas allows for all three usages.[31] The Pope, of course, could not have included these points in his discussion of the kind of metaphysics he had in mind without positively excluding non-Thomistic versions of metaphysics. But today's follower of Thomas's metaphysics can and should do so, whether he is simply studying it for its own sake, or whether he also wishes to put it at the service of theology in the latter's effort to arrive at a deeper understanding of revealed truth (*intellectus fidei*).

In conclusion, of all the kinds of metaphysics developed by human thought until this point in time, it seems to me that Aquinas's best meets the various requirements set forth in *Fides et Ratio* for one that is

---

[31] See, for instance, In *De Hebdomadibus*, lect. 2 (Leon. 50.273:234-51), where Thomas refers to Platonic forms (if they could exist) and to Aristotelian separate substances as participating in *esse commune*); In *De divinis nominibus*, c. 5, Pera ed. (Marietti, 1950), nn. 658-60) where he again refers to created existents as participating in *esse commune* and then to *esse creatum* or *esse commune* as participating in God; and In *De Heb.*, lect. 2, where after defining and dividing participation into different kinds, he refers to a kind of participation whereby an effect participates in its cause, especially if the cause is of a higher order (Leon. 50. 271:80-85). Participating in the First Cause would be the best example of this. See *De spiritualibus creaturis*, a. 1, where he refers to participation *per assimilationem* in the First Act, i.e., God, which ultimately accounts for the presence of participated *esse* in a created being (Leon. 24.2.13-14:379-85). Cf. my *The Metaphysical Thought*, 110-21. For the third usage see In *I Sent*, 19.5.2 (Mandonnet ed., vol. 1, 491): "...quaelibet res participat suum esse creatum, quo formaliter est, et unusquisque intellectus participat lumen per quod recte de re iudicat."

"consonant with the Word of God" and also most satisfying for the human intellect in its unending thirst for truth.

ST. THOMAS AND THE RENEWAL OF METAPHYSICS

Lawrence Dewan, O.P.[1]

1. Metaphysical Renewal as a Perennial Project

Let us begin by noting that there are here two considerations: (1) renewal of metaphysics, and (2) Thomas's ability to aid us. The renewal of metaphysics is a *perennial* problem. The *Republic* of Plato testifies to the need for metaphysical renewal in the Athens of the Fourth Century B.C. We might recall Protagoras's doctrine of man as the measure of all things, the teaching of Gorgias entitled "On Not-Being, or on Nature," whose first thesis is that "nothing is," and the traditionalist pragmatism of Isocrates.[2] However, far more serious is the larger situation described by Plato's Socrates in the *Republic*:

> ...I suppose that if the nature we set down for the philosopher chances on a suitable course of learning, it will necessarily grow and come to every kind of virtue, but if it isn't sown, planted, and nourished in what's suitable, it will come to all the opposite, unless one of the gods chances to assist it. Or do you too believe, as do the many, that certain young men are corrupted by sophists, and that there are certain sophists who in a private capacity corrupt to an extent worth mentioning? Isn't it rather the very men who say this who are the biggest sophists, who educate most perfectly, and who turn out young and old, men and women, just the way they want them to be?

---

[1] This paper first appeared in print in *Spirit et Esprit* 61 (2009): 5-17.

[2] Cf. Joseph Owens, *A History of Western Philosophy* (New York: Appleton-Century-Crofts, 1959), on Protagoras of Abdera, 490-420 B.C, 157-60; on Gorgias of Leontini, ca 480-380 B.C., 160-65; Isocrates of Athens, 436-338 B.C., 178-82.

Socrates is speaking of the general culture of the society; that is the sophistry which rules the roost in Athens, and produces the "philosophers" who give philosophy a bad name.[3]

There really does seem to be a permanent war about being (as Plato suggested in the *Sophist*).[4] We should expect to have to battle concerning purpose in nature, concerning substantial form and matter, concerning the immateriality of cognition, concerning the immortality of the human soul, and the existence of God, and creational causality, concerning our very ability to know being and truth. The Presocratics are always with us.[5]

If Plato has a bad theory of the state (as he has),[6] he is nevertheless right in seeing the need for an appropriate cultural setting for the well-being of the human spirit, the philosophical spirit. He is right in seeing the need for a turning of the soul from becoming to being.[7]

2. St. Thomas and Perennial Metaphysical Renewal

What does St. Thomas say about this situation? *Summa Theologiae* I, 1.1 should be our controlling text. There we learn why there is need for a teaching which *transcends philosophy*. Firstly and most important, human dignity, human nobility, the goal which the author of mankind

---

[3] Plato, *Republic*, VI, 492A-B, trans. Allan Bloom, in *The Republic of Plato* (New York: Basic Books, 1968). The whole of 489D-497A bears on the deformation of those having a nature fit for philosophy, thus giving philosophy a bad name.

[4] Plato, *Sophist*, 249D.

[5] Cf. also Aristotle on what is *always* the subject of controversy: "And indeed the question which was raised of old and is raised now and always, and is always the subject of doubt [*aei aporoumenon*], viz. what being is [*ti to on*], is just the question, what is substance [*tis he ousia*]? For it is this which some assert to be one, others more than one, and that some assert to be limited in number, others unlimited. And so we also must consider chiefly and primarily and almost exclusively what that is [*ti estin*] which *is* in *this* sense [*tou houtôs ontos*]." Aristotle, *Metaphysics* 7.1 (1028b2-7) [Ross translation].

[6] Cf. Charles De Koninck's essay on patriotism, "L'Amour de la patrie est-il donc dépassé?" in his book *Tout homme est mon prochain* (Quebec: Laval University, 1964), 109-11.

[7] Plato, *Republic*, VII, 518B-D.

has assigned for us, is beyond our investigative powers.[8] Yet the human being is meant to pursue known goals. Accordingly, God had to reveal to us what to pursue.

But secondly, as we remember, Thomas does not stop with that. There is truth about God, who is our goal, which human reason can discover. However, it is known only to a few, after a long time, and with an admixture of error. There is need for revelation by God even about such truth! The importance of that truth, "...the truth about God investigated by reason...," what we can call "philosophical truth," is strongly put by Thomas: "On knowledge of that truth [philosophical truth!] the entire salvation of man, which is in God, depends..."[9] This is where I take my beginning, and in so doing I am imitating Jacques Maritain,[10] as I will eventually show. We begin with faith in revelation, even as regards the philosophical truth implied by our ultimate goal.

We are speaking of the renewal of metaphysics. I mean by "metaphysics" what St. Thomas means, viz. the highest natural human knowledge, meriting the title of "wisdom:" a public knowledge, most difficult of access, but known on the basis of principles naturally known to all.[11]

Immediately we say "human," we must take into account the condition of the human being. That condition enters into this very first article of Thomas's *Summa Theologiae*. The picture of the human being as philosopher is very discouraging, as we begin to read St. Thomas.

Or rather, the picture of the human being as philosopher, considered strictly as to his own nature, is bleak, but the good news is

---

[8] The magnitude of human dignity is properly grasped only in the light of our true destiny. Cf. e.g., *ST* III, 57.6, ad 3: "...Christ, by ascending once into heaven, obtained for himself and for us the perpetual right and *dignity* [*ius et dignitatem*] of the heavenly dwelling." Cf. also III, 58.4, ad 1-2; I, 12 and I-II, 1-5, on beatitude; and I, 93.4 on the three levels of man's being "in the image of God."

[9] The Latin is: "...veritas de Deo per rationem investigate ... a cuius ... veritatis cognitione dependet tota hominis salus, quae in Deo est" [Ottawa ed., 2b11-17, in part].

[10] Henceforth "JM" for "Jacques Maritain."

[11] Cf. e.g., St. Thomas, *In Metaph.*, prologue.

that there is *revelation* of the very things which philosophy can know and seeks to know. Thus, with revelation, and with Thomas, we begin with wonderful *assurance* of the *truths* which philosophy seeks.

And how very *fruitful* is that situation, because, as St. Thomas later says, discussing the theological virtue of faith: "...when a man has *a prompt will to believe*, he loves the believed truth, and he thinks about it and looks at it from every angle, to see if some reasons for it can be found."[12] This surely applies not only to the revealed truths which are beyond philosophical demonstration but to those which reason can demonstrate.

We find Thomas speaking again of this *prompt will to believe* when he describes the contemplative life. Does that life have an affective dimension? Indeed, it does. One lives that life because one *intends* to do so. That intention, that vital drive, is an act of will, a *love* for the *truth*. As Thomas says:

> The appetitive power moves [us] to *inspect* something, whether sensibly or intelligibly, sometimes because of the love of the thing seen: because, as Matthew 6 [21] says: "where your treasure is, there also is your heart"; but sometimes because of a love of the knowledge itself which results from such inspection. That is why Gregory places the contemplative life in *charity toward God*: inasmuch as someone from love of God burns with desire to look upon his beauty. And because everyone delights when what is loved is possessed, the contemplative life also terminates in delight, which is in the affections, from which, again, the love is intensified.[13]

---

[12] Cf. *ST* II-II, 2.10: "Cum enim homo habet promptam voluntatem ad credendum, diligit veritatem creditam, et super ea excogitat et amplectitur si quas rationes ad hoc invenire potest."

[13] *ST* II-II, 180.1: "Movet autem vis appetitiva ad aliquid inspiciendum, vel sensibiliter vel intelligibiliter, quandoque quidem propter amorem rei visae, quia, ut dicitur Matth. VI, ubi est thesaurus tuus, ibi est et cor tuum, quandoque autem propter amorem ipsius cognitionis quam quis ex inspectione consequitur. Et propter hoc Gregorius constituit vitam contemplativam in caritate dei, inquantum scilicet aliquis ex dilectione dei inardescit ad eius pulchritudinem conspiciendam. Et quia unusquisque

It is surely the Christian philosopher's hope that his prompting, his call, arises from the charitable love of God.[14] The love for the knowledge itself pertains ultimately to our love of ourselves, a love which we hope, likewise, has the perfection of charity.[15]

We begin, then, in faith, and, as we hope,[16] in charity. However, we realize that with respect to naturally knowable truths, the goal is *to know them naturally*. Here there is no substitute for philosophical work. Some have worried about this step, as it seems to be a step away from

---

delectatur cum adeptus fuerit id quod amat, ideo vita contemplativa terminatur ad delectationem, quae est in affectu, ex qua etiam amor intenditur."

[14] In his more youthful *In Sent* III, 35.1, arg. 2 [ed. Moos, solutio 1, p. 1177, para. 32], Thomas provides more explanation concerning the twofold love: "Sed cum operatio sit quodammodo media inter operantem et objectum, velut perfectio ipsius operantis, et perfecta per objectum, a quo speciem recipit; ex duplici parte potest operatio cognitivae affectari. Uno modo inquantum est perfectio cognoscentis; et talis affectatio operationis cognitivae procedit ex amore sui: et sic erat affectio in vita contemplativa philosophorum. Alio modo inquantum terminatur ad objectum; et sic contemplationis desiderium procedit ex amore objecti: quia ubi amor, ibi oculus; et Matth. 6, 21: ubi est thesaurus tuus, ibi est et cor tuum; et sic habet affectionem vita contemplativa sanctorum, de qua loquimur. [But since operation is in a way in the middle, between the one operating and the object, thus being the perfection of the one operating, and being perfected by the object, from which it receives the specific likeness, the operation of the cognitive power can arouse affection from both sides: in one way, inasmuch as it is the perfection of the knower, and such affection for the cognitive operation arises from love of oneself: and the affection of the philosophers for the contemplative life was of that sort; in another way, inasmuch as (the cognitive operation) has its terminus at the object; and thus the desire for contemplation proceeds from love of the object: because where is love, there is the eye; and as Matth. 6.21 (says): 'where your treasure is, there also is your heart'; and the contemplative life of the saints, about which we are speaking, is such.]" Perhaps in his maturity he did not choose to conjecture concerning the hearts of those "philosophers" he distinguished from the "saints."

[15] On the charitable love for oneself, cf. *ST* II-II, 25.4; see also 25.7.

[16] Cf. *De Veritate* 10.10, that we cannot know with absolute certitude that we possess charity.

faith. Obviously, if we come to full intellectual vision of the truth, we can no longer merely believe that truth. And faith is a meritorious action (meritorious for eternal life!). Will we not lose precious merit by philosophizing about such truth? Thomas reassures us: if we do come to understand the demonstration of such a truth, this does not imply that we lose the merit of belief, as long as we have, in charity, the "will ready to believe." As St. Thomas teaches:

> ...demonstrative arguments leading to those [truths] which the faith holds, but which nevertheless are preambles to the articles, though they diminish the note of faith, because they make *apparent* what is proposed, still do not diminish the note of charity, through which *the will is ready to believe* those things even if they were not apparent. And so the note of merit is not diminished.[17]

3. The Difficult Human Condition: "A Wounded Nature"

These things I have recalled only as regards our situation in starting out as Catholics called to philosophize. Now I would repeat that our project is not new with the Christian. A primary interest of Plato in the *Republic* is precisely how to *breed* philosophers, how to *turn the soul towards being.*[18] Even before the issue of the philosopher is raised, Plato speaks of the importance of education, sound rearing. Later, as you remember, a whole course of studies is outlined, meant to turn the whole soul around, away from becoming and towards being.[19]

I am not here praising everything in Plato's particular answers, but wish to notice that this *is* the subject of discussion. The most apt students are seen as seduced by the society, which is *the greatest of all sophists*, for its own inferior ends. But if there is a hope, it is in good

---

[17] Cf. *ST* II-II, 2.10, ad 2: "...rationes demonstrativae inductae ad ea quae sunt fidei, praeambula tamen ad articulos, etsi diminuant rationem fidei, quia faciunt esse apparens id quod proponitur; non tamen diminuunt rationem caritatis, per quam voluntas est prompta ad ea credendum etiam si non apparerent. Et ideo non diminuitur ratio meriti."

[18] Cf. *Republic* VII (518B-519B).

[19] Cf. *Republic* VII (521C).

home formation and good intellectual guidance (Plato also explicitly mentions the need and possibility of divine help[20]).

Aristotle, in the *Nicomachean Ethics*, carefully notes the condition of the auditors suitable for his lectures.[21] He was a man of few words,[22] and so it is all the more notable when he says the same thing three times in succession. We read: "It makes no small difference ... whether we form habits of one kind or of another from our very youth; it makes a very great difference, or rather *all* the difference."[23]

St. Thomas teaches the dispositive role of the moral virtues relative to the contemplative life. The virtue of chastity is especially underlined, since the sexual inclination is judged to interfere most with rational judgment.[24]

---

[20] *Republic*, VI, 492A-B, quoted above, at n. 2.

[21] Aristotle, *Nicomachean Ethics* 1.3 (1094b28-1095a12).

[22] Thomas calls Aristotle "*breviloquus*," a man of few words; cf. *In De caelo*, 2.17 (457 [8]).

[23] Aristotle, *Nicomachean Ethics* 2.1 (1103b24-25) [trans. W. D. Ross]. Cf. Thomas, *In Eth*. 2.1.10: "Et ideo ulterius concludit quod non parum differt, quod aliquis statim a iuventute assuescat vel bene vel male operari; sed multum differt; quin potius totum ex hoc dependet. Nam ea quae nobis a pueritia imprimuntur, firmius retinemus."

[24] Cf. *ST* II-II, 180.2, ad 3: "Ad tertium dicendum quod pulchritudo, sicut supra dictum est, consistit in quadam claritate et debita proportione. Utrumque autem horum *radicaliter* in ratione invenitur, ad quam pertinet et lumen manifestans, et proportionem debitam in aliis ordinare. Et ideo *in vita contemplativa, quae consistit in actu rationis, per se et essentialiter invenitur pulchritudo.* Unde Sap. VIII de contemplatione sapientiae dicitur, amator factus sum formae illius. In virtutibus autem moralibus invenitur pulchritudo *participative*, inquantum scilicet participant ordinem rationis, et *praecipue in temperantia, quae reprimit concupiscentias maxime lumen rationis obscurantes.* Et inde est quod virtus castitatis maxime reddit hominem aptum ad contemplationem, inquantum *delectationes venereae maxime deprimunt mentem ad sensibilia*, ut Augustinus dicit, in libro *Soliloquiorum*. [...beauty...is found in a clarity and a due proportion. Both of these are to be found as to their root in reason, to which pertains a revealing light and a putting of other things in due order. And therefore beauty is found intrinsically and essentially in the contemplative life. Hence, *Wisdom* 8.2, speaking of the

In this same line, one should not neglect Thomas's teaching on the vice of pride [*superbia*], and the harm it does to us as beings who by nature desire to know. Why does the vice of pride, which has its seat in the irascible appetite or in the will, not in the intellect, nevertheless cause *blindness to the truth*? Thomas answers:

> ...knowledge of truth is twofold. One [is] purely speculative: and pride impedes this indirectly, removing the cause: for the proud person does not submit his intellect to God, so as to receive knowledge of truth from Him (in accordance with Matthew 11: "You have hidden these things from the wise and prudent," i.e. from the proud who consider themselves wise and prudent, "and you have revealed them to the little ones," that is, to the humble); nor [does the proud person] deign to learn from human beings (whereas it is said, in Ecclesiasticus 6: 34: "If you will incline your ear," that is, humbly listening, "you will receive a teaching.")
>
> The other knowledge of truth is affective, and pride directly impedes such knowledge of truth: because the proud, while experiencing delight in their own excellence, distain the excellence of truth (thus, Gregory says, in *Morals* 23, that "the proud, while they perceive by the understanding some hidden things, are unable to experience the sweetness of those things; and if they know how they are, they remain oblivious to how they taste"). Hence, 11.2 says: "Where there is humility, there is wisdom."[25]

---

contemplation of wisdom, says: 'I have become a lover of her form.' Beauty is found in the moral virtues by participation, inasmuch as they participate in the order of reason, and most especially in temperance, which represses those desires which most obscure the light of reason. And thus it is that *the virtue of chastity most of all renders a person apt for contemplation*, inasmuch as sexual delights most of all drag the mind down to sensible things, as Augustine says in the book *Soliloquies*.]" Cf. also II-II, 182.3 on the role of the moral virtues, and so of the active life, in forming the interior person for contemplation.

[25] *ST* II-II, 162.3, ad 1: "Ad primum ergo dicendum quod cognitio veritatis est duplex. Una pure speculativa. Et hanc superbia indirecte impedit, subtrahendo causam. Superbus enim neque Deo suum intellectum subiicit, ut

The difficulty we have with metaphysics is traced by Aristotle to the nature of the human mind, its inferiority to divine mind. Our mind is naturally ordered towards low-grade intelligibles, even to merely potential intelligibles.[26] While this is true, St. Thomas, in accordance with revelation, can appreciate another source of difficulty, located in the domain of our inclination. Our action is ordered by our natural inclination, that is, by natural law. As St. Thomas teaches, that law includes the inclination "to know the truth about God," i.e. the inclination to metaphysics.[27] Indeed, the very first sentence of Aristotle's *Metaphysics* testifies to the existence of this inclination.[28] Even more deeply, the inclination common to all substances is to love God more than themselves, and this inclination is found in the rational creature in the mode of willing, i.e. as natural law.[29] However, sin

---

ab eo veritatis cognitionem percipiat, secundum illud *Matth.* xi: 'Abscondisti haec a sapientibus et prudentibus,' idest a superbis, qui sibi sapientes et prudentes videntur, 'et revelasti ea parvulis,' idest humilibus. Neque etiam ab hominibus addiscere dignantur, cum tamen dicatur, *Eccli.* vi, 'Si inclinaveris aurem tuam,' scilicet humiliter audiendo, 'excipies doctrinam.' Alia autem est cognitio veritatis affectiva. Et talem cognitionem veritatis directe impedit superbia. Quia superbi, dum delectantur in propria excellentia, excellentiam veritatis fastidiunt, ut Gregorius dicit, xxiii *Moral.*, quod 'superbi et secreta quaedam intelligendo percipiunt, et eorum dulcedinem experiri non possunt, et si noverint quomodo sunt, ignorant quomodo sapiunt.' Unde et *Proverb.* xi dicitur: 'ubi humilitas, ibi sapientia.'"

[26] For Aristotle, cf. *Metaph.* 2.1 (993b7-11). Cf. Thomas, *ST* I, 79.3, ad 3: "The intelligible in act is not something existing in the nature of things, speaking of the nature of sensible things, which do not subsist apart from matter. [Intelligibile autem in actu non est aliquid existens in rerum natura, quantum ad naturam rerum sensibilium, quae non subsistunt praeter materiam.]"

[27] *ST* I-II, 94.2 (1226a3-14).

[28] Aristotle, *Metaphysics* 1.1 (980a21).

[29] *ST* I, 60.5, *sed contra* and the entire discussion. On our natural love having the mode of willing, cf. I, 60.1 (362b14-16): "...hence, in the intellectual nature the natural inclination is found in function of 'will [*secundum voluntatem*].'" On this "mode of willing" as presupposing the intellectual vision of the idea of goodness, cf. 1.59.1 (358a41-51): "Some are inclined towards the good with a knowledge by which they know the very idea of the good, which

weakens, though it cannot eradicate, the natural inclination.[30] The result is that without the help of supernatural divine grace the human being is not able to love God, even at the natural level of loving, more than its own self. The will of the human being is wounded to the extent of ordering things towards oneself rather than towards God.[31] In that way, one does not love one's true self, but is ordered towards the sensual self.[32]

If the love we ought to have for God is not there, we will not have that "prompt will" we saw Thomas mention, to seek the reasons for affirming those truths pertaining to our relation to God, i.e. *the properly metaphysical quest.* (As St. Thomas says: The whole of metaphysics is

---

[knowledge] is proper to intellect. And these are most perfectly inclined towards the good.... And this inclination is called "will.""

[30] *ST* I-II, 85.1-3.

[31] Cf. especially *ST* I-II, 109.3, in its entirety; note especially: "...man in the state of integral nature related his love of his own self towards the love of God as towards an end, and similarly the love of all other things. And thus he loved God more than himself and above all. But in the state of corrupt nature man falls short of this as regards the appetite of the rational will which because of the corruption of the nature pursues its own private good unless it is healed by the grace of God. And therefore it is to be said that man in the state of integral nature had no need of the gift of grace added over and above the natural benefits in order to love God naturally above all; though he needed the help of God moving him towards this. But in the state of corrupted nature man needs even for this the help of grace healing the nature."

[32] Thomas, in explaining the love that a sinner has for himself, sees sinners as loving a view of themselves which gives primacy to the sensitive and corporeal nature. Cf. *ST* II-II, 25.7 (1548b6-16). How does this fit a person such as Aristotle? One should consider that, in Thomas's view, no one is certain of actually having supernatural charity: cf. *De veritate* 10.10. Cf. *In Sent.* II, 21.2.3, ad 5: our affective habits are much more obscure than our cognitive habits. On the one hand, this gives us pause as to our own spiritual well-being. On the other hand, it should give us pause as to a conjecture, one way or the other, about e.g. Aristotle's spiritual well-being. Perhaps he had that divine help which Plato's Socrates mentions in connection with the philosophical vocation: *Republic* VI 492A.

ordered towards knowledge of God.)[33] The wounded nature of the human being adds a serious problem as to the rarity of metaphysics.

4. Maritain and the Role of Faith Relative to Philosophy

If I have insisted that the metaphysical vocation finds its full health only in the economy of grace, and thus that the Christian philosopher, partaking of the properly Christian virtues, is the best hope for the perennial task of metaphysical renewal, I am gratified to find similar observations from Jacques Maritain. He did, of course, address the topic of Thomism and renewal all through his career. In his book, *Antimoderne*, first published in 1922,[34] the third chapter, entitled "Some Conditions for a Thomistic Renaissance," is a paper read at Louvain in 1920. Maritain sets forth the reasons for the degeneration of scholasticism in order to prescribe the conditions which a Thomistic renaissance requires. Metaphysics is front and center in the prescription.[35]

Again, in 1924, JM published a short piece hailing the start of a magazine, *La Gazette Française*, and entitled: "The Return to Metaphysics." He sees this "return" as something already going on, but which is tending, particularly in Germany, towards a Buddhist irrationalism, and he seeks to give it the right direction. He says:

> It is up to Latin and Catholic intelligence to save the heritage of civilization, by restoring true wisdom. The spiritual mission of France is here very clear. Cured of the rationalist disease, and all the more faithful to reason, she has wonderful energy for bringing into the light of the *philosophia perennis* all the precious

[33] Cf. *Summa Contra Gentiles* III, 25.9 (ed. Pera et al, Rome\Turin, 1961: Marietti, #2063).

[34] Jacques Maritain, *Antimoderne*, Paris, 1922, Éditions de la Revue des Jeunes; new edition, reviewed and enlarged in 1926. Chap. III [in the collected works, 1009-1046] is entitled : *De quelque conditions de la renaissance thomiste*, and is the text of a talk given at the Institut Supérieur de Philosophie de Louvain, Jan. 26, 1920. Cf. Jacques et Raïssa Maritain, *Oeuvres complètes*, vol. II (1920-1923) (Fribourg, Suisse/Paris: Éditions Universitaires/Éditions Saint-Paul, 1922). (Henceforth I will simply refer to "OC" and the volume number.)

[35] Ibid. OC II, 1027: "History shows us, lastly, that the Thomistic intellectual breed [*race*] is before all else a metaphysical breed."

> fruits of ancient and modern reason. It is to this work that *the constructive minds of the new generation are convoked by history.* They will succeed, I am confident, if they take for guide the one whom the Church has chosen as its *Common Teacher* —a master whose thought and heart are fixed in pure truth —who disowns nothing pertaining to reason and nothing pertaining to grace, —who shows us how true spirituality crowns and elevates, far from destroying, the edifice of rational virtues, both speculative and moral, and of science properly so called, —who teaches us, finally, the true wisdom by which all that the West has found without knowing how to make right use of it is put in order, and by which we are given all that the East seeks without being able to find it. They [the new generation] will thus serve the sacred interests of the Universe.[36]

He never left off fighting this fight himself.

I might mention many other works of Maritain, but I will note only what might be called a preparation for *Le Paysan de la Garonne.* In December of 1964 Pope Paul VI sent Jean Guitton and Mgr. Pasquale Macchi (Pope Paul's personal secretary) to submit to JM a series of questions to discuss, looking towards the last period of the Second Vatican Council. One element of reply became JM's paper entitled: *On Truth.* He begins, writing to Pope Paul:

> It seems to me that what would answer to the most urgent needs of the Christian people today would be an encyclical on *Truth.* Because it is the significance [*le sens*] of truth which today is obliterated and menaced for a great number of people. I would certainly not presume to propose some sort of preliminary text for such an encyclical. I would like simply to indicate, in my style of "the old philosopher", a few thoughts which have come to my mind in reflecting on the needs of us, the poor faithful, concerning truth.

This is the introduction, published only in 1999 as a "memorandum" in the last volume [XVI] of OC.[37] The rest of the text had already been

[36] "Le Retour à la métaphysique," in OC XVI, 296-98, and dated May 3, 1924.

[37] Cf. OC XVI, 1085. The visit of the Papal emissaries occurred Dec. 27, 1964.

published in volume XIII because it had appeared as part of *Approches sans entraves*, as a paper read to the Little Brothers of Jesus, at Toulouse March 31, 1965, and entitled "On Truth".[38]

In it JM stresses that it is the very meaning of truth, the "*sens*," which is obliterated or threatened among many people. He sees this obliteration as also happening to the "*sens*" of the divine transcendence and of mystery. Here, it seems to me that "*sens*" is "sense" (a *feeling* for truth?). One has to do with *obliviousness* to these things, as to what they mean for authentic human living: truth, divine transcendence, mystery.

The beginning of JM's presentation is magnificent. He speaks of the importance of beginning with the *supernaturally revealed* truth, and this, as he puts it, "lived in act," *in actu exercito*. He says:

> In our reflections on truth I believe that it is appropriate to begin from on high, by the supernaturally revealed Truth [JM's capital "T"]. That is normal in the perspective of Christian thought. It is normal, for someone who has received the grace of faith, to begin these sorts of reflections with the faith, with what is most elevated and most precious in our intellectual equipment. The Christian has the privilege of being placed facing the *Absolute Truth*, the Truth who is God himself, and God himself revealing himself. In adhering to this absolute truth, he will set to work, spontaneously and in lived act, *in actu exercito*, the great things that philosophy discovers on its own concerning truth when it understands, for example, that truth is the adequation of the intellect and the real, or that being is the proper object of the intelligence, which finds its life and liberty in adherence to it.
>
> [514] Those things philosophy knows *in actu signato*, in signified act or by way of conceptualization. But there is an enormous advantage to have *lived*, experienced in exercised act, these great themes concerning truth *before* one has conceived them philosophically.

---

[38] Cf. OC XIII, 513-35.

> And it is in the faith in God who is subsisting Truth, in faith in the uncreated Truth and in the incarnate Truth, that we live them in a sovereignly eminent degree [513-514].

Accordingly, coming to St. Thomas and the renewal of metaphysics, I started with the first article of the *Summa Theologiae.*

5. St. Thomas and the Future of Metaphysics

In his encyclical letter *Fides et Ratio*, Pope John Paul II spoke of the demands that the word of God makes on philosophy today. First, it requires philosophy to recover its sapiential fullness [*sapientialem amplitudinem*] as a search for the ultimate and overarching meaning of life. Secondly, it must put on display the human capacity to know the very essence [*ipsam essentiam*] of things. Thirdly, and indeed the two previous demands themselves require it, there is need for a philosophy of a truly metaphysical nature [*opus est philosophia naturae vere metaphysicae*], one which is able to go beyond the merely empirical indications in such a way that, pursuing the truth, it arrives at some ultimate and fundamental absolute.

That the doctrine of St. Thomas already takes us along these three lines of work, there is no doubt. A philosophical ethics not having as principle the true ultimate end of the human being is unthinkable in his perspective, and such an ethics receives its principle from the metaphysician.[39] Moreover, as he teaches, the proper conception of the human intellect takes us beyond the objects of sense as such, to the "within" of things.[40] I will limit myself in the present talk to the third requirement, an ontology, which carries us to an "ultimate and fundamental absolute," the metaphysics of divine transcendence.

I once was asked (there was a shortage of "card-carrying" theologians at the moment) to give a short night-course on the Mystery of the Incarnation. At the conclusion, one of the rather mature students presented me with a little book, whose author I forget, but whose title

---

[39] Cf. my "St. Thomas, Our Natural Lights, and the Moral Order," in *Maritain Studies/Études maritainiennes* vol. 2 (1986): 59-92 [reprinted in *Angelicum* 67 (1990): 285-307].

[40] Cf. e.g. *ST* II-II, 8.1.

made my student's point: "Your God is too Small!"[41] Well, yes, I am sure most of us would admit that our poor efforts do not do justice to the Almighty. However, it is crucial that our metaphysics indicate the way our notions are both appropriate and infinitely inadequate.

Because there is general recognition of this need, metaphysicians in the Thomist fold have regularly worked to make the point. Fr. A. D. Sertillanges sometimes spoke of a "definitional agnosticism," so strongly did Thomas stress our ignorance relative to God.[42] Still, Thomas himself insisted that "then only does one know God truly when one knows that he is beyond anything one can conceive."[43] Nevertheless, that is part of the prescription for "*knowing* God *truly*".

In this context I wish to bring to Thomists' attention once more a teaching of the master that I think has been treated with insufficient seriousness (one thinks of Bañez's celebrated complaint: "Thomistae nolunt audire!"). In the *Summa Contra Gentiles* we read,

> ...those things which in creatures are divided are unqualifiedly one in God: thus, for example, in the creature essence and being [*esse*] are other; and in some [creatures] that which subsists in its own essence is also other than its essence or nature: for this man is neither his own humanity nor his being [*esse*]; but God is his essence and his being.
>
> And though these in God are one in the truest way, nevertheless in God there is whatever pertains to the intelligible role [*ratio*] of the subsisting thing, or of the essence, or of the being [*esse*]; for it belongs to him not to be in another, inasmuch as he is subsisting; to be a what [*esse quid*], inasmuch as he is

---

41 Google advises me that it is by J.B. Phillips, published in a Touchstone Edition, New York, 1997.

42 Cf. Étienne Gilson, *Le Thomisme,* 6th ed. (Paris: Vrin, 1965 [3rd printing, 1979]), 125 and n. 69, referring to the notes contained in Fr. Sertillanges's translation of Thomas's *Summa Theologiae* (Paris: Desclée and Co., 1926), t. II, 379-88.

43 *SCG* I, 5.3: "Tunc enim solum deum vere cognoscimus quando ipsum esse credimus supra omne id quod de deo cogitari ab homine possibile est: eo quod naturalem hominis cognitionem divina substantia excedit, ut supra ostensum est."

> essence; and being in act [*esse in actu*], by reason of being itself [*ipsius esse*].[44]

This is to say that even in the divine simplicity, or rather, especially in the divine simplicity, there are three ineluctable metaphysical dimensions or contributions. Since what pertains to them is found in the divine simplicity, they clearly name pure perfections. This is so even though in our mode of being, one has priority of perfection over another. Thus, if essence, as we know it, is potential with respect to the act of being, this is something which belongs to essence, not precisely as *essence*, but as *such* essence.[45] My point is that our metaphysics will benefit by intense interest in all three of these ineluctable and distinct contributions: the subsisting thing, the essence, and the act of being.[46]

The second point I wish to make about "metaphysics of transcendence" concerns another set of texts of Thomas that have not, to my knowledge, been taken seriously enough. Obviously, John Paul II was encouraging an interest in the metaphysics of creation and the Creator. Thomas, in that regard, presents God as the cause of being as being. Because that is presented by Thomas very much as the unity of a field of participants in the act of being, standing under the subsistent act of being, one may lose sight of how complete, how full, the divine product

---

[44] *SCG* I, 4.11 (para. 12-13; ed. Pera #3472-3473): "Ostensum est autem in primo libro ea quae in creaturis divisa sunt, in deo simpliciter unum esse: sicut in creatura aliud est essentia et esse; et in quibusdam est etiam aliud quod subsistit in sua essentia, et eius essentia sive natura, nam hic homo non est sua humanitas nec suum esse; sed deus est sua essentia et suum esse. Et quamvis haec in deo unum sint verissime, tamen in deo est quicquid pertinet ad rationem vel subsistentis, vel essentiae, vel ipsius esse: convenit enim ei non esse in aliquo, inquantum est subsistens; esse quid, inquantum est essentia; et esse in actu, ratione ipsius esse."

[45] Cf. *ST* I, 26.1, ad 2 on how beatitude is found in God, even though it is not there "the prize for virtue"; and cf. *De substantiis separatis* 7 (Leonine ed., lines 91-110): form is found in matter, not precisely because it is *form*, but because it is *such* form.

[46] I touched on this somewhat in my paper: "Nature as a Metaphysical Object." This paper was written for and read at the Summer Thomistic Institute, Maritain Center, University of Notre Dame (Indiana), July 13-20, 2001. It has been published only on their web page.

is. One may consider it as essentially relational, relative to the subsistent act of being. This is not quite correct. As Thomas explains, the relation to the first cause is a *property* of the creature, flowing from it as from a being by participation.[47] I.e. the doctrine of participation is not essentially relational, but entails a relation. This is important for an appreciation of the fullness of the divine effect, being as being.

So "full" is this effect that Thomas describes the Creator as the cause of "*totum ens*," being in its entirety. Were it not for a doctrine of analogy of being, there would be no room for calling the Creator "a being."[48]

That this is not an accidental aspect of Thomas's metaphysics of transcendence emerges very strongly in discussions of providence and the power of God as providence. It is well know that Thomas presents human free choice as inconceivable without the prior divine moving causality. However, it is not sufficiently stressed, I would say, that this prior causality is conceivable only inasmuch as God is the cause of being as being. Thomas regularly appeals to this doctrine to present God as the cause of the proper differences of being as being, viz. the possible or contingent, and the necessary.[49] I.e., it is being as a nature or essence that has the Creator and Universal Providence as its origin and constant source of events.

It is not enough to appeal to causal hierarchy in order to present God as prior to human freedom and to all contingent causality. No

---

[47] Cf. *ST* I, 44.1, ad 1.

[48] Cf. *ST* I, 45.1, speaking of creation: "...emanatio totius entis universalis a primo principio..." [...the emanation of the whole of being, taken universally, from the first principle...]. And cf. my "St. Thomas and Creation: Does God Create 'Reality'?," in *Science et Esprit* 51 (1999): 5-25.

[49] Cf. Thomas, *Commentary on the Metaphysics* 6.3 (1218-1220), and cf. my "Thomas Aquinas and Being as a Nature," *Acta Philosophica* 12 (2003): 123-35. Notice, for example, *Expositio libri Peryermenias* 1.14 (ed. Leonine, t. 1*1, Rome\Paris, 1989: Commissio Leonina\Vrin: "...the divine will is to be understood as standing outside the order of beings [ut extra ordinem entium existens], as a cause pouring forth being in its entirety [totum ens] and all its differences. Now, the possible and the necessary are differences of being [differentie entis], and so it is from the divine will itself that necessity and contingency in things have their origin..."

causal priority other than that which pertains to the cause of being as being will satisfy the mind in that respect.

I present these reflections on Thomas's metaphysics as calling us to look ever more carefully into what he has already seen. That is the way to any future for metaphysics.

FIDES ET RATIO AND JOHN PAUL'S CALL TO CATHOLIC PHILOSOPHERS: ORTHODOXY AND/OR THE UNITY OF TRUTH

John F. Morris

1. Introduction

John Paul II, often referred to as "the philosopher Pope," made it quite clear throughout his papacy that philosophy—far from being a detriment to faith and theology—was an integral part of the Catholic Church's Tradition, and that it remains an important tool for carrying out the mission of the Church as we move into the third millennium. For the Catholic Church, faith and reason have always been compatible. In *Fides et Ratio*, the late Holy Father chose to emphasize and expound upon this theme. As he explains in the "Introduction" to this letter:

> In my Encyclical Letter *Veritatis Splendor*, I drew attention to "certain fundamental truths of Catholic doctrine which, in the present circumstances, risk being distorted or denied." In the present Letter, I wish to pursue that reflection by concentrating on the theme of truth itself and on its foundation in relation to faith.... With its enduring appeal to the search for truth, philosophy has the great responsibility of forming thought and culture; and now it must strive resolutely to recover its original vocation. This is why I have felt both the need and the duty to address this theme so that, on the threshold of the third millennium of the Christian era, humanity may come to a clearer sense of the great resources with which it has been endowed and may commit itself with renewed courage to implement the plan of salvation of which its history is part (#6).1

And so, in *Fides et Ratio,* John Paul II carefully articulates the importance of reason within the faith life of the Christian, warning of the danger of separating faith from reason and pitting the two against each other. He

[1] The translation used throughout is taken from the Vatican website at http://www.vatican.va/edocs/ENG0216/_INDEX.HTM.

also discusses the dual and complementary roles of theology and philosophy within the Tradition of the Church.

It is worth noting that in this discussion of faith and reason, theology and philosophy, John Paul II holds up St. Thomas Aquinas as a special model and example for Catholics. He writes that:

> ...Thomas had the great merit of giving pride of place to the harmony which exists between faith and reason. Both the light of reason and the light of faith come from God, he argued; hence there can be no contradiction between them.... More radically, Thomas recognized that nature, philosophy's proper concern, could contribute to the understanding of divine Revelation. Faith therefore has no fear of reason, but seeks it out and has trust in it.... Although he made much of the supernatural character of faith, the Angelic Doctor did not overlook the importance of its reasonableness; indeed he was able to plumb the depths and explain the meaning of this reasonableness. Faith is in a sense an "exercise of thought"; and human reason is neither annulled nor debased in assenting to the contents of faith, which are in any case attained by way of free and informed choice (#43).

Now John Paul II is quick to point out that in recommending St. Thomas as a model, neither he nor the Church as a whole intends to restrict the search for truth to any one particular philosophical approach or system. In keeping with the tradition of his predecessors, John Paul II notes that "The Church has no philosophy of her own nor does she canonize any one particular philosophy in preference to others" (#49).

This last quotation, however, raises some confusion over the whole point of this particular encyclical. If the Church has no "official" philosophy, then why write a letter on the subject? If the letter is not meant to "canonize" a particular philosophical approach, then what is its purpose? Attempting to discuss the full meaning of *Fides et Ratio* is simply beyond the scope of one paper. However, I want to focus in on one of the central points of the larger message of the letter: the role of philosophy within the Catholic Tradition. Of special importance will be John Paul II's "challenge" or "call" to philosophers in *Fides et Ratio* to help people "come to a unified and organic vision of knowledge" (#85). This call is summarized in the conclusion of the letter:

> I appeal also to philosophers, and to all teachers of philosophy, asking them to have the courage to recover, in the flow of an enduringly valid philosophical tradition, the range of authentic wisdom and truth-metaphysical truth included-which is proper to philosophical enquiry. They should be open to the impelling questions which arise from the word of God and they should be strong enough to shape their thought and discussion in response to that challenge. Let them always strive for truth, alert to the good which truth contains. Then they will be able to formulate the genuine ethics which humanity needs so urgently at this particular time (#106).

In sum, John Paul II, with lament over the current state of philosophy in the contemporary world, uses *Fides et Ratio* in part to urge philosophers to renew the very task of philosophy itself—the search for truth and wisdom—and to do so in earnest and without fear!

But what are the theoretical and the practical implications of John Paul II's "call," specifically for one who identifies her or himself as a "Catholic philosopher"? On the one hand, the Catholic philosopher as a "philosopher" must confront the contemporary world in which Christian philosophers as a whole are often subjected to criticism because of their religious background, given our pluralistic culture. Although the concept of "pluralism" ought to open the door for philosophers of all backgrounds, in practice it is more often than not used in an exclusionary fashion to marginalize the religious voice, even when that voice is not attempting to be explicitly religious. On the other hand, the Catholic philosopher as a "Catholic" must be mindful of the demands of her or his faith. The reality of religious orthodoxy seems, at times, to put limits upon the philosophical quest. There is much concern within the Church regarding orthodoxy, including concerns from Catholic philosophers themselves over what can actually be spoken or written under the title of "Catholic." Working under both sets of pressures is difficult, to be sure. But, because of his fidelity to the unity of truth, John Paul II is confident that philosophy and the Christian faith are, and always will be, compatible: "philosophy must obey its own rules and be based upon its own principles; truth, however, can only be one. The content of Revelation can never debase the discoveries and legitimate autonomy of reason" (#79).

And so, in reflecting upon John Paul II's call to Catholic philosophers and attempting to come to an understanding of the theoretical and practical implications of that call, three themes from *Fides et Ratio* will be examined. First, I will examine what John Paul II says in the letter about philosophy in and of itself. I will then explore what the Pope says about the interaction between philosophy and theology. And finally, I will reflect upon the implications of the first two points for the Catholic philosopher, especially in light of the tension between religious orthodoxy and the unity of truth. In examining these issues, I will argue that the Church is asking Catholic philosophers to continue to engage in genuine philosophical enquiry with confidence in the unity of truth. Concerns for orthodoxy must not be ignored, but the defense of the faith belongs primarily to the Church as a whole, and more specifically to the Magisterium working within the guidance of the Holy Spirit. Thus, part of the message of *Fides et Ratio* is that Catholic philosophers need to take assurance that, if we do our work well, we can only promote truth.

2. Philosophy and the Catholic Tradition

Whereas the overall discussion of *Fides et Ratio* is cast under the heading of faith and "reason," John Paul II focuses specifically on the discipline of philosophy, rather than other ways of human knowing, and its special function in the search for truth. Thus, in the "Introduction," he notes that:

> Men and women have at their disposal an array of resources for generating greater knowledge of truth so that their lives may be ever more human. Among these is philosophy, which is directly concerned with asking the question of life's meaning and sketching an answer to it. Philosophy emerges, then, as one of the noblest of human tasks. According to its Greek etymology, the term philosophy means "love of wisdom." Born and nurtured when the human being first asked questions about the reason for things and their purpose, philosophy shows in different modes and forms that the desire for truth is part of human nature itself (#3).

With this focus upon truth—indeed, upon ultimate truth—philosophy can clearly stand in harmony with faith, and, therefore, philosophy is in harmony with theology as well. This is one of the unique aspects of

Catholic Christianity. "Faith" and "Reason" are not at odds with one another, but rather are intimate allies in the search for truth. Thus, John Paul II specifically rejects both rationalism and fideism as extreme and incomplete views, especially within the Church's theology. Instead, he emphasizes that:

> On her part, the Church cannot but set great value upon reason's drive to attain goals which render people's lives ever more worthy. She sees in philosophy the way to come to know fundamental truths about human life. At the same time, the Church considers philosophy an indispensable help for a deeper understanding of faith and for communicating the truth of the Gospel to those who do not yet know it (#5).

Throughout the letter, the late Pope continuously emphasizes the compatibility of faith and reason, and more specifically philosophy's contribution to helping the believer reflect upon faith.

However, even though philosophy can complement faith, it is in itself an autonomous and independent discipline. John Paul II is quite clear about this, pointing out that:

> ...even when it engages theology, philosophy must remain faithful to its own principles and methods. Otherwise there would be no guarantee that it would remain oriented to truth and that it was moving towards truth by way of a process governed by reason. A philosophy which did not proceed in the light of reason according to its own principles and methods would serve little purpose. At the deepest level, the autonomy which philosophy enjoys is rooted in the fact that reason is by its nature oriented to truth and is equipped moreover with the means necessary to arrive at truth (#49).

None of this is meant to imply that philosophy represents a perfect human activity that is immune to error—far from it. The philosopher, Catholic or other, must always maintain a certain humility in exercising the autonomy of her or his discipline, given the natural limitations of human reason.

This is also why the Church, through the teaching authority of the Magisterium, intervenes at times in philosophical matters. John Paul II explains:

> ...history shows that philosophy—especially modern philosophy—has taken wrong turns and fallen into error. It is neither the task nor the competence of the Magisterium to intervene in order to make good the lacunas of deficient philosophical discourse. Rather, it is the Magisterium's duty to respond clearly and strongly when controversial philosophical opinions threaten right understanding of what has been revealed, and when false and partial theories which sow the seed of serious error, confusing the pure and simple faith of the People of God, begin to spread more widely (#49).

Thus, the Church's stance is not to become the font of the one, true philosophy, but it rather safeguards the faith from the implications of philosophical errors. In this light, John Paul II emphasizes that when the Church intervenes in philosophical matters, its actions should not be viewed as punitive or negative, but rather as "a humble but tenacious ministry of service which every philosopher should appreciate, a service in favour of *recta ratio*, or of reason reflecting rightly upon what is true" (#50), which is "intended above all to prompt, promote and encourage philosophical enquiry" (#51).

Now there will be some who will scoff at the late Holy Father's sentiments that all the Church wants to do is promote open philosophical enquiry, but the teaching of the Church here in *Fides et Ratio* is clear: philosophy is the independent and autonomous human search for truth, and it should remain so for the common good of humanity! Perhaps the true spirit of John Paul II's message is best captured in his bold exhortation to philosophers in Chapter V of his letter:

> ...I cannot but encourage philosophers—be they Christian or not—to trust in the power of human reason and not to set themselves goals that are too modest in their philosophizing. The lesson of history in this millennium now drawing to a close shows that this is the path to follow: it is necessary not to abandon the passion for ultimate truth, the eagerness to search for it or the audacity to forge new paths in the search (#56).

These are not the words of a person who wants to control and dominate philosophy—indeed, they are quite the opposite. John Paul II calls philosophers of every background to philosophize, and to do so with all of their intellectual might!

3. The Interaction Between Philosophy and Theology

As his discussion in *Fides et Ratio* unfolds, John Paul II turns to the specific question of the relationship between philosophy and theology. Right from the outset, the Pope is clear that within the Catholic Tradition, theology and philosophy are interconnected. His words here are telling:

> As a reflective and scientific elaboration of the understanding of God's word in the light of faith, theology for its part must relate, in some of its procedures and in the performance of its specific tasks, to the philosophies which have been developed through the ages. I have no wish to direct theologians to particular methods, since that is not the competence of the Magisterium. I wish instead to recall some specific tasks of theology which, by the very nature of the revealed word, demand recourse to philosophical enquiry (#64).

In this light, John Paul II identifies three areas of theological discourse that depend upon the contributions of philosophical enquiry.

First, there is dogmatic theology. The Pope emphatically states that, "Without philosophy's contribution, it would in fact be impossible to discuss theological issues such as, for example, the use of language to speak about God, the personal relations within the Trinity, God's creative activity in the world, the relationship between God and man, or Christ's identity as true God and true man" (#66).

Second, fundamental theology, which seeks to give an account of the faith, also makes use of philosophy. As John Paul II explains:

> ...the First Vatican Council pointed to the existence of truths which are naturally, and thus philosophically, knowable; and an acceptance of God's Revelation necessarily presupposes knowledge of these truths. In studying Revelation and its credibility, as well as the corresponding act of faith, fundamental theology should show how, in the light of the knowledge conferred by faith, there emerge certain truths which reason, from its own independent enquiry, already perceives. Revelation

> endows these truths with their fullest meaning, directing them towards the richness of the revealed mystery in which they find their ultimate purpose (#67).

Finally, there is moral theology. As it seeks to help believers apply the basic principles of Christian morality to "the particular circumstances of individual and communal life, Christians must be able fully to engage their conscience and the power of their reason. In other words, moral theology requires a sound philosophical vision of human nature and society, as well as of the general principles of ethical decision-making" (#68).

In the end, John Paul II illustrates the interaction between theology and philosophy with the concept of a circle:

> In the light of these considerations, the relationship between theology and philosophy is best construed as a circle. Theology's source and starting-point must always be the word of God revealed in history, while its final goal will be an understanding of that word which increases with each passing generation. Yet, since God's word is Truth (cf. Jn 17:17), the human search for truth—philosophy, pursued in keeping with its own rules—can only help to understand God's word better. It is not just a question of theological discourse using this or that concept or element of a philosophical construct; what matters most is that the believer's reason use its powers of reflection in the search for truth which moves from the word of God towards a better understanding of it. It is as if, moving between the twin poles of God's word and a better understanding of it, reason is offered guidance and is warned against paths which would lead it to stray from revealed Truth and to stray in the end from the truth pure and simple. Instead, reason is stirred to explore paths which of itself it would not even have suspected it could take. This circular relationship with the word of God leaves philosophy enriched, because reason discovers new and unsuspected horizons (#73).

In this way of thinking, philosophy and theology can be affirmed as mutually compatible and mutually supportive, without taking anything away from the autonomy of philosophy as an independent human discipline, and without degrading the lofty nature of theology. John

Paul II is emphatic on this point. Philosophy is not perfect; it never has been and never will be. Philosophy is limited, because the human beings that engage in it are limited. But human beings are capable of attaining truth, at least in some measure, and careful, philosophical enquiry is an indispensable tool in the search for truth, including the theological search of the Church.

4. The Three Stances of Philosophy

Towards the end of his discussion of the interaction between philosophy and theology, John Paul II suggests that "...from this brief sketch of the history of the relationship between faith and philosophy, one can distinguish different stances of philosophy with regard to Christian faith" (#75). He goes on to identify three such "stances," each of which is worthwhile to reflect upon in terms of what *Fides et Ratio* asks of the Catholic philosopher.

First, John Paul II recognizes a philosophical approach that stands completely outside of faith and revelation. What is worth noting is that whereas he points out the limitations of what we might call a "purely" rational approach to philosophy, John Paul II still extols such a philosophical approach: "We see here philosophy's valid aspiration to be an autonomous enterprise, obeying its own rules and employing the powers of reason alone. Although seriously handicapped by the inherent weakness of human reason, this aspiration should be supported and strengthened. As a search for truth within the natural order, the enterprise of philosophy is always open—at least implicitly—to the supernatural" (#75). Once again, we find the Pope recognizing and supporting the autonomous nature of philosophical inquiry for its own sake. Philosophy is an important human endeavor, even outside the specific realm of faith.

The second "stance" involves the concept of a specifically "Christian" philosophy, still a much debated issue today. For his part, John Paul II argues that there can indeed be such an endeavor. His understanding, however, bears careful consideration. First, it is once again pointed out that in discussing a "Christian" philosophy, this "...in no way intends to suggest that there is an official philosophy of the Church, since the faith as such is not a philosophy" (#76). Nonetheless, John Paul II states that there can be a genuine "...Christian way of philosophizing, a philosophical speculation conceived in dynamic union with faith" (ibid). But what would such a "Christian" philosophy entail? As he supports his position here, John Paul II argues that "Christian" philosophy:

> ...does not therefore refer simply to a philosophy developed by Christian philosophers who have striven in their research not to contradict the faith. The term Christian philosophy includes those important developments of philosophical thinking which would not have happened without the direct or indirect contribution of Christian faith (#76).

Yet, lest some fear that this notion of "Christian" philosophy blurs the line between philosophy and theology, John Paul II adds that:

> In speculating on these questions, philosophers have not become theologians, since they have not sought to understand and expound the truths of faith on the basis of Revelation. They have continued working on their own terrain and with their own purely rational method, yet extending their research to new aspects of truth. It could be said that a good part of modern and contemporary philosophy would not exist without this stimulus of the word of God (#76).

In short, the "Christianity" of the "Christian" philosopher opens reason to new areas of thought and new realms of action by lifting the intellect beyond physical reality, all the while remaining within the proper sphere of philosophical enquiry.

Finally, John Paul II discusses a third and final "stance" of philosophy in regards to Christian faith, which he identifies as, "when theology itself calls upon it" (#77). In this paragraph, a clearer vision of the proper role of philosophy within the Church, both in its past and for its future, is put forth. First, John Paul II reaffirms much of what the previous chapters of the encyclical have been putting into place. He notes that:

> Theology in fact has always needed and still needs philosophy's contribution. As a work of critical reason in the light of faith, theology presupposes and requires in all its research a reason formed and educated to concept and argument. Moreover, theology needs philosophy as a partner in dialogue in order to confirm the intelligibility and universal

> truth of its claims. It was not by accident that the Fathers of the Church and the Medieval theologians adopted non-Christian philosophies. This historical fact confirms the value of philosophy's autonomy, which remains unimpaired when theology calls upon it; but it shows as well the profound transformations which philosophy itself must undergo (ibid).

In reading the above passage, some might assume that the late Holy Father is about to lower the boom on philosophy by harkening back to the Patristic and Medieval notions that philosophy is nothing more than the "handmaiden of theology"—all of the fine rhetoric about the autonomy of philosophy in the earlier pages of the letter, notwithstanding. Any that might think this would, however, be wrong. As John Paul II goes on to explain:

> It was because of its noble and indispensable contribution that, from the Patristic period onwards, philosophy was called the ancilla theologiae. The title was not intended to indicate philosophy's servile submission or purely functional role with regard to theology. Rather, it was used in the sense in which Aristotle had spoken of the experimental sciences as "ancillary" to "prima philosophia". The term can scarcely be used today, given the principle of autonomy to which we have referred, but it has served throughout history to indicate the necessity of the link between the two sciences and the impossibility of their separation (#77).

Now, while some may quibble over his explanation of the attitude towards philosophy in the Church's past, the message for the future could not be clearer. Taking the Pope at his word, *Fides et Ratio* emphatically reminds us of the autonomy of philosophy, even in light of the role that it can—and must—provide to theology.

5. The Unity of Truth and Orthodoxy

Thus far, I have quoted extensively from John Paul II's encyclical letter, *Fides et Ratio*, to illustrate what he has set forth as the Catholic Church's stance towards philosophy, and its proper role within the Tradition of the Church, as well as the continued need of philosophical enquiry for the future evangelization of the Church in the third millennium. Even still, I have only scratched the surface of the late

Holy Father's message in *Fides et Ratio.* Nevertheless, I believe it is important to read John Paul II's own words, given that many viewed him and his papacy as anything but "open-minded." Even during his last days, and throughout his funeral services, the media would constantly refer to his "traditional" ways, his "ultra-conservative" policies, his "unbending control" of the bishops and cardinals—all, of course, in polite and deferential tones. I would submit that such attitudes towards John Paul II's papacy are unfair and misguided, largely coming from a lack of understanding of the Catholic Tradition. His writings tell the real story. The truth is that John Paul II loved the truth and encouraged every man and woman to pursue it without fear! In fact, the easier path would probably have been to use *Fides et Ratio* to go ahead and "canonize" whatever the Pope held to be the one, true philosophy and be done with it. Such a move has often been the temptation down through the ages, and we have seen countless other institutions and governments attempt to codify thought, shut down free enquiry, and establish a very narrow vision of what is perceived at the time as *the* "truth." Yet, the Church has not made such a move in its history, although it often speaks to the errors of various philosophies and ideologies. John Paul II did not make such a move in his papacy either. But why not? Is it simply that the Church cannot make up its mind? Has the Holy Spirit failed the Church in this one area?

To address these questions, and to fully understand the "openness" of the Church here with its resistance towards "canonizing" one particular philosophy for all believers, one must recall the Catholic Tradition's perpetual belief and confidence in the unity of truth. This is the ultimate foundation upon which the wisdom of the Church in all of its teachings is based, and it is clearly at work in *Fides et Ratio.* To begin with, John Paul II recognizes that, "The unity of truth is a fundamental premise of human reasoning, as the principle of non-contradiction makes clear" (#34). But saying that truth is one does not imply that there is only one path to the truth: this is a common mistake that must always be corrected. For his part, John Paul II explains instead that "There are many paths which lead to truth, but since Christian truth has a salvific value, any one of these paths may be taken, as long as it leads to the final goal, that is to the Revelation of Jesus Christ" (#38). Thus, any one of the paths to truth may be taken, which leaves philosophical enquiry open. In fact, philosophical enquiry must remain open, given the limitations of human reason:

> ...it is necessary to keep in mind the unity of truth, even if its formulations are shaped by history and produced by human reason wounded and weakened by sin. This is why no historical form of philosophy can legitimately claim to embrace the totality of truth, nor to be the complete explanation of the human being, of the world and of the human being's relationship with God (#51).

No one philosophy, and no one philosopher as a "philosopher," will ever be able to attain the totality of truth.

In sum, God is Truth. Thus, the search for truth through either theology or philosophy will always lead to the same end, God (even when the seeker is unaware of the real Truth she or he is seeking!). Confidence in the unity of truth is what grounds the Church's openness to philosophy. Confidence in the unity of truth is also what grounds John Paul II's personal urging towards philosophers to recover philosophy's "original vocation" (#6) and "not to set themselves goals that are too modest in their philosophizing" (#56).

But what about maintaining Catholic orthodoxy? What of the dangers of a particular philosophical argument, or even a whole philosophical system, contradicting the faith? In recognizing the autonomy of philosophy, has John Paul II opened the door to relativism? After all, if there are many paths to truth, does this mean all paths (i.e. all philosophical approaches) are on an equal par with one another? Is everyone free to choose what works best for him or herself? Careful reading of *Fides et Ratio* makes it clear that the late Holy Father was not developing a relativistic attitude. As noted earlier, this is where the intervention of the Magisterium comes into play:

> In the light of faith, therefore, the Church's Magisterium can and must authoritatively exercise a critical discernment of opinions and philosophies which contradict Christian doctrine. It is the task of the Magisterium in the first place to indicate which philosophical presuppositions and conclusions are incompatible with revealed truth, thus articulating the demands which faith's point of view makes of philosophy. Moreover, as philosophical

> learning has developed, different schools of thought have emerged. This pluralism also imposes upon the Magisterium the responsibility of expressing a judgment as to whether or not the basic tenets of these different schools are compatible with the demands of the word of God and theological enquiry (#50).

It is the Church, through her proper teaching authority, guided by the Holy Spirit, that is the determinant and defender of orthodoxy. And even for the Church, John Paul II admits this is a daunting task:

> Today, then, with the proliferation of systems, methods, concepts and philosophical theses which are often extremely complex, the need for a critical discernment in the light of faith becomes more urgent, even if it remains a daunting task. Given all of reason's inherent and historical limitations, it is difficult enough to recognize the inalienable powers proper to it; but it is still more difficult at times to discern in specific philosophical claims what is valid and fruitful from faith's point of view and what is mistaken or dangerous. Yet the Church knows that "the treasures of wisdom and knowledge" are hidden in Christ (Col 2:3) and therefore intervenes in order to stimulate philosophical enquiry, lest it stray from the path which leads to recognition of the mystery (#51).

We must keep these points in mind, then, when we consider the role of a Catholic philosopher. It is the Church as a whole that clarifies what falls outside of Catholic orthodoxy.

What I find particularly interesting here, however, is that throughout all of the discussion regarding the intervention of the Magisterium in philosophical matters, nowhere does John Paul II withdraw his stance regarding the autonomy of philosophy or alter his position that philosophy is integral to the work and mission of the Church. Rather, he emphasizes the positive role that even erroneous philosophical positions have made in developing the understanding of the Christian faith and the official teachings of the Church throughout its Tradition. Citing the Dogmatic Constitution from the First Vatican Council, *Dei Filius*, John Paul II states that:

> Even if faith is superior to reason there can never be a true divergence between faith and reason, since the same God who

> reveals the mysteries and bestows the gift of faith has also placed in the human spirit the light of reason. This God could not deny himself, nor could the truth ever contradict the truth (#53).

There it is—truth cannot contradict the truth! Thus, we might say that for one who recognizes the unity of truth, the philosophical search for truth—when done openly, honestly, and sincerely—becomes consonant with Catholic orthodoxy.

6. Conclusion: *Fides et Ratio* and the Catholic Philosopher

In the end, *Fides et Ratio* has much to say to many different groups of people. I have focused on but one group, Catholic philosophers. I believe that, in this letter, John Paul II extols the beauty and dignity of our discipline both for itself and for its role within the mission and teaching of the Church. At the same time, John Paul II extols the religious faith of Catholic philosophers as well. In so doing, he affirms that a "Catholic philosopher" is not a walking paradox or a living contradiction for those inside as well as outside of the Church. As I reflect upon what all of this means for myself as a Catholic philosopher, two statements from *Fides et Ratio* keep coming back to me, washing over my thoughts.

First, there is John Paul II's urging all philosophers:

> ...to trust in the power of human reason and not to set themselves goals that are too modest in their philosophizing. The lesson of history in this millennium now drawing to a close shows that this is the path to follow: it is necessary not to abandon the passion for ultimate truth, the eagerness to search for it or the audacity to forge new paths in the search (#56).

Even in the midst of discussing the role of the Magisterium in seeking to defend and preserve the truth of the Catholic faith from philosophical errors, John Paul II turns to the philosopher and says, "philosophize!" His confidence in the unity of truth and faith in the Holy Spirit prompt his boldness. As he urged from the beginning of his papacy: be not afraid! Nor does the Pope simply call for renewing the old philosophical arguments. Rather, he explicitly calls for the boldness to forge new enquiries and new arguments. Philosophers of every ilk ought to be asking themselves, "Have I become complacent in my philosophy?," "Do I need to be awoken from my dogmatic slumbers?," and, "What more can I do, what new enquiries can I begin?"

I believe the above quote (#56) provides more than enough food for thought for any philosopher, and we could justly stop right here to ponder the implications of it alone. However, the second quote that keeps coming back to me becomes a lens that intensifies John Paul II's specific "call" to Catholic philosophers. I am thinking of the passage in which he addresses the question of Christian philosophy. In his discussion, John Paul II notes that the concept of Christian philosophy "...does not therefore refer simply to a philosophy developed by Christian philosophers who have striven in their research not to contradict the faith" (#76). Now I do not believe that any philosopher that claimed to be Catholic, and who was a committed believer, would ever knowingly want to contradict her or his faith or the official teaching of the Church. But John Paul II, I believe, is pointing out that if one's primary standard as a Catholic doing philosophy is simply to avoid anything that might appear to be unorthodox, then one is not engaging in the fullness of philosophical enquiry. The encyclical explicitly states that philosophy, including Christian philosophy, ought not to be constrained by such limits. What is more, Catholic philosophers who believe that this is all their philosophy should do ought not to project the same demands upon other Catholic philosophers who are attempting to forge new paths towards the truth. If we limit our philosophical work too much in this regard, the ability of the Church as a whole to contribute to the moral growth of our culture will be severely hampered. Thus, towards the end of his letter, John Paul II specifically exhorts Catholic philosophers, noting that:

> Philosophical thought is often the only ground for understanding and dialogue with those who do not share our faith. The current ferment in philosophy demands of believing philosophers an attentive and competent commitment, able to discern the expectations, the points of openness and the key issues of this historical moment. Reflecting in the light of reason and in keeping with its rules, and guided always by the deeper understanding given them by the word of God, Christian philosophers can develop a reflection which will be both comprehensible and appealing to those who do not yet grasp the full truth which divine Revelation declares. Such a ground for

> understanding and dialogue is all the more vital nowadays, since the most pressing issues facing humanity—ecology, peace and the co-existence of different races and cultures, for instance—may possibly find a solution if there is a clear and honest collaboration between Christians and the followers of other religions and all those who, while not sharing a religious belief, have at heart the renewal of humanity (#104).

In the end, the Church asks much of Catholic philosophers, both as "philosophers" and as "Catholics." This is because, within the Catholic Tradition, philosophy is not merely an esoteric sideline, but rather it is an integral part of the work of the Church in breaking open the Wisdom of God for both believers and non-believers alike. Nor must we forget that, in doing this work, the Church does not ask the Catholic philosopher to become a theologian. *Fides et Ratio* tells us that the Church needs both theology and philosophy. Now, some Catholic philosophers will make a much closer use of theology in their efforts than others, and such approaches are perfectly legitimate. But equally important are Catholic philosophers whose work is much less explicitly religious. All such efforts are needed in metaphysics, natural theology, philosophy of mind, bioethics, aesthetics, philosophy of the human person, and so on. Catholic philosophers need to be supportive of each other in all of these various works, even ones that fall outside of our own particular preferences for how philosophy ought to be done in general, and more specifically as members of the Catholic Church. As John Paul II reminds us in *Fides et Ratio*: "It must not be forgotten that reason too needs to be sustained in all its searching by trusting dialogue and sincere friendship. A climate of suspicion and distrust, which can beset speculative research, ignores the teaching of the ancient philosophers, who proposed friendship as one of the most appropriate contexts for sound philosophical enquiry" (#33). I do not take this to mean that we ought to be soft on each other in our philosophical exchanges—that would not really be of much help to the Church as it faces critics within society. However, by continuing to support each other in our work, and by challenging each other to argue well and to argue wisely, Catholic philosophers can answer John Paul II's "call" in *Fides et Ratio*. For my part, I believe that it is a privilege to engage in this role as part of the saving mission of the Church. In this effort, we must not be afraid.

Part IV

Contemporary Challenges

Humanism and Bioethics: The Prophetic Voice of Jacques Maritain (1882-1973)

Edmund D. Pellegrino, M.D.

1. Introduction

Jacques Maritain was, among 20th Century philosophers, the most prescient about how the changing relationships between science and philosophy would affect our presuppositions about what it means to be human, and therefore what the good for humans might be. He was fully cognizant and respectful of the knowledge empirical science was gaining about man's physical and psychological constitution. But he was also fearful that the truths of man's nature which came from religion and philosophy beyond the experimental method would be lost. The resulting damage to the ontological unity of our idea of man would, he predicted, have irreparable consequences on our moral and social lives.

This dissonance in our idea of man was, he felt, the central cultural crisis of modernity. Maritain knew this crisis would reach into our 21st Century and beyond. He posed his prophecy succinctly in these words: "*The peculiar problem of the age lying before us is to reconcile science and wisdom in a vital and spiritual unity.*"[1] He spelled out the nature of this "peculiar problem" in a substantial portion of his own thinking and writing. First and foremost, he distinguished the congruence and the conflicts between the ways of knowing and thinking of science,

[1] Jacques Maritain, *Science and Wisdom* (New York: Charles Scribner's Sons, 1954), 32.

philosophy and theology.[2] He also foresaw the profound influence of these changing relationships on man's social and political life.[3]

Maritain hoped for an "integral humanism"—one that could provide a unified idea of human beings and in their physical, psychological, rational and spiritual dimensions. Maritain sought this ontological unity in a Christian humanism, one fully in communion with the Christian tradition yet responsive to the positive elements in modern culture.

Maritain could not foresee how prophetic his notion of an integral humanism would be for today's bioethics. But nothing could be more relevant for the growing debates in bioethics between those who hold to an anthropocentric and those who hold to a theocentric humanism. Both groups draw of the presuppositions underlying their version of humanism to respond to the questions of how to use the powers of biotechnology over human life both wisely and well. The differences in the way our presupposition of man and his destiny shape our bioethical reasoning are creating serious rifts within the bioethics community as well as the general public.

I will summarize the ways in which Maritain's humanism provides a prophetic voice that bears attention in our present debates about the ends to which our new-found powers can be used to enrich or endanger our humanity. I will do this under four headings: (1) Maritain's relationship with biological science; (2) The importance of our idea of man, i.e., the "anthropological question" in today's bioethics; (3) The outlines of Maritain's Christian Humanism; and (4) The potential place of Maritain's hope for a retrieval of the philosophy of nature in today's bioethical discourse.

---

[2] See Jacques Maritain, *The Degrees of Knowledge*, translated from the French edition under the supervision of Gerald B. Phelan (New York: Charles Scribner's Sons, 1959); *Science and Wisdom* (New York: Charles Scribner's Sons, 1954); *True Humanism* (New York: Charles Scribner's Sons, 1950); and *The Philosophy of Nature* (New York: Philosophical Library, 1951).

[3] See Jacques Maritain, *Man and the State* (Chicago: University of Chicago, 1951); *Scholasticism and Politics*, trans. Mortimer Adler (New York: Image Books, 1960); *Christianity and Democracy* (London: Geoffrey Bles, 1946); and *Reflections on America* (Garden City, New York: Image, 1964).

2. Maritain and Biology

Maritain devoted his scholarly life to philosophy in almost all its branches. He produced works of originality in epistemology, metaphysics, aesthetics, social and political philosophy as well as moral philosophy. He saw each of these topics as differing ways of knowing reality, each in its way distinct, but also related to the others. He carefully, and *in extenso*, made these connections in his seminal work *Degrees of Knowledge*. In his *Moral Philosophy* he recognized the importance of taking all perspectives and ways of knowing into account since all contributed in its own way to our knowledge of man.[4]

Maritain's philosophical perspective in all these works was the moderate realism of his intellectual guides, Aristotle and St. Thomas Aquinas. By this method he brought these thinkers into congruence with modern sciences—physical, biological and social—as well as with modern social and political thinking. In all his work, Maritain's Catholic and Christian faith infused his thought and gave it the spiritual unity his "true humanism" demanded. His true humanism was unapologetically a Christian Humanism.

Maritain, however, never forgot his early experiences as a student of biology. In fact he began his studies at Heidelberg as a student of Hans Driesch. Driesch was a pioneer experimental embryologist. Maritain was formally a student of biology for only a short time (1907-1908). His diary records that he eventually pawned his microscope in the summer of 1908, in order to help Léon Bloy in his penury.[5] Maritain, however, continued as a friend of Driesch after he left Heidelberg. In his own philosophy of biology, he strongly supported Driesch's embryogenetic neo-vitalism.

In 1921 Maritain wrote the preface to Driesch's *La Philosophie de l'organisme*.[6] Later he cited Driesch's experiments to support his own strong contention that the ontologic status of animals could never be

---

[4] Jacques Maritain, *Moral Philosophy: An Historical and Critical Survey of the Great Systems* (New York: Charles Scribner's Sons, 1964).

[5] Jacques Maritain, *Notebooks*, trans. J. J. Ryans (New York: Magi, 1984), 48.

[6] Hans Driesch, *Le Philosophie de l'organisme* (Paris: Beauchesne, 1921).

explained by physico-chemical mechanisms alone.[7] He argued that a methodological separation should be made between the empirical study of living organisms and the ontological investigations proper to philosophy. This paralleled his conviction that he should never use a revealed premise in a philosophical proposition.[8]

Although his life's work was in philosophy, Maritain never lost his original interest in the relations between philosophy, science, and biology. He recognized full well how significant they were for any comprehensive view of what it means to be human. He retained that interest to the closing years of his life, when he wrote a strongly worded criticism of Teilhard de Chardin's attempt to fuse the biological sciences with theology. Maritain, perhaps too harshly, thought Teilhard's synthesis of evolution, cosmology, and theology was a kind of Christian Gnosticism. For Maritain, Teilhard's work was more mystical and poetic than philosophically or theologically sound.[9] It veered from Maritain's own integral humanism by a wide margin.

3. Maritain's Humanism and Modern Bioethics

In the brief 35 years or so of its existence, bioethics has expanded from its earlier focus on medical ethics to the larger issues of how to use the capabilities of modern biotechnology wisely and well. Humans can now alter their ways of reproduction, re-engineer their present and future genetic endowment, modify the germ plasm, create and abort life at will, clone animals and perhaps themselves, etc. It is now obvious that the most profound and relevant question is deciding what is good for man. To answer that question, we need to know who man is and the meaning of his existence. Without some answer to these questions, we cannot judge how to use the expanding power of modern biomedicine without being overwhelmed by it.

---

[7] Jacques Maritain, *Bergsonian Philosophy and Thomism*, trans. Mabelle L. Andison in collaboration with J. Gordon Andison (New York: Philosophical Library, 1955), 244.

[8] See Yves R. Simon, "Jacques Maritain, The Growth of a Christian Philosopher," in *Jacques Maritain, The Man and His Achievement*, ed. Joseph M. Evans (New York: Sheed and Ward, 1963), 23.

[9] Jacques Maritain, *The Peasant of the Garonne: An Old Layman Questions Himself about the Present Time* (New York: Holt Rinehart and Winston, 1968), 119-20.

We need a moral template against which to measure our answer to the question John Paul II asked all mankind in his first Encyclical: "*Does the progress which has man as its author and promoter make human life on earth more human in every aspect of that life?*"[10] That question occupied him as a young Bishop at the Vatican Council. It was the focus for the philosophical anthropology of his colleagues at Lublin.[11] That question is the reason his biographer called him "...the Pope of a New Humanism...."[12] The same question now engages both anthropocentric and theocentric philosophers and theologians today.[13] It is also the question at which bioethical discourse must begin and end.

"Humanism" is, however, at one and the same time, an attractive and a troublous term in bioethics as elsewhere in modern culture. On the one hand, it suggests a sensitivity to the more spiritual dimensions of the personal, the existential, and the humane dimensions of our existence. On the other, it is symbolic of a man-centered universe in which God plays a minor or absent role. For Christians, humanism is God-centered and other-world oriented. Its telos is the beatific vision and not a biotechnological utopia here on earth.

The idea we hold of man is the foundation stone for our normative guidelines in bioethics, as in any system of ethics. It is the unavoidable starting point, explicit or implicit, for any moral line of reasoning. Without a stable foundation point, our arguments about right and wrong, good and bad, will end in endless regress or endless circularity. Whether we are speaking of the common good in social medicine or the individual good of the patient in clinical medicine, our deepest convictions about what is a good or authentic human life ground our moral choices.

---

[10] John Paul II, *Encyclical Redemptor Hominis* #15 (March 4, 1979).

[11] Mieczylaw A. Krapiec, *I-Man, An Outline of the Philosophical Anthropology*, trans. Andrew Woznicki and Theresa Sandok et al. (New Britain, Connecticut: Mariel Publications, 1983).

[12] George Weigel, *Witness to Hope, A Biography of John Paul II* (New York: Cliff Street, 1999).

[13] Edmund D. Pellegrino, "Toward a Richer Bioethics," in *Health and Human "lourishing,* eds. Carol Taylor and Roberto Dell'Oro (Washington, D.C.: Georgetown University, 2006).

Maritain understood this fact clearly. He said:

> The fact is I believe that in the background of all of our moral difficulties there is a fundamental problem which is ineluctably posed for each of us... the problem of the relation of man to the human condition or of his attitude in the face of the human condition.[14]

This is the ineluctable problem which is today the force behind the growing and widening rift in bioethical discourse. As Maritain said:

> It is clear that whoever uses the word humanism brings into play at once an entire metaphysic and that the idea we form of humanism will have wholly different implications according to whether we hold or do not hold there is in the nature of man something which breathes an air outside time and a personality whose profoundest needs surpass the order of the universe.[15]

The metaphysics we bring into play will determine the way we ground the justifications we use for our moral choices.

There are many "humanisms" today, e.g., the classical-renaissance version of the humanist as a scholar learned in the ancient languages and cultures, the atheist humanism of many moderns who see man as the center of the universe, the Hegelian-Marxist humanism of dialectical materialism, the humanisms of the major religions, and the humanism of scientistic modernists. For the purposes of moral philosophy, they are reducible to two, based on whether or not they accept a source of moral authority beyond man in a personal God, or whether they see man only as the sole determinant of right and wrong, good and bad. The disparity in the bioethics resulting from each presupposition becomes more evident daily.

Anthropocentric humanism explains man in terms of his chemical and physical constitution, or his psycho-social formation or his subjective values and preferences. On this view, his ethics is his to fashion, by law, public policy, and social construction. It exalts the

---

[14] Jacques Maritain, *Moral Philosophy: An Historical and Critical Survey of the Great Systems* (New York: Charles Scribner's Sons, 1964), 452.

[15] Jacques Maritain, *True Humanism,* xii.

pragmatic, relativistic, and autonomous choice, without need of metaphysics. Its roots were well laid in the ancient world by Democritus and Lucretius. It enjoys a revival among many influential writers of the day, who hold both religion and metaphysics discredited by modern science.[16] They are the modern children of Descartes' most ardent mechanist disciple, de La Mettrie.[17]

On this view, human dignity, mind and soul are mere epiphenomena: i.e., a manifestation of the complexity of our physical structure. The normal or the demented patient or the embryo and infant, therefore, have no greater moral claim on us than any other living being in the biosphere. The implications of such presuppositions for human life-questions—embryonic stem cell research, abortion, euthanasia, human enhancement, genetic engineering, neuroethics, etc.—are profound. There is no moral distinction in belonging to the natural kind to which human nature belongs.

Anthropomorphic humanism is not, as its adherents attest, the only scientifically valid conclusion about who and what we are. Many credible scientists do hold both to a divine source of morality, as well as to the legitimacy of science—each in its own sphere.[18] Elsewhere, I have contrasted the way anthropocentric philosophies of man result in divergent and conflicting systems of bioethics.[19]

It is necessary to point out, as Maritain did, that to speak of humanism is to introduce metaphysics into the discussion. The anthropocentric perspective cannot claim to be free of metaphysics.

---

[16] See James D. Watson and Andrew Berry, *The Secret of Life* (New York: Alfred Knopf, 2003); Edward O. Wilson, *Consilience,The University of Knowledge* (New York: Alfred Knopf, 1998), 235; and Daniel C. Dennett, *Breaking the Spell, Religion as a Natural Phenomenon* (New York: Viking Penguin, 2006).

[17] Julien Offray de La Mettrie, *L'Homme Machine, A Study of the Origins of an Idea* (Princeton, New Jersey: Princeton University, 1960).

[18] Francis Collins, *The Language of God: A Scientist Presents Evidence for Belief* (New York: Simon and Schuster, 2006).

[19] See Edmund D. Pellegrino, "Toward A Richer Bioethics"; see also Arthur Peacocke, *Paths from Science Towards God: The End of all Exploring* (Oxford: One World, 2001), Chap. 1-2, and John Polkinghorne, *Belief in God in an Age of Science* (New Haven, Connecticut: Yale University, 1998), 92.

Instead, it is grounded in a covert metaphysics, one open only to the insights of positive and empirical science. This covert metaphysics is inescapably itself a metaphysics, because it claims an exclusive grasp of reality, a grasp of the ultimate truth of things, but one open only to the methodology of empirical and experimental science.

4. Maritain's True Humanism

Maritain's thinking about the crisis of humanism was triggered initially by his concern for the fundamental atheism inherent in Marx and Lenin's materialist foundations for Soviet Communism. Maritain, however, recognized a certain truth in the Marxist idea of man as a being in a collectivity. He wanted to preserve some of this truth, but cleanse it of its materialist bias. He saw man's fulfillment as a human being not in contradiction of God but in one with God:

> ...The creature should be respected in his connection with God because he is totally dependent upon Him; a humanism indeed but a theocentric humanism rooted in what is radical in man; integral humanism, the humanism of the Incarnation.[20]

In *Science and Wisdom*, Maritain summarized his humanism and the dignity of man in the law of Incarnation.[21] For Maritain, it follows that:

> ...to love a being in and for God is not to treat him as a mere means of a mere occasion for loving God, but to love and cherish their being as an end, because it merits love, in the degree to which that merit and their dignity spring from the sovereign love and the sovereign loving-kindness of God.[22]

Maritain's humanism grounds man's dignity not only in Genesis but in the Incarnation. What better evidence can there be for man's inherent dignity among created things than God's choice of man as the being in whom, and among whom, He sent His only Son? This is radically different from the neutral or non-existent dignity that accords the same worth to every creature in the biosphere, man included! Here, Maritain's humanism moves in the direction of Wojtyła's Christian

---

[20] Jacques Maritain, *True Humanism*, 65.

[21] Ibid.

[22] Ibid.

personalist humanism.[23] Speciesism is for Maritain not the mortal sin against Darwinian evolution condemned by the materialist, but a recognition of man's transfiguration by grace—man so changed by grace that he strives to become the new man.[24]

These differences between opposing ideas of man become apparent whenever we must as professionals, individuals, or societies decide whether or not to adopt a new or particular biotechnological "advance." The idea of man we espouse defines the good man as man and of *this* patient in the clinical encounter. The idea of man is therefore far more than a theoretical preoccupation for the physician and other health workers. The same is true of policy makers who cannot avoid having a vision, implicit or explicit, of what it means to be truly human when they fashion a policy or regulation. These differences in perceptions of what is authentic human existence have, in recent years, come to divide the bioethics community itself. Scholars and practitioners are being classified, or classify themselves, as "progressive" or "conservative" on the basis of their preferences for one or the other version of humanism.

As bioethics moves into the public sphere, increasingly the differences I have been describing are dividing public opinion and complicating efforts to legislate, regulate or promote a particular version of humanity's future. Witness the contrast between the Christian humanism of the *Pastoral Constitution of the Church in the Modern World*, on the one hand, and that of the *Humanist Manifesto*, on the other.[25] Both, with sincerity, seek a world that is more "humane," but their logical presuppositions of how to judge that world are often far apart. Consider only the humanism of John Paul II's existential personalism with the "humanism" of those legislators in California,

---

[23] Andrew N. Woznicki, *Karol Wojtyła's Existential Personalism* (New Britain, Connecticut: Mariel, 1980).

[24] Jacques Maritain, *True Humanism*, 86.

[25] See *Gaudium et Spes, Pastoral Constitution on the Church in the Modern World*, 1965, and Paul Kutz, *Humanist Manifesto* (New York: Prometheus Books, 2002).

New Jersey, and elsewhere who are willing to sacrifice human embryos for their vision of a new utopia built on stem cell research.[26]

The debate grows more contentious every day. Bioethics does, of course, have profound political implications, but partisan bioethicists do discredit their claims to expertise in ethics. At this moment, the gap is growing and the chances for some sort of political reconciliation are becoming more remote. Honest and civil dialogue has deteriorated into vicious polemics, often personal in their attack.[27]

This brings me to the last of the three issues in Maritain's prophecy pertinent to bioethics—the need for a conceptual bridge between metaphysics and experimental science, a bridge of language and dialectical methodology that he subsumed under the rubric of the philosophy of nature. Retrieval of a vital philosophy of nature is potentially an instrument of mediation through which theocentric and anthropocentric humanism might find some common ground. If the dichotomy of anthropological perspectives is not to divide bioethics further, some medium is needed through which they can communicate without immediate mutual rejection. Could this be a retrieval of the idea of a philosophy of nature as Maritain proposed? Could it be the ultimate higher truth to which empirical science aspires? Is there a philosophical realm between science and metaphysics?[28]

5. Ought there to be a distinct philosophy of Nature?

Maritain asked this question out of his concern, even in his early studies of biology with Driesch, for a bridge between the knowledge claims of experimental science and those of philosophy, especially metaphysics. Maritain strongly supported Driesch's neo-vitalism: the doctrine that life is not totally explicable in terms of physics and

---

[26] See Andrew N. Woznicki, *Karol Wojtyła's Existential Personalism* and Karol Wojtyła, *The Acting Person*, translated from the Polish by Andrzej Potocki in collaboration with Anna-Teresa Tymieniecka (Dordrecht: D. Reidel, 1969).

[27] See Edmund D. Pellegrino, "Bioethics and Politics: "Doing Ethics" in the Public Square," *Journal of Medicine and Philosophy* 31, no. 6 (2006): 569-84.

[28] Matthew S. Pugh, "Maritain and Post Modern Science," in *Post Modernism and Christian Philosophy*, ed. Roman T. Ciapolo with an introduction by Jude P. Dougherty (Washington, D.C.: American Maritain Association, 1997), 181.

chemistry. He did so against the insistent claim of many empirical scientists then, as now, that they possessed the only valid source of knowledge of nature. On their view, the answer to the question "What is man?" could only be answered by an ever more detailed study of man's physical being. On their view, an ontological grasp was not possible.

The impact of modern science on philosophy was a recurrent theme in Maritain's work, particularly in *Science and Wisdom, True Humanism* and the *Philosophy of Nature*. And in these works he argued that there must be harmony between wisdom (infused wisdom, theology and metaphysics) and knowledge of what he called the "special sciences." He developed these epistemic relations with great care in *The Degrees of Knowledge*. Maritain held that there was a hierarchy of distinct degrees of knowledge each with its definitive style of explanation and none of which can be substituted for the other.[29] Both science and philosophy have their own methodology. Each has a just place of each in the order of wisdom. Defining these places and their hierarchical relationships was a challenge for modern epistemology.

In such a hierarchy, experimental and empirical science was suited to explain nature in terms of its sensible, observable and measurable characteristics. Metaphysics, on the other hand, while not constituting the whole of philosophy, does deal with the being of things in a higher order of abstraction. Yet, between empirical science and metaphysics, there also exists a realm of reflection which constitutes the philosophy of nature, which knows the same world as the physical sciences, but knows it philosophically: that is, conceptually and as intelligible being.[30]

A philosophy of nature differs from empirical science. It starts with the same sensible world but, unlike empirical science, it abstracts from that world to a conceptual level, to probe the more general meaning of change, motion, causality, time, soul, and life as they underlie the measurable phenomena of human life. On this view, it would be an error to expect philosophical criteria to emerge directly from scientific

---

[29] Jacques Maritain, *Science and Wisdom* op cit., 33.

[30] Jacques Maritain, *Scholasticism and Politics* (New York: Image, 1960), 58.

observation and equally erroneous to expect to construct a philosophy of nature without scientific fact.

Metaphysics is necessary for a philosophy, for without it there is no philosophy, no contact with being as such. But philosophy of nature is also necessary for metaphysics, for without it there is no connection with the real world of observable and measurable phenomena. Philosophy of nature fulfills the "ontological aspiration" of the sciences. Maritain summarizes his view of the role of mediation a philosophy of science might play:

> It [a philosophy of nature] is an indispensable mediator which reconciles the world of the particular sciences (which is inferior to it) with the world of metaphysical wisdom, which it obeys. It is here at the basis and beginning of our human knowledge, in the heart of the sensible and the changeable manifold that the great law or hierarchical and dynamic organization of knowledge comes into play. And on it depends for us the appetite and the good of intellectual unity.[31]

Perhaps the most incisive and informed evaluation of Maritain's notion of philosophy of nature in reference to modern philosophy of science is that of William Wallace.[32] Wallace connects Maritain's thought to the Jesuits Peter Hoenen and Filippo Selvaggi. He includes the revisions Yves R. Simon made in Maritain's thought. He also points to a renewed interest in a philosophy of nature among philosophers of science today. For the present author, philosophy of science is a reflection on the philosophical problems arising in the doing of science, and in defining its status as an area of knowledge. Philosophy of nature has as its object not science nor the philosophical problems involved in experimental science as a way of knowing the world per se, but the meanings of the phenomena of nature itself.

In any case, it remains to be seen if serious attention to a philosophy of nature as defined by Maritain and Simon can serve as the much needed bridge between the Scientistic perspectives of today's

---

[31] Jacques Maritain, *Science and Wisdom*, 69.

[32] William Wallace, *The Modeling of Nature* (Washington, D.C.: Catholic University of America, 1990), 197ff.

materialists, and those who hold to the importance of scientific method, but see it as insufficient for a full understanding of man and the natural world.

Could a strengthened and clarified philosophy of nature save the contending factions from the descent from dialectics to polemics in bioethics? Could it serve as the intellectual bridge for a productive dialectic between a more traditional realistic metaphysics and the enormous powers of experimental science? Can the balance between science and wisdom be restored in the arena of bioethics? Could the prophetic voice of Maritain serve as the springboard for a more civil and productive dialectic?

William Wallace has suggested that a retrieval of philosophy of nature might also bring it into closer convergence with contemporary philosophy of science. To this end he suggests that:

> ...a realist and up to date view of the philosophy of science, as opposed to a Humean or Kantian view brings it very close to a philosophy of nature so much so that philosophy of science can be seen with proper qualifications as itself a part of the philosophy of nature.[33]

This is a great deal to hope for. But if this can come about, it would go a long way towards healing the divide between contemporary and traditional epistemology.

6. Humanism, Medicine and Bioethics

The anthropological question and Maritain's cogitations come to a very sharp and practical point in modern medicine. Medicine has always centered on an idea of man and what is good for mankind.[34] The first truly moral principle of the Hippocratic ethos is the moral obligation of the physician to act for the well being, i.e., the good, of his patient. But the "good" of the patient is not subsumed entirely by his medical good—that which is attainable by the art and science of medicine. The good of the patient also includes his perceptions of his

---

[33] Ibid., 227.

[34] Edmund D. Pellegrino, "Medicine, History and the Idea of Man," *Annals of the American Academy of Political and Social Sciences* 346 (March 1963): 9-20.

own good, his good as a human being and his spiritual good, whatever he might conceive that to be.[35]

Comprehensive medicine requires attention to each of the levels of the patient's good. What physicians think it means to be human is pertinent to the decisions at each level of human good. Since medicine in one way or another will be the conduit for decisions about the application of the latest in biotechnologic advance, what we think humans are *for* will condition our assessment of whether, as Maritain and John Paul II surmised, it is "good" for man as man, whether it sustains and deepens his flourishing as man, or whether it makes him ultimately a victim of his own inventiveness.

The only measure by which to calibrate how much of genetic, regenerative and enhancement medicine or nanotechnology and re-engineering of the human species are morally permissible is our idea of man. We must not forget, believer and non-believer alike, the warning of Henri de Lubac: "It is not true, as is sometimes said, that man cannot organize the world without God. What is true is that, without God, he can ultimately organize it only against man. Exclusive humanism is inhuman humanism."[36]

The difficulties of the reconciliation of science and wisdom for which Maritain wished is today complicated by the need for philosophy itself first to be reconciled with its own intellectual tradition. Post modern and post metaphysical philosophy has, as Theodor Adorno pointed out, abandoned having answers to "questions regarding the personal or even the collective conduct of life."[37] It has become a melancholy science as a result.[38]

---

[35] Edmund D. Pellegrino and David Thomasma, *For the Patient's Good* (Oxford: Oxford University, 1987).

[36] Henri de Lubac, *The Drama of Atheistic Humanism* (San Francisco: Ignatius, 1995).

[37] Jürgen Habermas, *The Future of Human Nature* (Cambridge: Polity, 2003).

[38] Theodor Adorno, *Minima Moralia, Reflections from Damaged Life*, trans. E. F. Jephcott (London: New Left Books, 1974), 15; cited in Habermas, *The Future of Human Nature*, 1.

This defection on the part of philosophy, i.e., from what Maritain would have classified as "wisdom," is something he did not envision. Its implications for bioethics are not apt to be remedied by a philosophy of nature. Only a partial resolution of the "peculiar problem" at the heart of Maritain's concerns seems possible. That resolution would make a renewal of the philosophy of nature a bridge which might allow a passage of ideas over the rifts between anthropocentric and theocentric ideas of man now roiling the bioethical waters.

A philosophy of nature might also be influential in ameliorating the malaise of modern philosophy as Habermas has diagnosed it:

> The new technologies make a public discourse on the right understanding of cultural forms of life in general an urgent matter. And philosophers no longer have any good reasons for leaving such a dispute to biologists, and engineers intoxicated by science fiction.[39]

Although he does not use the word, Habermas seems to be restating Maritain's "peculiar problem" in postmodern terms. Without the reconciliation Maritain sought between science and wisdom, de Lubac's "inhuman humanism" will continue to plague any attempt to discern what it means to be human.

Thirty years after his death, Maritain's prophetic voice remains ever more clear and relevant. His plea for an integral humanism resonates closely with what has become the central conundrum of bioethics. Though Maritain had no direct contact with bioethics even in its nascent years, it has become a beneficiary of his wisdom.

---

[39] Jürgen Habermas, *Human Nature,* 15

VOCATION, FAMILY, AND THE ACADEMY: *SIGNA PERSCRUTANDI*[1]

James G. Hanink

1. Introduction

Vatican Council II bids us to search out the "signs of the times" (*Gaudium et Spes*, #4). Doing so has never been easy. Of old, the Pharisees sought a "sign," only to hear Jesus say, "You know how to interpret the appearance of the sky, but you cannot interpret the signs of the times" (Matthew 16.3). Even *Gaudium et Spes* prompts questions about how it reads the signs of *its* times. Joseph Ratzinger noted early on that the document has little to say about how grace makes freedom possible. In his words, freedom "does not consist in abstract selection between different possibilities of behavior, but by its very nature lives in the presence of God and can only be really understood in relation to this vis-à-vis."[2] More recently, Tracey Rowland has argued that the document is ambiguous about the structural flaws of liberal culture.[3] With such high stakes, John Paul II's advice to "look truth in the eye and to call things by their proper name" remains our best guide in searching out the signs of *our* times (*Evangelium Vitae*, #58).

The Catholic thinker reads the signs of the times in the light of the sacraments, each of which is a "sign and instrument of grace."[4] Yet something like a conspiracy obscures the perspective that matrimony provides. We are thus impoverished because, as John Paul II points out,

---

[1] I thank Michael Berg, Anne Barbeau Gardiner, and Carroll Kearley for their help with this essay.

[2] *Commentary on the Documents of Vatican II: Volume V. Pastoral Constitution on the Church in the Modern World*, ed. Herbert Vorgrimler (New York: Herder and Herder, 1969), 139.

[3] Tracey Rowland, *Culture and the Thomist Tradition: after Vatican II* (London: Routledge, 2003), 9-34.

[4] *Compendium of the Social Doctrine of the Church.* Libreria Editrice Vaticana. Pontifical Council for Justice and Peace (Washington, D.C.: United States Conference of Catholic Bishops, 2005), 99.

"The social role that belongs to every family pertains by a new and original right to the Christian family ... based on the sacrament of marriage (*Familiaris Consortio,* #73)." In this essay, I argue that academic life, even in the Catholic university, occludes this sacramental perspective. My analysis is critical in that it indicts two patterns that are obstacles to the vocation of matrimony and family life. Both patterns reflect a liberal theory of institutions. My analysis, however, is constructive in that it identifies a pair of resources helpful in confronting these obstacles. We need not witness the "dying of the light."[5] As *Gaudium et Spes* #52 insists, it is a duty of public authority "to recognize, protect and promote" the dignity of marriage and the family.

2. Secular "Bracketing"

The university's first occlusive pattern is *systemic.* It is the "bracketing" of the sacramental vocation of spouse and parent. The university does so in how it constructs its policies and goals. To be sure, the university is made up of flesh and blood people, of husbands and wives and sons and daughters. But the vocation of spouse and parent plays no public role in the structure or governance of the university.

This bracketing is symptomatic of a deep *hubris.* We search in vain for signs that the academy recognizes its own limits or admits that anything but the State is more basic than it is. At the same time, this *hubris* is often coupled with bewilderment about what matters most. Such is the consequence of an academic skepticism that invites the triumph of procedure over substance. Harvard's *Veritas* died the death of a thousand doubts. But no university would proclaim the *Humilitas* on which depends the truth about our very selves. Indeed, St. Augustine, once a restive and ambitious academic, sees humility as the key to the unity of the virtues. "Do you propose," he asks, "to raise the great fabric of high virtue? Then attend first to the foundation of humility."[6] Everywhere today, we instead find the touting of excellence. But who promotes this mantra of excellence? It is

---

[5] See James Tunstead Burtchaell, C.S.C., *The Dying of the Light: The Disengagement of Colleges and Universities from their Christian Churches* (Grand Rapids, Michigan: Eerdmans, 1998).

[6] Sermon LXIX, I. PL 38, 44.

institutions that do, and they largely seek excellence through the efficiency of "value-neutral" procedures and secular goals duly accredited by a liberal ethos.

There is a vast literature on the meaning and methods of secular liberalism. Here we could not do better than to focus on what the deeply influential John Rawls, a premier theorist of liberalism, writes about spouses and their families. (Indeed, even the recent and welcome study, *The Future of Family Law*, appeals [naïvely] to Rawls in its advocacy for the natural family.[7]) In his early *A Theory of Justice*, Rawls casually allows that "in a broader inquiry the institution of the family might be questioned, and other arrangements might indeed prove to be preferable."[8] What he tells us in his posthumous *Justice as Fairness: A Restatement* is twofold: first, the family belongs to the basic structure of society with which justice directly concerns itself; and, second, when we articulate the basic principles of justice, we must *bracket* our status as spouse, parent, and child.[9] Our personal history must retreat behind a veil of ignorance. If we resist this bracketing, we unreasonably impose on our fellow citizens. We must keep in mind that they might not be spouses or parents. If they do not share our life circumstances, why should they share our particular social and economic interests?

Rawls observes, too, that disputed questions about either monogamous marriage or same-sex unions raise no special considerations concerning the principles of justice or how we might best apply them.[10] Of course, what counts as parenthood and family membership becomes deeply problematic, given new reproductive technology. Though silent

---

[7] *The Future of Family Law: Law and the Marriage Crisis in North America.* A Report from the Council on Family Law, 2005. Dan Cere, Principal Investigator, 12-13.

[8] John Rawls, *A Theory of Justice* (Cambridge, Massachusetts: Belknap Press of Harvard University, 1971), 463.

[9] John Rawls, *Justice as Fairness: A Restatement*, ed. Erin Kelly (Cambridge, Massachusetts: Belknap Press of Harvard University, 2001), 162-67. At one point, intriguingly, Rawls had suggested that contractors behind the veil of ignorance might think of themselves as representatives of families and, as such, caring about members of the next generation; see *A Theory of Justice*, 128.

[10] Ibid., 163.

on this point, Rawls does emphasize that family law should prevent the care of children from undermining women's equality of opportunity.[11] Thus, he finds it unreasonable to restrict first-trimester abortion.[12] What he plainly rejects, in any case, is the differential treatment of rational contractors in virtue of marriage and family. To insist on a distinct role for contractors as spouse or parent, much less to do so in terms of vocation, imperils the liberal polity. The requisite civility for such an order sternly mandates something like an "abstraction of self from self."[13]

Let us imagine, as easily we might, that the secular academy aspires to the Rawlsian model. To be sure, Rawls notes that the bonds of justice apply indirectly to the university in a context of just background institutions. But such bonds still bind tightly. In his *Political Liberalism*, Rawls insists that parents prepare their children, even in their early education, for compliance with "the public culture."[14] When one turns to the university, largely a creature of the State, these indirect bonds prove very strong.[15] Insofar as the academy aspires to such a model, it brackets spousal and familial identity.

But does the *Catholic* university aspire to so compartmentalized a model? Not without qualification. "Campus Ministry" continues its orbit, and here and there it lights the paths of some. In practice, though, spousal and family identity plays a minimal role in the policies of the Catholic university, whether they bear on curriculum or on professorial recruitment, compensation, and moral leadership. There are, to be sure, the exceptions of medical insurance and family tuition remission. With regard to the former, ironically, the State can and does intervene to decide critical policy matters. California law, for example,

---

[11] Ibid., 11.

[12] John Rawls, *Political Liberalism* (New York: Columbia University, 1996), 243.

[13] For this condition, see Walker Percy's *Love in the Ruins: the Adventures of a Bad Catholic at a Time near the End of the World* (New York: Farrar, Straus & Giroux, 1971), esp. 30-34. Percy's hero, Dr. Tom More, describes his diagnostic tool, the Qualitative Quantitative Ontological Lapsometer and its measurement of how sufferers from this disease allow theories to supplant reality.

[14] Rawls, *Political Liberalism*, 200.

[15] Rawls, *Justice as Fairness: A Restatement*, 10-11, 164.

purportedly requires that Catholic universities share insurance costs for homosexual domestic partners.[16] With regard to the latter, the university—with economic parsimony—supplements its employee compensation plan.

But there is a deeper bracketing at work. In both Rawlsian theory and actual practice, the liberal polity eschews any sense of the sacred. The secular polity is constructivist; thus, in the context of our institutions, we fashion justice through our self-regulating political processes. Privately, one might affirm that human law participates in a natural law grounded in God's creative love. Nonetheless, private affirmation should play little or no role in public deliberation.

A corollary of this contructivism is that a sense of vocation becomes attenuated. In the secular university one has a *career* rather than a *calling*. Insofar as the Catholic university is constructivist, its self-understanding markedly changes. Success, in its public measure, is professional success. And how does one's profession measure success? It does so in terms of the visible and preferably quantifiable productivity that brings institutional prestige. What, then, becomes of fidelity to one's *vocation* as a professor? That is a personal matter. What becomes of one's sacramental vocation as spouse and parent? That is *a fortiori* personal and bracketed.

3. On Instrumentalizing an Intrinsic Good

The second of the university's occlusive patterns is *strategic*. It chooses, on occasion, to relax its own bracketing of marriage and family. When it suits its own institutional purposes, the university selectively acknowledges marriage and family. Yet, in doing so, it keeps them at a regulated distance from its academic identity and "on message" with its own agenda.

John Rawls offers a rationale for this instrumentalization of an intrinsic good. He notes the obvious: "Reproductive labor is socially necessary," and the family has been its established source.[17] Hence, the

---

[16] For one university's eager compliance with this law, see "A Clear Mixed Signal," by Christopher Zehnder, in *Los Angeles Lay Catholic Mission* (January, 2005), 1.

[17] Rawls, *Justice as Fairness: a Restatement*, 162.

family is to arrange "in a reasonable and effective way" for the "raising and caring for children, ensuring their moral development and education into the wider culture."[18] Yet the political trumps the familial, even if subsidiarity is made forfeit. Justice, the celebrated and sovereign political virtue, must shape and restrict the familial virtue of piety. Rawls continues, "[T]he spheres of the political and the public, and of the not-public and the private, take their shape from the content and application of the conception of justice and its principles."[19] If the Catholic university follows the Rawlsian model, it too deploys the family in the service of its own goals. The family becomes a tool that has its appropriate place.

A pair of examples illustrates this reductionism. Consider, first, that the secular university professes to serve the State. Yet the State can be (notoriously) at odds with the needs of the family, as philosophers from Plato to our own day have remarked. Families strive to have their own homes; families need a sense of place. Both are requisite for establishing roots; both are critical for children. All of us, moreover, are children long before we are students or professors. Typically, however, the *prestigious* university exploits the local to serve the national and the international. In doing so, the university cheerfully uses the stable family as a strategic recruit-pool. The academic apparatus displaces students and professors, as well as their families. In time it can even overwhelm the places they call home.

Wendell Berry, a professor *and* a farmer, addresses this deracination. Writing of the "vandalism" of the elites, he cites the standard requirements for membership therein. The first is that the aspirant be a careerist; the second is a university education. Yet how often, he observes, "these professionals have been educated ... in colleges or universities that had originally a clear mandate to serve localities or regions—to receive daughters and sons of their regions, educate them, and send them home again to serve ... their communities. The outcome

---

[18] Ibid., 163.

[19] Ibid., 166.

shows, I think, that they have generally betrayed this mandate ....”[20] Family and community become resources for the university's own ends.

For the second example, we can point to often repeated university complaints about parent interference in student orientation.[21] Some parents, no doubt, are too fretful. Nonetheless, the “pay and go away” strategy is insulting.[22] Parents, moreover, wonder about comments like the one that a colleague of mine recently offered the local press. “Students can leave my class believing the same as they did when they came into the class, but I want them to understand exactly why they believe what they believe.”[23] It is *hubris* for a teacher to think that student beliefs are somehow his or hers to allow; it is also naïveté to suppose that a student's beliefs could become transparent, even to the student, on demand. Secular academics have scant reason to assume that they know more about the moral, much less religious, growth of their students than do the parents of these students. Yet, Rawlsian liberalism fosters this *hubris*. While Rawls admits that “at some point society has to trust to the natural affection and goodwill of parents,” many parents wish, too often in vain, that they could safely trust the secular State and its universities.[24] It can, moreover, often be presumptuous for academics to assume that they know more about what is intellectually critical for students than do the parents of their students. Here Christopher Lasch is bracing. He applauds Orestes Brownson's claim that the real work of educating the young takes place

---

[20] Wendell Berry, “Higher Education and Home Defense,” in *Home Economics* (Berkeley: North Point, 1987), 51-55.

[21] For campus orientation tensions, see Sue Shellenbargar, “Colleges Ward Off Overinvolved Parents,” in *The Wall Street Journal Online* (July 29, 2005).

[22] More worrisome is the message “Pay and Stay.” One Jesuit university's introduction to its new web portal, under the rubric “General Challenges to Overcome,” lists “Creating an online community from ‘cradle to endowment.’ The portal is ‘forever.’”

[23] L. Arik Greenberg, as cited by Meredith Grenier, “Dawn Unity Group offers 2 religion classes,” *Daily Breeze*, Section B, 1 (August 23, 2005).

[24] Rawls, *Justice as Fairness: a Restatement*, 165.

not in schools but rather in their families and communities and, indeed, through nature itself and the very passions of the young.[25]

The university's efforts to serve *in loco parentis* have more than one source, and as a result they are apt to be uneven and erratic. Courts play a decisive role, and sometimes the university abdicates its responsibility for students in order to avoid lawsuits. When the legal climate shifts, the university might revisit its responsibility for students, and often for the same reason. Coupled with legal concerns, there is an effort to instill "progressive thinking" about select social issues.[26] However alert the university is to shifting legal and social dictates, it is the family itself that ought chiefly to define, and delegate, the service of *in loco parentis.* To do so with any authority, there must be effective family councils with the capacity to intervene. When the court and the university override the family, as they often do, the family is diminished and, in turn, less able to challenge its increasing usurpation by these public institutions.

The Catholic university involves a further dimension. A religious and even intellectual *cura personalis* often persists in the Catholic university, although a recent Higher Education Research Institute study suggests that Catholic universities are not much different from secular schools in how they affect student belief and conduct.[27] But the authority for such a role has its basis in the teaching authority of the Church. To the extent that the Catholic university separates itself from the teaching Church, parents must all the more insist that, because of the sacramental character of their vocation, they are the first teachers of their sons and daughters. Vatican Council II speaks to the point: "Graced with the dignity and office of fatherhood and motherhood, parents will energetically acquit themselves of a duty which devolves primarily on them, namely education and especially religious education

---

[25] Christopher Lasch, *The Revolt of the Elites and the Betrayal of Democracy* (New York: W.W. Norton & Co., 1995), 157.

[26] See David Weigel's "Welcome to Fun-Free University," *reasononline*, October 2004.

[27] Patrick Reilly, "Are Catholic Colleges Leading Students Astray?," *The Catholic World Report* (March 2003), 38-46. Most welcome is the inaugural issue of *The Bulletin of Catholic Higher Education*, vol. 1, no. 1, (October 2008).

(*Gaudium et Spes*, #48)." This parental duty is in service of the salvation of their sons and daughters. How, then, can education in a Catholic university fail in its responsibility to serve the family?

4. A First Resource for Renewal

My negative thesis, as I have developed it, is that insofar as the Catholic university follows the model of the secular academy, especially in the context of Rawlsian liberalism, it brackets the sacramental vocation of parents. When, in secondary matters and for its own strategic ends, the university relaxes this bracketing, it often instrumentalizes the family. It is time now to turn to my constructive thesis and to identify two resources that can help us challenge the *status quo*.

The sacramental character of marriage and family transforms their natural dimension; in doing so, this character exemplifies how grace transforms nature. This transformation advances the common good. To be sure, clarity about the common good is pivotal. With this clarity, we can better engage the established *dis*order. Let us understand by "common good" the whole range of material and cultural conditions that enables us to pursue the basic personal and shared goods, together with their realization. Vatican II presents the common good as "the sum of those conditions of social life which allow social groups and their individual members relatively thorough and ready access to their own fulfillment (*Gaudium et Spes*, #26)." We realize our integral fulfillment in freely participating in the common good, which itself includes the goods of specific institutions. The family is one such institution; the university is another.

The family, however, is the primordial community. As Jacques Maritain notes, one "is constituted a part of the family society before [one] is constituted part of the political society."[28] But the liberal polity, as distinct from the political order itself, is a social product. The secular university, in turn, is an artifact of the liberal polity. The common good of the family embraces the unitive good of marriage and the nurturing of children, as well as the conditions that enable the family to realize

---

[28] Jacques Maritain, *The Person and the Common Good*, trans. John J. Fitzgerald (Notre Dame, Indiana: University of Notre Dame, 1966), 75.

these goods. The common good of the university includes the good of knowledge and the conditions that support it. Often the material and cultural conditions that advance both the ends of the family and the university are interwoven. Beyond this, since the family and the university are both dimensions of the common good, to diminish either diminishes both. Thus, for the university to bracket the family undermines the common good.

How, then, might we best promote the dynamic of the common good as it integrates both the goods of the family and of the university? We should enter the Public Square to develop this integration and to show how the bracketing of the family undercuts the university's integrity and authority. With respect to its *integrity*, when the university equates same-sex unions with the family, it violates justice. Rather, the University should affirm that the family is the matrix for life; from this it follows that every other right demands the recognition and protection of the family. With respect to *authority*, we should highlight its erosion by confronting the university's own growing obeisance to the economic sphere. Without the strength of families that would welcome its service, the university hires itself out to those who will pay its way. Expanding all the while, and hustling rather than slouching, the military-athletic-corporate complex is already within the gates of the university.

5. A Second Resource for Renewal

My constructive analysis, then, looks first to the family, a natural institution which grace transforms, and then to the university, a developing social product. If we understand both family and university in terms of the common good, we can and should insist on their right ordering.

The next step is to show how the common good calls for an integrated pursuit of the virtues that enable us to achieve our ends. Specifically, we cannot pursue knowledge, the basic good of the academy, apart from the virtues of piety and fidelity that have their start in the family. In turn, piety and fidelity thrive in the light of the knowledge, both theoretical and practical, which the academy fosters.

Consider some links in this interplay of virtues. Piety is a potential part of justice; it has the character of justice but falls short of full justice.[29] Why is this so? Keep in mind that while justice seeks what is due to others, in some cases we cannot fully render others what is in fact their due. This is manifestly so with respect to a connatural principle of our being: that is, with respect to God, our political order as such, and our parents. Piety is in order, too, with respect to our intellectual inheritance; once again, we cannot fully render those who have given us that inheritance what is their due. The university, moreover, plays a key role in how we share in and develop this inheritance. Thus piety, as an expression of justice, has a place in serving the good of the university. Fidelity, too, has a place in honoring the integrity of our intellectual inheritance and sustaining our participation in it.

How is it, though, that we come to acquire piety and fidelity? The family is where they are first and best taught. The bracketing of marriage and the family weakens the academy itself. If we recognize how this occurs, we can better identify its bitter fruit in university life: the tyranny of the calculative and the commercial over the contemplative and the humane. Exposing its etiology, we can better confront the academy's increasingly established *dis*order.

To be sure, the family needs the university insofar as it advances the good of knowledge. The family faces grave economic and political crises and the challenge to build a true "politics of the family" is daunting.[30] But only if the university honors its own heritage can it encourage the piety and fidelity that sustain the family. Justice in the structuring of the university is incompatible with the "bracketing" of the vocation, much less its sacramental source, which gives birth to familial piety and fidelity.

How might we best act on the basis of the unity of the virtues to pursue the common good? A modest proposal comes to mind. We should encourage public debate to understand the virtues and, in doing so, to integrate each virtue with its allied virtues—as we note in the interplay of piety, fidelity and justice. We must also press home a sobering truth. It is a standing temptation of the university to give way

---

[29] Aquinas follows Cicero in locating piety as a potential part of justice. See *ST* II-II, 101.3.

[30] On "family politics," see John Paul II, *Familiaris Consortio*, #44.

to elitist economic forces. When the university does so, it divorces knowledge from wisdom. Without wisdom, the university becomes a blind guide and, worst of all, is the corruption of the best.

6. Envoi

Jacques Maritain indicts the denizens of the academy who detach themselves from so much of what animates the search for truth. "[T]he condition of the professor who is nothing more than a professor, retired from existence ... is precisely opposed to the genuine condition of the metaphysician."[31] He warns that "[t]he scholarly pedagogue ... must perpetually triumph over his own intimate adversary, the Professor."[32]

In this battle, Raïssa Maritain often rescued her spouse, and he often spoke of his debt to her for doing so. They shared a vocation to marriage and wisdom, and their reading of the signs of the times set their course. Together they found the Sorbonne hostile to their search for truth; so together, they initiated Thomist study circles centered on truth. In both peace and war, they bore witness to this truth. As both patriots and cosmopolitans, they practiced civic friendship.

And what of today? How might the Maritains fare at our secular universities and the Catholic universities which so often imitate them? This we cannot know, at least not in any detail. There is one truth, however, that we can know: they would surely weep were we not to read, wisely and with a view to action, the signs of our own times.

---

[31] For this citation, translated from Maritain's *Sept leçons sur l'être et les premiers principes de la raison speculative*, see Francesca Aran Murphy, *Art and Intellect in the Philosophy of Étienne Gilson* (Columbia, Missouri/London: University of Missouri, 2004), 168.

[32] Ibid.

CHOSEN FOR GLORY: AQUINAS ON VOCATION TO THE SUPERNATURAL

Heather McAdam Erb

Thomas Aquinas' rich notion of the supernatural is tied to his theory of vocation. Philosophical reasoning about the Providence whereby intellectual beings are called to beatitude reveals two facts. First, the freedom and possibility of human response flows from the gratuity of the divine invitation to glory. Second, the vocation to the supernatural signals a radical reorientation of human nature and its capacity for goodness, such that a secular life in full rejection of this call is nothing short of a kind of living death.[1] The secular vision of humanity diminishes the scope of vocation by characterizing human persons as private, autonomous centers of choice who seek piecemeal temporal fulfillment while experiencing neither the conscious deprivation of sin nor the specificity of a supernatural call.

The title of this essay points to the union of approaches Aquinas takes with respect to our knowledge of God. "*Chosen for glory*" suggests the way of God's *descent* to us through revelation, especially in the Incarnation. "*Vocation to the supernatural*" signals the way of *ascent* from creatures to God. St. Thomas' statement that these two ways are in fact "the same"[2] can be explained by reference to the order of finality. In the natural desire for perfection, the principle from which the thing originates is also its end. The outpouring of divine love that summons man to eternal life is the same Trinitarian life that is his glory. Thomas Hibbs formulates the key principle: "descent precedes ascent and

[1] If humans possessed only a natural (not a supernatural) end, they would be less noble than all creatures, since they would fail to return to their source, through their unique route of rationality, and their natural desire would not come to rest (*SCG* III.25). Unlike beasts, we reach a more noble end with assistance, which is more perfect than achieving a less noble end on one's own (*ST* I-II 5.5 ad 2).

[2] *SCG* IV, 1.

transcendence is not an escape but rather a return (*reditus*)."[3] The vocation to the supernatural can be fulfilled because a personal relation to, and participation in, the transcendent is already inscribed in the invitation to eternal life. The divine liberality expressed in the twofold gift of creation and redemption, we will see, already points to the glory of participation in the interior life of God, even as the Passion of Christ contains the seeds of *His* glory, as the manifestation of God's inner life of supreme love as Self-gift. Thus, the notions of "vocation," "divine liberality" and "glory" are interdependent ideas for St. Thomas. The soul's natural capacity for grace[4] in the actual order of Providence is made possible through the Incarnation, the "splendor of the Father's glory,"[5] a glory whose original seal is stamped upon its model, conforming us to Himself.[6]

In this paper we will study the affinities present in the notions of vocation, glory and the supernatural, by looking at three aspects of "vocation" in his thought: first, the treatment of the Biblical theme of "call"; second, the levels of call to the spiritual life; and third, the metaphysical foundations for man's general call to the supernatural. We shall begin with an introductory look at Aquinas on the concept of the supernatural.

1. On the Concept of the "Supernatural" in Aquinas

If "nature" signified that which is possessed *by birth*,[7] or that which exists in virtue of a thing's essential principles, then the "supernatural" is that which originates *outside* a thing's essence, signifying a divine operation that surpasses the operation of nature, namely, creation and

---

[3] Thomas Hibbs, "Transcending Humanity in Aquinas," *Proceedings of the American Catholic Philosophical Quarterly* 66 (1992), Suppl.: 198.

[4] An idea inherited from Augustine: *ST* I-II, 113.10, with reference to *De Trinitate* XIV, 8, 11.

[5] Hebrews 1.3. See his treatment of this in *In ad Rom.* VIII, l. 6 #703-06.

[6] *De pot.* 10.4: "We read in Sacred Scripture that 'we are configured to the Son by the mediation of the Holy Spirit'...Now, nothing is conformed to a model except by means of its own seal...Consequently, we say of Christ: 'He has stamped us with his seal...he has given us in pawn the Holy Spirit present in our hearts.'"

[7] E.g., *ST* III, 2.12.

miracle.[8] For Aquinas, the supernatural has both an ontological and a moral sense—theology is said to deal with "supernatural substances," namely, God, angels and the human soul, all of which transcend nature, but also concerns those means proportioning man to his ultimate end, lying beyond his natural operations. Thus, the "supernatural" includes several divisions,[9] starting with the division between the supernatural *entity* that is God, and His supernatural *effects* begun at creation. Within creation, there is another distinction, namely, of that which is *essentially* supernatural, such as the sanctifying grace necessary for salvation, and that which is only *modally* supernatural; namely, the preternatural gifts (not equivalent to the "sevenfold gifts" of the spirit, but rather Paul's charismatic list) and miracles, neither of which are strictly necessary for salvation. In his review of the issue, Père Garrigou-Lagrange summarizes these divisions, adding that an abyss exists between the two basic forms of the supernatural:

> The *intrinsically* supernatural (*supernaturale quoad substantiam*), characteristic of the intimate life of God, of which sanctifying grace, or "the grace of the virtues and the gifts," is a participation, and the *extrinsically* supernatural or preternatural (*supernaturale quoad modum tantum*) which is the character of the signs or extraordinary phenomena that the devil can imitate.[10]

Within the domain of the intrinsically or *essentially* supernatural, we can note the element of passivity on the side of the human person in that the virtues and especially the gifts of the Spirit involve passivity and docility[11] in contrast to the modern stress on extraordinary paranormal spiritual feats. Prophecy is not prayer, as one patristic noted. Turning to the first and central instance of the supernatural,

---

[8] See: Johann Auer, "Inwieweit ist im 13. Jahrhundert der Wandel des Begriffes 'supernaturalis' bedingt durch den Wandel des Naturbegriffes?" in Auer, *La Filosofia della natura* (Milan, 1966), 331-49.

[9] A good illustration of these divisions is found in Reginald Garrigou-Lagrange, *Christian Perfection and Contemplation According to St. Thomas Aquinas and St. John of the Cross*, tr. Sr. M. Timothea Doyle (London: Herder, 1937), 347.

[10] Garrigou-Lagrange, *Christian Perfection*, 19.

[11] *ST* I-II, 68. The mystical state is identified with the passive way, says Père Garrigou-Lagrange (*Christian Perfection*, 346 #1).

namely, *Divine Being*, we can discern three notes in the concept: As a supernatural agent, God's causality is *extrinsic* to the creature and *gratuitous*[12] (meaning unmerited and not contained in the creature's essential principles, but rather supplied as a gift elevating man to attain an end beyond his nature) as well as *immediate* or *unassisted*.[13] The *extrinsically* or *modally* supernatural phenomena, which involve ordinary miracles, gratuitous graces or charismatic gifts such as prophecy, carry only one of these notes, namely, that of *extrinsic efficient causation*, thus falling short of a first order supernatural event.

2. The Biblical Theme of "Call"

The notion of 'call' draws together related themes such as predestination, glory, mission, the good shepherd, charity, and the relation of humility to truth. The Old Covenant's emphasis on Israel's being set apart for an instrumental role in salvation history is replaced by the New Covenant's stress on the call to adoptive sonship, such that by living in faith, hope and charity, the Christian believer partakes in the divine nature and is called into eternal glory. While focusing on the New Testament understanding of the term, Aquinas also drew from the Jewish understanding of vocation in its 'active' sense, which united the divine invitation with the "naming" activity of God and the new 'being' resulting from it. In his treatment of vocation, Aquinas spares no effort to elaborate on the nature of the divine initiative which establishes a new way of existing in Christ. We will limit our discussion of his views to a few examples: the '*apostolic call*' and the '*good shepherd*' texts; the parables of the '*banquet*' and the '*workers in the vineyard,*' and finally, the text in Romans 8, which links vocation to predestination and justification.

In his Gospel commentaries, Aquinas presents the *call of the fishermen* as an invitation to the spiritual life through detachment from temporal goods. In the commentary on Matthew, the apostles are called to an

---

[12] *ST* I, 62.2.

[13] We attain our supernatural end only through a supernatural agent (God), whose action is gratuitous (*ST* I, 62.2), who infuses a perfection or principle of operation (*lumen gloriae*) that surpasses our natural powers in order to attain the end that exceeds the proportion of any created nature. (Cf. *De virt. in communi*, q. un., a. 10.)

imitation of Christ through the perfection of charity more than through mere renunciation, for the latter is a mere means, a prerequisite, to following Him,[14] and the same is said of Jesus' conversation with the rich young man. In his commentary on John,[15] Aquinas glosses the initial conversation between Jesus and his disciples. The Lord's first words to those following after him on the road were, "What are you looking for?" which Thomas takes to imply the possibility of either temporal or spiritual goods. Alluding to Exodus 33.23, they are said to follow after Him because in this life we only see God's back, that is, His effects, and not His face. To their reply, "Rabbi, where are you staying?" Aquinas applies first the *mystical* and then the *moral* sense. According to the former, Christ is peace, and we will find perfect peace in the fullness of the sevenfold gifts of the Spirit and in glory. Applying the *moral* sense, the disciples are asking the qualities of those who dwell with Him. Jesus' reply, "*come and see*," is given great weight—Jesus is saying that glory and grace cannot be known except by experience—"*Veni,*" come, by believing and acting; "*videte,*" see, by experiencing and knowing. Further, there are *four modes* of coming to this knowledge—through good action, through attaining a 'quiet mind,'[16] through supernatural wisdom or a 'taste of the divine sweetness,' and through prayerful devotion.

The theme of vocation is continued in lectio 16, where the call of Philip and Nathaniel provides the opportunity for detailing the modes of responding, or converting, to Christ. This takes place, he says, either through an exterior source, namely, miracles, or through interior inspiration, where the latter is more likely to have a divine source. As he says elsewhere,[17] the exterior source could also be preaching, direction or reading, working in tandem with the interior light of

---

[14] *In Matt. IV*, 22, l.2, #373.

[15] *In Joann.* I, l.15. The Johannine commentary is a *reportatio* (a summary of his lectures taken by his Dominican brother Reginald of Piperno, between 1270 and 1272).

[16] "*per mentis quietum, seu vacationem*" (Ps. 45.11).

[17] E.g., *In Sent.* I, 41.1.2, ad 3; *In Sent.* IV, 17.1.1.2.

grace, a movement towards the good[18] to effect a general call to the spiritual life.

In his commentary on the *"good shepherd"* text in John, chapter 10, Aquinas clarifies the conditions of response to the divine invitation. Versus Chrysostom, who identified Scripture as the door, Thomas adopts Augustine's interpretation of Christ as the door of the sheepfold, for a door both protects and "leads in" the sheep. The Christological emphasis recurs here, where Christ is at once the shepherd, the door and the way through the door to salvation. As a participated light of the truth which is Christ, we are called to imitate His self-gift and humility. The divine initiative gives a context to vocation, for the good shepherd both opens the door, leads them from evil and teaches them by example, thus "opening a path before them." Christ is the gate to God's interiority, Thomas says, in which intimacy the sheep are protected and defended in their going in and going out—the invitation to freedom in Christ thus gives joy even amidst persecution and results in both good conscience and good exterior actions through the virtues. If one puts this text beside others in the *Summa* and the commentary on the Apostles' Creed, we can conclude that, despite the supernatural origin of vocation, its path of response is through the Passion of Christ, the model of which we are the imperfect image. As Aquinas says in the Biblical commentary, the sheep know His voice but only through a veil, for their participation in the divine life is only by similitude or participation.

The parable of the *banquet*[19] reveals Aquinas' continued emphasis on the quality of *humility* necessary for responding to the divine call to the spiritual life, and the greatness of God's mercy in extending the universal call. Through his authorities, Aquinas juxtaposes human pride in the traditional "symbolism of the excuses," whether it be in the form of bodily goods (one's farm), or the yoke of the five senses or even the Law (the oxen), with the magnitude of divine mercy and condescension to those excluded from the world, who dine, as Clement says, on the eternal word of God in the "rational feast of charity."

---

[18] See Garrigou-Lagrange, *Christian Perfection*, 337-38.

[19] *Cat. Aurea In XXII Matt; Cat. Aurea In XIV Luc.*

Often we are compelled to enter the banquet through bad fortune and scourges, as lost sheep are pulled homeward.

In his commentary on the parable of the *workers in the vineyard* in Matthew,[20] Aquinas interprets the various hours of the day as either various times in salvation history, or as the stages of man's life on earth. God invites all to faith from the moment of birth, and his family is the whole world, with special emphasis on the rational creature. In terms of the ages of salvation history, the first hour represents the time from Adam to Noah, or the "childhood" of man. Here, the invitation is through apparitions and messengers, it is extended to all and received without a great deal of initiative by obeying the Law. The third hour corresponds to the age from Noah to Abraham, or the "adolescence" of man. Here, the invitation is through angels, and emerges through the light of intellect, thus entailing more personal responsibility for response, although it is clouded by the passions. The sixth hour signifies the time from Abraham to David, which corresponds to the Jews and to the "young adulthood" of faith. The conditions of this invitation are grouped together with that of the ninth hour, signifying the time from David to Christ, the fullness of time represented by "old age." God's mercy condescends to the sinner, as in the last hour, where the owner finds workers standing idle. These last represent the Gentiles, who, like the unconverted elderly, replace the true God with worship of idols, thinking they still have time to repent. The final ones represent those nourished with the sacraments, to whom the greatest grace is given, just as the ones closest to death attain their reward more quickly.

Divine liberality is shown by the extent of divine mercy, which, like vocation,[21] requires distance between the giver (of grace) and the receiver (in a state of sin). In this sense, "vocation" is Christ working within us and a call to remission from sin, where the distance caused by pride is left behind. "'Being called' refers to God's help moving and exciting our mind to give up sin, and this motion of God is not the

---

[20] *In Matt*, XX, 1.1.

[21] Cf. *In Sent.* IV, 17.1.1, qc. 2, arg. 3.

remission of sins, but its cause."[22] To the objection that all should obtain equal glory, he replies by distinguishing beatitude from the side of the object and the subject. Objectively speaking, there is only one silver coin, or one river of life, beatitude; but from the side of the subject, there are different sizes of vessels, and thus degrees of participation in beatitude, because some hearts are more filled with (opened by) charity.[23] One could apply the distinction between the remote or general call to the spiritual life and the proximate, individual call, to this parable, as expressed in the mystery of predestination.[24] In his commentary on Matthew, Aquinas balances Gregory's emphasis on the great depths of divine mercy initiating the call, with the divine distinction of pride from charity and humility.

In his commentary on Romans, Aquinas links the notion of call, justification and predestination to glory. Paul speaks of God predestining those He foreknew to be conformed to the image of His Son (Rom. 8.28). He continues, "and those whom He predestined He also called; and those whom He called He also justified; and those whom He justified He also glorified" (Rom. 8.30). Christians are reconciled and united with Christ, then, with an eye to the glory of eternal life, in that the divine invitation already involves the "planned sending of a rational creature to the end of eternal life."[25] The assurance of the end is already inscribed in the call of grace, since the vocation to glory flows from the order of providence directing things to their ends.[26] The omnipresence of divine causality implied in this text, however, does not deny the presence of intermediary secondary causes and creatures' own operations in response to the divine call.[27]

The Biblical theme of "call" presents Aquinas with a variety of opportunities to express the dominant idea that God in His grace calls

---

[22] *ST* I-II, 113.1, ad 3; cf. *Quodl.* II, 4.1, ad 1, on the interior movement of Christ in the soul.

[23] "*sic qui animam habet caritate magis dilatam, magis accipiet...*"; cf., *Super Heb.* IV, l.2, on the interior stimulus of love by which we recognize the call.

[24] See Garrigou-Lagrange, *Christian Perfection*, 340.

[25] *ST* I, 23.1.

[26] *ST* I, 22.3ff.

[27] *ST* I, 105.5.

men to forsake a sinful life and to enter Christ's kingdom. Aquinas treats the divine initiative and mercy, as well as the promise of divine union through progress in charity through imitation of Christ. This reveals Aquinas' balance and interplay between primary and secondary causes in his theory of vocation.

3. Levels of Call to the Spiritual Life

Regarding the mode of response to the call to the spiritual life, Aquinas' position is sharply contrasted with the Pelagian *denial* of an interior supernatural principle that would cause assent.[28] In order to answer the call to conversion and accept the elevated beatitude that God has prepared as our fulfillment, a supernatural interior principle (grace) is needed. Aquinas also rejects the pagan method of response to the divine, which is either *indifference*, as in the case of Epicureans, who reject prayer and sacrifice in the face of the inflexibility of the divine plan, or *manipulation and control*, which is the Stoics' solution, an attempt to change the divine will by placating it.[29] Aquinas emphasizes grace as a divine initiative and the human powers of intellect and will as responsive in structure to this invitation, not as autonomous or alienated capacities but as summoned and empowered to a personal and transforming union. The call to the supernatural is through the divine initiative cooperating with our natural powers, which raises two questions. First, "how is the general and universal call to the supernatural distinct from that call established in baptism, and from the more specific call to a more intense degree of spiritual perfection, exhibited in some persons?" And second, "what are the conditions of response to the call to the supernatural?"

---

[28] Pelagians claimed that assent is caused by human free choice; Aquinas responds that "this is false, for since, by assenting to what belongs to faith, man is raised above his nature, this must needs come to him from some supernatural principle moving him inwardly; and this is God" (*ST* II-II, 6.1).

[29] See *De Ver.* 6.6, on whether predestination can be helped by prayers of the saints: "...the view of the Stoics, who maintained that all things are governed by certain spirits, which they called gods. And when they had decided on something, prayers and sacrifices could win a change in their decision, so they claimed, by placating the gods' minds..." Aquinas also attributes this view to Avicenna in the same article.

To answer the first question, Aquinas distinguishes levels of appetite in relation to ends, ranging from the natural love of the end found in inanimate objects, to the rational form of love proportioned to divine being, in the case of men and angels. "Appetite," the tendency of a thing towards its end, presupposes a proportion and suitability of the end to the subject,[30] which itself signals a certain anticipation of the end, its beginning preexisting in the subject.[31] There is a natural love of inanimate objects towards their ends, as even these have a principle of the inclination towards what is suitable to them.[32] On a higher level, sensitive appetite moves towards its end through sense knowledge, and rational appetite, or will, directs itself towards the end, operating in tandem with the lower appetites to achieve it, such that the degrees of appetite attain varying degrees of union through gradations of universality in scope and intensity or power.[33]

Things are also directed to the final end according to the diversity of operations.[34] First, all things tend towards the preservation of their being, and in this they implicitly desire the likeness with God, and God Himself.[35] Second, with respect to sensitive and rational souls, they also strive towards the ultimate end by means of producing their form, or their likeness, in the diffusion of goodness. Thus, in the giving of being to another, things assimilate themselves to divine causality.[36]

Humans are drawn towards the beatific vision in exactly the same way, Aquinas says, as every creature is moved towards some kind of unity with God—by expressing in their own way their origin from God in their tendency towards Him.[37] Rational souls attain a more intense

---

[30] *ST* I, 63.2. On this topic, see Jan Aertsen, *Nature and Creature: Thomas Aquinas's Way of Thought* (Brill: Leiden, 1988), 342-45.

[31] *De Ver.* 14.2.

[32] *De Ver.* 22.1.

[33] Appetites form an inclusive hierarchy (where the higher includes the lower). See Aertsen, *Nature and Creature*, 344.

[34] *SCG* III, 22.

[35] *De Ver.* 22 ad 2.

[36] *Comp. Th.* 103.

[37] *SCG* III, 25; cf., John Milbank, *The Suspended Middle* (Grand Rapids, Michigan: Wm. B. Eerdmans, 2005), 26-28.

union through understanding and love.[38] Milbank says "*as spirits,* [angels and humans] are innately called to the beatific vision," referring to this as our "latent mystical condition."[39] Thus, the supernatural is not a superadded "extra" in the soul, but an ontological dynamism striving for full realization in the life of glory. Our call to glory is paradoxical: the natural desire belongs to all and cannot be frustrated, yet cannot by itself be fulfilled.[40] So, for Aquinas, the universal call is best answered by the *Christian believer*, who forms a response through being elevated and perfected by the second gift, sanctifying grace. Thus we find embedded in Aquinas' treatment of the supernatural the problem of reconciling the natural desire for the supernatural and the historical offer of grace in Christ. But the principle expressed above, that the end is in a way present in the subject by its suitability, means that the unbeliever still lives in a state of anticipated grace. We could say that the perfection of the believer's response to the supernatural, in contrast to the unbeliever's response, is analogous to the perfection of the spiritual proficient's response in comparison with that of the ordinary believer. In both cases, the divine invitation initiates the degree of union.[41]

---

[38] God bestows on rational creatures a "special love, by which he draws the rational creature above its natural condition to have a part in the divine goodness. And it is by this love that he is said to love someone simply speaking, because by this love God simply speaking wills for the creature that eternal good which is himself" (*ST* I-II, 110.1).

[39] Milbank, *The Suspended Middle*, 28.

[40] See *The Suspended Middle*, 30; cf. Paul Waddell, "Faith and Reason in the Wake of Milbank and Pickstock," *International Philosophical Quarterly* 48 (2008): 381-96.

[41] Here the issue of predestination and the "principle of predilection" are at work (*ST* I, 23.5, ad 3), and, in both, the degree of receptivity to the call is at work. A thing is perfect insofar as it attains to its principle (*ST* I, 12.1). Garrigou-Lagrange puts it succinctly: "A proximate, efficacious vocation to the mystical life is not necessarily an efficacious vocation to the highest degrees of the mystical life or to a high perfection; that depends on predestination in the order of the divine intentions, and on the fidelity of the soul in the order of execution" (*Christian Perfection*, 340).

God is prepared to give grace to all, but unbelievers provide in themselves an obstacle to its reception.[42] Once in a state of sin, they cannot remove the active impediment to grace without divine help, and yet are responsible, in the way a drunk is still guilty for a homicide he commits,[43] or a man covering his eyes while the sun is shining, is still responsible for his actions.[44] Although humans cannot even form a good act of will apart from grace, they can nonetheless control whether or not they refuse this grace,[45] in willing not to be open to the possibility of detesting one's sin and desiring divine goodness. In a sense, then, the disbelief of many pagans is like the faith of the devils. Both may know the truth of the propositions of faith through their intellect, but their wills are turned from grace—although the pagan will may not be informed by malice and the sheer desire for power apart from truth (as in the case of the devils[46]), it is nonetheless not necessarily informed by charity or cooperative with its influence. Such is the case of the unbeliever who has heard of God's revelation but has not received the gift of faith. His will is voluntarily turned away from a desire for divine goodness, thus impeding the assent proper to the virtue of faith. And, with respect to the non-hostile pagan, the Christian believer's adherence to the truths of faith signals he has entered another world than the one revealed by the path of human discovery, inaugurating him into future beatitude[47] through a sure and direct path.[48]

---

[42] *SCG* III, 159.

[43] *SCG* III, 160.

[44] *SCG* III, 159.

[45] He is arguing against the Pelagian view, *SCG* III, 159: "...one must consider that although a person cannot merit or produce grace by a motion of free will, he can nonetheless impede himself from receiving grace.... And so this is in the power of free will: to impede the reception of the divine grace or not to impede it. For this reason the person who provides an obstacle to the reception of divine grace merits the blame imputed to him... the only people deprived of grace are the ones who provide in themselves an obstacle to grace."

[46] *ST* II-II, 5.2, ad 3.

[47] *Comp. Th.* 2.

[48] *ST* II-II, 2.4. Thus, the necessity for Biblical revelation.

What about the relationship between the ordinary believer and the spiritually advanced Christian? In the spiritual proficient and Christian mystic, the mysteries of faith are not only believed but *lived* in a habitual, not transitory manner, exhibited clearly in the superhuman mode of the Spirit's gifts prevailing over their merely human mode, as found in the virtues.[49] And, with respect to the latter, it is the heroic degree of the virtues, and not the mystical form of prayers that lead up to them, which is an index of holiness for Aquinas. The gratuity of the proximate, individual call to the mystical life, as distinct from the universal, remote call, is affirmed by the metaphysical underpinnings of predestination. Among things ordered to the end, some are nearer to it, namely, those that participate in the divine goodness more fully and require less mediation to reach it than do lower beings.[50]

The degrees of perfection in the universe are mirrored in the personal order, in that sizes of vessels (or different grades of spiritual perfection) mirror the abundance of divine goodness[51] and are dependent on its will. The full flowering of the mystical life in many can be explained by the dictum that "what is received is received according to the mode of the receiver," such that lack of detachment, courage or perseverance slow the journey and impede its fulfillment. This brief survey of the various degrees of call to the life of holiness reveals Aquinas' ability to balance the infallible workings of the divine will with human autonomy in the attainment of the end.[52]

We can now turn to the second question: namely, "what are the conditions of response to the call to the supernatural?" It requires a combination of *reason* and *humility.* As an application of *synderesis* and conscience through free will, our response to the vocation to the supernatural must be a rational deduction of conclusions from the

---

[49] *ST* I-II, 68.1-2.

[50] *Comp. Th.* 148: "...everything is ordered to the divine goodness as to its end, and since of those things that are ordered to this end some are nearer to the end, namely, those that participate in the divine goodness more fully, it follows that those things that are lower in creation... are somehow ordered to the higher beings as to their ends..."

[51] *ST* I, 23.5, ad 3.

[52] *De malo* 6.1, ad 3, for example.

principles of natural law, according to Aquinas. *Synderesis* is the natural habit of the human soul through which it knows principles of action, which are the universal principles of natural law.[53] The central meaning of *conscience* is the application of habit or knowledge to a particular act, by which one judges the rightness or wrongness of an act to be done.[54] Thus, starting with the principles grasped by *synderesis*, we add judgments about particular actions; the drawing of the conclusions is called "conscience" (*conscientia*[55]), a knowledge directive of action, as prodding, urging or binding.[56]

Since our choices are about means to an end, the wisdom called *prudence* ("right reason about things to be done"[57]) determines both the rightness of an act and its performance, adapting the person to his true end through the correct means.[58] Just as prudence directs the lower moral virtues, so *charity* completes and directs prudence, by setting the mean of prudence in the context of union with God, such that all actions strive towards complete union under the command of charity.[59] The vocation to the supernatural is the current saturating the particular forms of vocation, and the grasp of neither one requires private revelation or intuition. In a text on prophecy,[60] Aquinas describes a divinely imprinted intellectual light by which the mind discerns truthfully and efficaciously what is to be done—a sort of prophetic revelation for action. But in the determination of one's specific vocation the mind is not a mere instrumental agent elevated in

---

[53] *De Ver;* 16.1, *ST* I, 79.12; I-II, 94.1.

[54] *De Ver.* 17.1; *ST* I, 79.13.

[55] For example, by *synderesis* one recognizes that murdering one's father is bad; one then recognizes that a particular action is a case of such a murder; and finally, by conscience, one concludes that this action is bad. See *ST* I-II, 76.1.

[56] *De Ver.* 17.1.

[57] *ST* I-II, 57.4; cf. *ST* II-II, 47.1.

[58] *ST* I-II, 57.5. Here, Aquinas explains the way in which rightness of choice involves two factors, namely, a due end and something suitably ordained to that due end.

[59] *ST* II-II, 27.6, ad 3, on reason and charity as two measures of acts.

[60] *ST* II-II, 173.2.

a transient way by the principal agent,[61] but rather it is an agent moving out of its own powers, abiding in the principles of its nature and applying them consciously to a set of concrete life circumstances, while subject to love without measure.

In addition to reason, *humility* is a necessary condition of response to our vocation to the supernatural, for Aquinas. It is the dependence upon God signified by humility that makes both the reception of vocation and its response possible. Moral failure, on the other hand, has its root in pride, the self-aggrandizement that rejects subordination and bears a sense of inordinate entitlement to great things.[62] Pairing humility with magnanimity and opposing both to pride, Aquinas writes, "a twofold virtue is necessary with regard to the difficult good: one, to temper and restrain the mind, lest it tend to high things immoderately, and this belongs to the virtue of humility; and another to strengthen the mind against despair, and urge it on to the pursuit of great things according to right reason; and this is magnanimity."[63] Thus, humility and magnanimity balance each other in the pursuit of virtuous action, both operating according to right reason and avoiding the extremes of presumption and despair. Although some have argued that Aquinas sets up an impossible alliance here between Aristotelian magnanimity and the dependence of humility,[64] the pairing of these virtues seems particularly fitting in light of popular ideas of vocation today, providing a corrective to both fundamentalist *certitudes* about the particularities of the divine call and damnation (a type of presumptuous entitlement) and the sense of *despair* among the faithful in the face of spiritual adversity and the dominant culture, even within the Church. Magnanimity is not opposed to humility but tempers the

---

[61] Cf. *ST* II-II, 173.4.

[62] *ST* II-II, 162.1.

[63] *ST* II-II, 161.1.

[64] See Pierre Manent, *The City of Man*, trans. Marc A. LePain (Princeton, New Jersey: Princeton University, 1998) and Eileen Sweeney, "Vice and Sin (I-IIae, qq. 71-89)" in *The Ethics of Aquinas*, ed. Stephen Pope (Washington, D.C.: Georgetown University Press, 2002), 167 #37.

awareness of dependence with the noble attempt to perfect our natural and acquired abilities.[65]

4. Metaphysical Foundations of Aquinas' Notion of Vocation

Among the various metaphysical ideas at work in the broad notion of vocation, we will treat four: the dimension of *activity and passivity* (*or receptivity*); *love* as both source and response to the divine call; *likeness* as conformity to Christ as the final cause of vocation; and the *totality of self* required by the first commandment, definitive of vocation as self-gift. The previous section on the degrees of call to the spiritual life already detailed the nature and role of love, while the section on humility touched on the interplay of action and passivity.

The balance between *action and passion* (or *reception*) in the response to divine invitation finds expression in the Biblical commentaries. In the Gospel of John's analogy of the good shepherd, the imitation of Jesus involves passing through the door of humility and Christ's passion towards eternal life, entailing a love of God even in the poverty of His Incarnation.[66] Love combines with humility here in the requirement of forgetfulness of self to follow the good shepherd, who Himself enters through the door and opens it before us through humility. But reception extends to the arena of *action*, for believers must follow the example of one who teaches through deeds, not mere words. In his commentary on John, Aquinas invests the analogy of the "door," which is fundamentally Christ Himself, with a dynamic of activity and passivity. Christ, as the door, is the gate to the interiority of God, and a "gate" is "that through which things must pass, in order to go within, and find peace."[67] Passivity also operates in the supernatural gifts, which perfect the theological virtues through increasing docility to the Spirit.[68] While *active* purification is self-

---

[65] See *ST* II-II, 129.3, ad 4: "magnanimity makes a man 'esteem himself worthy of great rewards' in view of the gifts he possesses from God.... Humility, on the other hand, makes a human esteem himself low in view of his own natural defects.... Thus magnanimity and humility are not contrary to each other."

[66] *In Joann.* X, 1.1.

[67] *In Joann.* X,. 1.2.

[68] *ST* I-II, 68.

initiated, the nobility of *passive* purification lies in its origin not in the self but in God, as seen especially in the gift of understanding.[69] This sense of passivity is not opposed to human action, but is a radical receptivity to God in the awareness of the need for grace on the part of the human person. Further, it is not a question of pure passivity or receptivity to divine grace, since infused charity works with already activated moral virtues.[70] As one author expressed it:

> If through the effect of charity people become friends of God, two things must happen: (1) God acts in them and (2) they make themselves available to the affairs of God in the world by means of their natural capacities.[71]

On the philosophical level, Aquinas provides the ground for understanding the theological dimension of receptivity. As an intrinsic principle of motion, "nature" has a twofold origin: an active and a passive principle. Thus, a thing is determined by its own activity as well as through the influence of a higher nature *(natura superior)*.[72] Things are assimilated to God both from within and through a higher influence, and the twin dimensions present in nature, action and passion, are at work in the inclination to ultimate ends. By nature taken as a *passive* principle, man naturally inclines to the vision of God. By nature taken as an *active* principle, he cannot 'naturally' attain this end, for natural powers have no proportion to it. Thus, man's nature requires a higher nature for fulfillment of his natural receptivity toward it.[73]

This leads us to the role of *love as both source and response* in Aquinas' theory of vocation. Divine love is the *source* of man's free response, in that out of His infinite love God draws all creatures in accord with their

---

[69] *ST* II-II, 8.7. Cf. *ST* I-II, 69.2, ad 3: "In this life...the [mind's] eye being cleansed by the gift of understanding, we can, so to speak, see God."

[70] Paul J. Waddell indicates that charity permeates the moral virtues as its "strategies." (See Waddell, *The Primacy of Love: An Introduction to the Ethics of Thomas Aquinas* [New York: Paulist, 1992], 90.)

[71] Eberhard Schockenhoff, "The Theological Virtue of Charity (IIa IIae, qq. 23-46)," in *The Ethics of Aquinas*, 251.

[72] *ST* II-II, 2.3.

[73] *De virt. in comm.* 10, ad 2.

own dignity back to Himself as their end: "grace, which directs us to the final vision of God, *causes* the love of God within us."[74] Quoting the first letter of John, he explains that it is only through God's love for us that we can return love: "*His love consists in this: it is not we who have loved God, it is He who loved us first.*"[75]

Yet the grace that elevates us to supernatural beings does not destroy but preserves our nature, such that through faith we are partakers of the divine knowledge, and through charity our will partakes of the divine love.[76] Since spiritual creatures desire to return to God in a spiritual way, they are ordered to their end freely through intellect and will,[77] but, as Milbank recalls, "there can be no spiritual existence without grace," such that intellectual creatures without grace would be less than other creatures: that is, radically disordered.[78]

Although proportioned to our nature, the human response to the supernatural call culminates in conformity to the actions of Christ—"Christ's action was our instruction."[79] Striving for a fulfillment of the demands of charity and having nothing in oneself that is contrary to the love of the Father and of Jesus is what permits union or "abiding" with God.[80] This response occurs not through God's self-sufficiency or power, but through Christ's Passion, which shows man the depth of God's love, thus evoking man's love in return, which is that in which his salvation consists.[81] Thus, the aspects of *humility, love, receptivity* and *likeness* as conformity dovetail in the theological analysis of vocation. On the side of God, man's response to his vocation is possible through being ordered to Him as an end; on the side of the rational creature, it is possible inasmuch as he is made a rational creature in the *image or*

---

[74] *SCG* III, 151 [*my emphasis*].

[75] 1 John 4.10, as found in *In Joann XV* l.2 #2002-3.

[76] *ST* I-II 110.4; I, 62.7 on grace preserving nature. Cf. *In Boeth. De Trin.* II, 3.

[77] *SCG* III, 112; cf. *ST* I, 8.3.

[78] Milbank, *The Suspended Middle*, 98.

[79] *ST* III, 40.1 ad 3: "*Christi actio fuit nostra instructio.*"

[80] *In 15 Joann.* l.2 #2002-03.

[81] *ST* III, 46.3.

likeness of God.[82] Man is naturally capable of receiving this grace in part due to this original imaging, which culminates in a transformation of self in conformity to Christ. Two types of similitude exist for Aquinas, each being a cause of love in its own degree. The first type obtains between the original and its image when both have the same thing in *act*, such as two things having whiteness. This first type of similitude is the principle of the love of *friendship*. The *second* type is between something that has in potency that which the other has in act, this type causing the love of *concupiscence*, or a friendship of utility or pleasure.[83]

The first type of similitude can exist between God and man only with the help of a supernatural elevation of his nature through grace and is fulfilled in eternal life through the *lumen gloriae*, a form which perfects man's intellect, making it commensurate with God's being, although not comprehensive of it.[84] In this life, it is the increase in charity, not knowledge, which unites us to God.[85] This gradual perfection of "imaging" is a sign of our status as wayfarers capable of advancing in the way of love[86] through ever-increasing docility and fervor with respect to the Spirit's promptings.

The fourth and final foundation of vocation is the notion of *self-gift* demanded by the First Commandment.[87] The love of God above all things and of one's neighbor as oneself are the two main precepts of charity, in which the love of God, self, and neighbor are bound in an inner unity.[88] Aquinas adopts the Gospel sense of *agape* as the love of God for humans, the responsive love of humans for God and, included in that love, the love among humans. Charity, the infused gift whereby God is loved in Himself as the end of all our actions, is the foundation of

---

[82] *ST* III, 9.2, ad 3.

[83] *ST* I-II, 27.3.

[84] *De Ver.* 10.11. Comprehensive knowledge of God's essence is not possible, even for the blessed. On this general topic, see John Wippel, *The Metaphysical Thought of Thomas Aquinas: From Finite Being to Uncreated Being* (Washington, D.C.: Catholic University of America, 2000), 501-75.

[85] *ST* II-II, 24.4.

[86] Ibid.

[87] Deut. 6.5; cf. *ST* II-II, 184.3.

[88] *ST* II-II, 25-26; 44.

growth for all the virtues and gifts and the gauge of their perfection.[89] Because it is not subject to limits or measure, he can say that our perfection consists in observance of this commandment,[90] which for the wayfarer is the removal of obstacles to the primary love of God.

Against the Franciscans, Aquinas says that perfection consists not in renunciation, which is a mere means and is more external, but in charity.[91] The voluntary forfeiting of externals is a means to self-renunciation, however,[92] in that putting these things aside opens a space to answer the call, "*come, follow me.*"[93] In this way, he will be perfect in charity who loves God to the point of renouncing himself[94] in an analogous manner to God's own Self-gift in the sending and sacrifice of His own Son, and in Christ's obedience to the Father.[95]

Vocation as self-gift is possible, then, only for those who possess charity, which presupposes the gifts as uniquely and to a varying degree exercised by individuals.[96] This self-gift that represents the free creature's response to the divine invitation is marked by a "love of friendship" shared imperfectly with God and extended outwards to self and others. Although self-love is ontologically prior, in that "being a unity" is prior to "becoming one with another,"[97] the natural movement of love by which the end is inchoately present in the subject[98] means that there is one motive for charity. This motive flows out of the love of God in Himself towards those things that this love contains

---

[89] *ST* II-II, 184.1.

[90] *ST* II-II, 184.3.

[91] *In Matt IV*, 22 l. 2 #373.

[92] *In Matt. XIX*, 21 #1593.

[93] Ibid.

[94] Ibid.

[95] *De perfect.* 8.

[96] *ST* I-II, 68.5, ad 3.

[97] Cf. Schockenhoff, "The Theological Virtue of Charity," 253: "If it is occasionally stated that each one loves oneself more than the other, Thomas intends neither a diminishment of the biblical commandment of love nor any concession to egoism (II-II, 27.4)."

[98] *ST* II-II, 180.4.

virtually as its end. However, for Aquinas, love for others is *not* characterized as a mere means towards the end of loving God. Rather, it is a continuation of the original movement of *caritas*, as a response to the original Self-gift of creation, toward the Creator who calls things into existence from nothingness because He is love.[99]

Moreover, the forms in which the primary love appears extend to the domain of action *and* contemplation. The contemplative life provides an opportunity for self-gift in that by it man "offers" or "sacrifices" the first and highest of his goods to God, namely his own soul.[100] Joining contemplation to prayer, he says that it is more acceptable to God that "one apply one's own soul and the souls of others to contemplation than to action,"[101] where action is understood as an external gift radiating out of the plenitude of a contemplative center.[102]

The principle that binds the contemplative and active forms of vocation is in fact the same principle that binds together the two dimensions of charity in action. In his analysis of the human act, Aquinas states that the specification of human acts follows the formal aspect under which they attain their object. An act that is related to a general object is specifically identical with any act directed to an individual object under the same aspect.[103] For instance, there is one act of eyesight encompassing both light and the colors of individual objects. As applied to *charity,* there is a unity of love of God and neighbor, since friendship with *God* encompasses as its concrete object the neighbor, who is called to the same end. Applied to contemplation and action, there is a unity of *friendship with God,* encompassing the objects of knowledge and goodness, for it is charity that unites the diverse acts of the active and contemplative lives and directs them to

---

[99] See the development of this notion by Pope John Paul II, "*Creation as Fundamental and Original Gift*" (General Audience, January 2, 1980) #4, and "*Revelation and Discovery of the Nuptial Meaning of the Body*" (General Audience, January 9, 1980) #1-2. See also *Familiaris Consortio* #11.

[100] *ST* II-II, 182.4, ad 1.

[101] *ST* II-II, 182.4, ad 1.

[102] *ST* II-II, 188.6.

[103] *ST* II-II, 25.1.

their proper end by effecting an inner transformation of the acting subject.

5. Conclusion

Having sketched some key aspects of Aquinas' theory of "vocation to the supernatural," we see the interdependence of the terms in their philosophical, theological, and Biblical significations. From our human longing for the beatific vision arises our ongoing transformation by grace, just as God's call of the intellectual creature to accept His loving gift of Himself also provides the means and powers for receiving it. Aquinas' treatment of vocation in his Biblical commentaries focused on the New Testament's notion of filial adoption and the vocation of conformity to Christ, through whom we approach God as imperfect mirrors reflecting the divine original. The texts concerning the "apostolic call," the "good shepherd" and the parables of the *banquet* and the *workers in the vineyard,* open up numerous vistas on the notion of call.

In contrast to both pagan and Pelagian forms of denial of the supernatural, Aquinas admits both the native sphere of the rational creature and the gratuity of its God-like life and destiny. Without making the supernatural a spontaneous emanation out of the natural order, he nonetheless refuses to make grace an extrinsic accident superimposed on a purely natural human beatitude. There is a tension between divine providence and personal freedom reflected in the three levels of participation in the divine life: the unbeliever, the ordinary Christian, and the spiritual proficient.

The metaphysical foundations of Aquinas' notion of vocation draw upon "nature" taken as both an active and as a passive principle for understanding the return to God. Aquinas showed the foundation of similitude or likeness for the "love of friendship" between men and God. The Christological model in Aquinas' theory of self-gift infuses both the realms of action and contemplation.

The richness of Aquinas' teaching on vocation to the supernatural reveals that post-medieval philosophy's concept of the supernatural has developed in a historical and theological vacuum, and in its forgetfulness has failed to give an account of the source and summit of the life of the spirit. Thus, the importance of Aquinas' theory of that vocation lies less in its fidelity to a long-buried but vital tradition before him, than in its power to effect spiritual renewal by clearing the ground and reinvesting both the supernatural and "vocation" with their full and persuasive credentials.

INDEX OF NAMES

CONTRIBUTORS

Sister Prudence Allen, R.S.M., is a member of the Religious Sisters of Mercy of Alma, Michigan; professor in the department of philosophy, St. John Vianney Theological Seminary, Denver, Colorado; and distinguished professor emeritus, Concordia University, Montreal, working in the areas of the philosophy of the person, with emphasis on woman and man, and of the school of personalism. Her two volume work on *The Concept of Woman in Western philosophy from 750BC-1500 AD* is published by Eerdmans, and she is presently working on the third volume (1500-2000+). She has lectured widely in Canada and the United States, and published in such journals as *Communio, Thought, New Blackfriars, American Catholic Philosophical Quarterly, Homelitic and Pastoral Review, Seminary Journal, International Philosophical Quarterly*, and *Maritain Studies.*

Lawrence Dewan, O.P., is professor of philosophy at the Dominican University College, Ottawa, Canada, and a member of the Pontifical Academy of St. Thomas Aquinas, Rome. A native (1932) of North Bay, Ontario, Canada, he studied philosophy at the University of Toronto, the University of Paris, and the Pontifical Institute of Mediaeval Studies (PIMS). His teaching career has also included periods at the University of Ottawa, the University of Toronto and PIMS, and the Catholic University of America. He received the Maritain Medal for Scholarly Excellence in 2006 (conferred by the American Maritain Association). In 2007, he gave the Aquinas Lecture at Marquette University; cf. *St. Thomas and Form as Something Divine in Things*, Milwaukee, Wisconsin, 2007: Marquette University Press [The Aquinas Lecture, no. 71].

Heather McAdam Erb is assistant professor of philosophy at Lock Haven University of Pennsylvania. With degrees from Leuven (Belgium) and the University of Toronto, she has taught philosophy and religious studies at the undergraduate and graduate levels at several universities. In addition to traditional students, she has taught teachers, seminarians, and religious. Her publications focus on the nexus between metaphysics and spirituality in the thought of St.

Thomas Aquinas, and on the relevance of these topics to issues in Catholic culture.

Rev. Daniel B. Gallagher, M.A., Ph.L., S.T.L. is a priest of the Diocese of Gaylord, Michigan, and has taught philosophy and theology at Sacred Heart Major Seminary. His areas of interest include metaphysics, aesthetics, and fundamental theology. He has published in *Topics on General and Formal Ontology, Fellowship of Catholic Scholars Quarterly, The Linacre Quarterly, Social Justice Review, The New Oxford Review, Journal for Christian Theological Research, The Latin Americanist*, and other scholarly journals. A regular contributor to the *Philosophy and Popular Culture* series and the editor of *Values in Italian Philosophy*, Father Gallagher is currently assigned to the Vatican Secretariat of State.

James G. Hanink is professor of philosophy at Loyola Marymount University in Los Angeles. He has taught there for the past 34 years. His academic interests and publications center on personalist metaphysics, realist epistemology, natural law ethics, and Roman Catholic political philosophy. He is active in University Faculty for Life and, with his wife Elizabeth, pro-life advocacy work. They have five adult children and are now grandparents of four children.

John P. Hittinger is a graduate of the University Of Notre Dame (1974). He enrolled in the School of Philosophy at The Catholic University of America, where he completed a master's thesis on "Reason and Intellect in Two Texts of Thomas Aquinas," and a doctoral dissertation on "Natural Law in Locke's *Essay Concerning Human Understanding*." He has held faculty positions at: Benedictine College in Atchison, Kansas; the College of St. Francis in Joliet, Illinois; the United States Air Force Academy; St. Mary's College of Ave Maria University in Orchard Lake, Michigan; and Sacred Heart Major Seminary in Detroit, Michigan. From 2006 to 2008, Dr. Hittinger served as the Vice President for Academic Affairs at the University of St. Thomas, Houston. He presently serves as a full professor in its department of philosophy and is a member of its Center for Thomistic Studies. John has published three books: he was co-editor of *Liberalism at the Crossroads: An Introduction to Contemporary Liberal Theory and its Critics* (Rowman and Littlefield, 1994) and *Reassessing the Liberal State: Reading Maritain's Man and the State* (American

Maritain Association, 2001), and he authored *Liberty, Wisdom and Grace: Thomism and Modern Democratic Theory* (Lexington Press, 2002). John has published articles and presented papers on a variety of topics, including John Locke, Jacques Maritain, military ethics, liberal education, political philosophy, and the thought of John Paul II.

John F. Morris is professor of philosophy at Rockhurst University in Kansas City, Missouri. His specialties include medieval philosophy, as well as contemporary ethics and medical ethics. Dr. Morris has also served since 2005 as the Special Advisor to Bishop Robert Finn for the Diocese of Kansas City/St. Joseph on the issues of Stem Cell Research, Cloning, and Human Embryos. Dr. Morris has presented and published numerous papers on these topics. Most recently, Dr. Morris published an anthology on medical ethics from the Catholic perspective titled *Medicine, Health Care & Ethics: Catholic Voices* (The Catholic University Press of America, 2007), which he edited and in which he authored a chapter on stem cell research.

Ralph Nelson was professor emeritus of philosophy and political science at the University of Windsor, Ontario. His research and publications were in the areas of French, moral, social, and political philosophy, and in democratic theory. He was author of numerous articles on Yves R. Simon and Jacques Maritain and the co-editor of Simon's *Foresight and Knowledge*.

Edmund D. Pellegrino, M.D., is senior research scholar at the Kennedy Institute of Ethics at Georgetown University. He is the author of over 600 published items in medical science, philosophy, and ethics and a member of numerous editorial boards. He is the author or co-author of twenty three books, and the founding editor of the *Journal of Medicine and Philosophy*. Dr. Pellegrino is a Master of the American College of Physicians, Fellow of the American Association for the Advancement of Science, member of the Institute of Medicine of the National Academy of Sciences, and recipient of fifty two honorary doctorates, in addition to other honors and awards, including the Benjamin Rush Award from the American Medical Association, the Abraham Flexner Award of the Association of American Medical Colleges, and the Laetare Award of the University of Notre Dame.

Richard Schenk, O.P., is professor of systematic theology and philosophy in Berkeley at the Graduate Theological Union and its Dominican School of Philosophy and Theology. He is former director of the Hannover Institute of Philosophic Research (1991-2000) and of the Intercultural Forum for Studies in Faith and Culture at the Pope John Paul II Cultural Center in Washington, D.C. (2004-2006). Having completed his doctorate in theology *Summa cum laude* at the University of Munich in 1986, he was chosen as a member of the European Academy of Sciences and Arts in 1991 and as Master of Sacred Theology in 2004.

Michael D. Torre is associate professor of philosophy at the University of San Francisco. He edited the American Maritain Association volume *Freedom in the Modern World: Jacques Maritain, Yves R. Simon, Mortimer J. Adler* (1989, second printing: 1990), and has contributed numerous articles to its series, of which he has been the General Editor since 2009. That same year, his *God's Permission of Sin: Negative or Conditioned Decree?* was published by Fribourg University Press. He has served as Vice-President of the Institut International Jacques Maritain.

John G. Trapani, Jr., is professor of philosophy at Walsh University in North Canton, Ohio. During his 36 years at the university, he has served as chair of the philosophy department and Humanities Division. In addition, he is also the Founder and Director of the university's annual Philosophy-Theology Symposium, now in its 35th year. The current President of the American Maritain Association, John has written extensively on Maritain's philosophy and his book, *Poetry, Beauty, and Contemplation: The Complete Aesthetics of Jacques Maritain*, will be released by Catholic University of America Press in 2011. In the AMA book series, he was the editor of *Truth Matters* (2004). John is also a professional musician, and leader of the 17-piece John Trapani Big Band, founded in 1977.

Cornelia Tsakiridou is associate professor of philosophy at La Salle University, Pennsylvania. Her areas of expertise are aesthetics, social and political philosophy (nationalism, modernity, radical ideologies). She has most recently published the article "The Connatural Eye: Photography Without Representation," *Philosophical Inquiry*, vol. XXIX, Summer-Fall 2007, No. 3-4, 41-57. She has also produced a translation (with M. Spanos) of *Elder Paisios of Mount Athos: Spiritual Counsels*, vol. I (Thessaloniki: Holy Monastery of St. John The Theologian, 2006).

Msgr. John F. Wippel is professor of philosophy at The Catholic University of America. He was recently awarded the Aquinas Medal by the American Catholic Philosophical Association. In addition to numerous articles and papers, Wippel has authored, coauthored, or edited several books, including *Metaphysical Themes in Thomas Aquinas* and *The Metaphysical Thought of Godfrey of Fontaines*, both published by CUA Press.

CPSIA information can be obtained at www.ICGtesting.com
260296BV00002B/2/P

9 780982 711903